The
DEEPENING
DIVIDE

D0322118

The
DEEPENING
DIVIDE

Inequality in the Information Society

Jan A. G. M. van Dijk
University of Twente, Netherlands

SAGE Publications
Thousand Oaks ▪ London ▪ New Delhi

For information:

Sage Publications, Inc.
2455 Teller Road
Thousand Oaks, California 91320
E-mail: order@sagepub.com

Sage Publications Ltd.
1 Oliver's Yard
55 City Road
London EC1Y 1SP
United Kingdom

Sage Publications India Pvt. Ltd.
B-42, Panchsheel Enclave
Post Box 4109
New Delhi 110 017 India

Printed in the United States of America on acid-free paper.

Library of Congress Cataloging-in-Publication Data

Dijk, Jan A.G.M. van.
The deepening divide : inequality in the information society / Jan A.G.M. van Dijk.
   p. cm.
Includes bibliographical references and index.
ISBN 1-4129-0402-1 (cloth) — ISBN 1-4129-0403-X (pbk.)
   1. Information society. 2. Equality. I. Title.
HM851.D55 2005
303.48'33—dc22

                                        2004022909

05   06   07   08   09   10   9   8   7   6   5   4   3   2   1

Acquiring Editor:	Margaret H. Seawell
Editorial Assistant:	Jill Meyers
Project Editor:	Claudia A. Hoffman
Copy Editor:	Catherine M. Chilton
Typesetter:	C&M Digitals (P) Ltd.

Contents

1

Introduction

At the end of the 1990s, the issue of the so-called digital divide was suddenly put on the agenda of public, political, and scholarly debate, starting in the United States and spreading to Europe and the rest of the world. Previously, the ancient problem of information inequality was framed in more abstract terms, such as *knowledge gap, computer literacy,* and *participation in the information society.* See Gunkel (2003) and Mossberger, Tolbert, and Stansbury (2003) for the exact American origins of the term *digital divide* in the mid-1990s. Around the turn of the century, hundreds of conferences of computer professionals, social scientists, and government policy experts worldwide were dedicated to the issue. It was also put on the agenda of public opinion, political discussion, and mass media attention. Commonly, the digital divide was defined as the gap between those who do and those who do not have access to computers and the Internet. *Access* first of all meant physical access: having a personal computer and Internet connection.

It is rather peculiar that this critical issue of the rise of information and communication technology appeared on the scene at the climax of the Internet hype. It seemed as if the last shadows hanging over the digital revolution had to be removed before everyone could benefit from its limitless opportunities. The statistics of computer and Internet access revealed such unequal distributions that they could not be ignored. In the 1980s, unequal access to the new digital media was only acknowledged as a problem of the future. At that time, only a small part of the Western populations, consisting of young academics and technicians, was using these expensive and complicated media. With the arrival of the World Wide Web and multimedia computers, the technology reached mass diffusion, and the problem of particular parts of the population not having access was put on the agenda of societies worldwide.

It is even more curious that, after the Internet bubble was dissolved in the year 2001 and the boundless opportunities of the digital era swiftly grew dim, the optimistic message was pronounced that the digital divide was over, that it had been a myth or a hugely overrated problem. In the developed countries, computer and Internet diffusion rapidly reached the majority. These media were getting cheaper and simpler by the day. Thus many observers reached the conclusion that, apparently, the diffusion of the new media was another instance of the so-called trickle-down principle. This principle holds that some parts of the population always get access to new media first, buying the new technology when it is expensive and forcing the prices to drop. These segments of the population thus pay for the access of others who only get the new media a little later. The observers argued that the market was doing its work and would finally solve access problems. Those who did not gain access did not really want it or need it. In the United States, the Bush administration canceled many federal funds that had been dedicated to new media infrastructure and skills development in the Clinton years.

The first purpose of this book is to show that the digital divide is far from closed. In most parts of the world, it is still widening. The gap between developed and developing countries is extremely wide, and it is growing. Even in the most developed high-tech societies, where the division in physical access has stopped broadening, about one quarter, or even one third, of the population has no access to computers and the Internet. However, the main message of this book is that *the digital divide is deepening where it has stopped widening.* In places where most people are motivated to gain access and physical access is spreading, differences in skill and usage come forward. The more information and communication technology is immersed in society and pervades everyday life, the more it becomes attached to all existing social divisions.

It tends to strengthen them, as it offers powerful tools for everyone engaged. This occurs in the context of the evolving information society and network society. This type of society makes both digital and social divisions even more critical issues, as it is characterized by differential information and communication skills and might lead to an increase of unequal (network) positions in society.

In the past 5 years, I have often considered dropping the concept of the digital divide altogether and replacing it with the general concept of information inequality and a number of more specific terms. It has caused so many misunderstandings (see the next section of this chapter). Particularly, it has led to the misconception of the digital divide as a primarily technological problem. It spurred the narrow interpretation of the digital divide as a physical access problem: of having computers and networks and being able to handle them. As a reaction, dozens of authors on this topic have urged passage beyond access or beyond the digital divide and redefinition or rethinking of the concept. In this book, the digital divide is conceived of as a social and political problem, not a technological one. Physical access is portrayed as only one kind of (material) access among at least four: motivational, material, skills, and usage.

Nevertheless, I have chosen to maintain the concept of the digital divide for strategic reasons. It has managed to be put on the public and political agenda. It should not be moved from the table and smashed to pieces by scientific hairsplitting and political opportunism. It is a long-term problem that will mark all future information societies. However, to reach a better understanding of this problem, the concept of the digital divide has to be reframed.

❖ THE PITFALLS OF A METAPHOR

The strength of a metaphor is that it offers a vivid expression by a clear image or model that is similar to something we know from more familiar circumstances. In English, a *divide* is both a point or line of division or disagreement and a specific term indicating a geographical dividing line, such as a watershed. In other languages, *digital divide* is translated in more figurative terms, such as gap or gorge. The comparison made is to the well-known social division between people or a two-tiered society. This image appeared to be very successful in putting the issue on the agenda of social, political, and scholarly discussions.

Apparently, such a simplification is required to bring a complex and abstract issue to our attention. However, it does so at the risk of several misunderstandings.

First, the metaphor suggests a simple division between two clearly divided groups with a yawning gap between them. However, in contemporary society, we may observe an increasingly complex social, economic, and cultural differentiation. The image of an extended spectrum of positions stretching across populations might be more appropriate. If any demarcation were required, a tripartite distribution might be a better distinction than a two-tiered society. On one side we would find an information elite and, on the other, the digitally illiterate or truly excluded, but in between would be the majority of the population, which has access in one way or another and uses digital technology to a certain extent (see van Dijk, 1999, 2000).

The second wrong connotation of the term *digital divide* is that the divide is unbridgeable. This does not seem to be the case at this early stage of diffusion of digital technology. There appears to be a scope for policy making by governments, corporations, and civil societies; that is, policy making with the intent to prevent inequalities becoming unbridgeable structural divides. In this book, I want to contribute to this policy.

A third misunderstanding might be the impression that the divide is about absolute inequalities, such as between those included and those excluded. In reality, most inequalities of access to digital technology are of a more relative kind. This means that some people are earlier or faster than others in accessing new technologies; that some people possess more hardware, software, and skills than others; or that one group uses the technology more or in different ways than another. It should be granted that this does not make these relative inequalities of a lesser importance, certainly not in an information or network society, as I show in this book.

A fourth wrong impression is that there is only a single digital divide; the actual picture is much more complex. There are several divides running in parallel to the four successive kinds of access distinguished in this book: motivational, physical or material, skills, and usage divides. This relates to the next wrong connotation: the suggestion that the divide is a static condition. In fact, all kinds of access are continually moving. In this book, I demonstrate that motivational and physical access divides may diminish, while skills and usage access divides may grow. In doing this, particular inequalities are coming forward as others disappear (van Dijk & Hacker, 2003).

Three other remarks should be added to put the discussion about the digital divide into perspective. The term *digital* suggests that the digital divide is a technical issue. Most people emphasizing the digital divide as a problem are driven by a kind of technological determinism (Gunkel, 2003; Warschauer, 2002, 2003b). Some suppose that people not using digital technology are missing many opportunities and are excluded from society. Others blame digital technologies, such as the computer and the Internet, for inequalities that are in fact much older than these technologies. In fact, it still has to be demonstrated that people cannot live as normal citizens in contemporary society without using digital technology. Numerous old technologies and media still seem to be able to serve the same purposes they always did. Presently, many jobs, studies, domestic lives, and leisure activities can be managed without the use of computers, the Internet, or any other digital media. It must also be proven that digital technologies really are improving these activities.

The ensuing remark is that people framing the digital divide as a technological problem suggest that access to the technology concerned is able to fix existing social problems, among them problems of social inequality, democracy, freedom, social relationships, and community building. This is a remnant of the Internet hype of the 1990s. Giving someone a computer and an Internet connection does not solve any of these problems. It might be more correct to say that that is when they begin! "Just as the ubiquitous presence of other media, such as television and radio, has done nothing to overcome information inequality in the United States, there is little reason to believe that the mere presence of the Internet will have a better result" (Warschauwer, 2003a, p. 297).

A last remark: Most observers emphasizing the importance of the digital divide insufficiently distinguish this supposed new kind of inequality from old inequalities. In examining the background variables of the digital divide, they always turn up the same old demographical inequalities of income, education, employment, age, gender, and ethnicity. What is new about them, if it is not the inequality of technical command of the digital media? To quote the famous Indian moral economist Amartya Sen (1992): "Equality of *what?*" (p. ix). Is it (in)equality of opportunities, life chances, freedoms, capital, resources, positions, capabilities, skills, or what? The answer is largely absent in almost every book, article, and investigation about the digital divide.

The result is that the causes and effects of the observed digital divides are not sufficiently articulated and clarified. Are the observed divides simply a byproduct of old social inequalities? Is digital technology intensifying these inequalities in some way or another? Or are new inequalities appearing in the context of the information and network society? Unfortunately, analyses and empirical investigations of these kinds of potential new inequalities are very scarce. Still, the answer to these questions will decide the policy lines to be adopted if the attempt is made to close particular digital divides. Is it just a matter of policy in the fields of income, education, gender, age, and ethnicity, or should special policies be invented to confront apparently new problems of computer anxiety, lack of digital skills, and unequal computer use? In this book, I give a positive answer to all three questions posed here: Divides *are* byproducts of old inequalities, digital technology *is* intensifying inequalities, and new inequalities *are* appearing. Both old and new inequalities are shown to be working, and it becomes clear that digital technology has its own enabling and defining role to play.

❖ REFRAMING THE DIGITAL DIVIDE

In this book, I want to make both a theoretical and a practical contribution to the digital divide discussion and research. It offers a framework for understanding this phenomenon that is based on an explicit theory of inequality in the information and network society. This framework is applied in a comprehensive overview of current problems of access to the new digital media—first of all, computers and the Internet. The framework and the empirical analysis of access problems lead to a number of policy options that may help in solving the digital divide problem. The book ends with a list of 26 policy instruments that may be specified by others in an action plan appropriate for a particular country, situation, or field of action.

To accomplish this ambitious task, the current discussion and problematic of the digital divide have to be reframed substantially. They simply are too superficial. More in-depth analysis is required. This appears in the five clusters of basic questions I attempt to answer in this book.

1. As nothing is taken for granted here, the first question entails whether unequal access to information and communication technologies is actually a problem. Are these technologies really necessary for life in modern society? Are the old mass media and face-to-face

communication no longer appropriate for work, study, communication, and recreation in this society? This is the first cluster of questions. If unequal access is shown to be a problem, how should it be defined? Is it mainly a technological problem, of development and diffusion of a particular technology that is too slow? Is it primarily an economic problem, of a new market of hardware, software, and services that is too small and of a part of the population that has no stake in innovation? Or is it, first and foremost, an educational problem of inadequately skilled workers, citizens, and consumers? Finally, it might principally be a societal problem of unequal participation in particular fields of society.

2. An important part of the conceptual framework elaborated in this book is a distinction between four successive kinds of access that indicate the full appropriation of the new technology: motivational, material (physical), skills, and usage. What are the main stimuli and barriers to gaining these kinds of access? This is the question about the causes of the digital divide. In this book, these stimuli and barriers are understood as the presence or absence of particular resources. What are the main resources determining every kind of access? The following question is how the distribution of these resources can be explained. In this book, I look for explanations in a large number of personal and positional inequalities that define relations between categorical pairs such as old and young, male and female, manager and employee, employed and unemployed, high and low levels of education, teacher and student, and ethnic majority and minority.

3. A third cluster of questions asks about the consequences of the digital divide. What are the stakes in unequal access? Are those without access missing the opportunities of the new technology in all its applications? Does unequal access mean a narrower base for economic growth, innovation, and competition in a particular country? Or is the main risk unequal participation in a number of fields of society, such as politics, education, culture, social relationships, and communities?

4. A fourth cluster of questions relates to the context of the digital divide issue. Is this a new phenomenon? Doesn't information inequality apply to all ages? Isn't the digital divide simply a matter of old inequalities reproduced in the appropriation of a new technology? Aren't different wealth and education, or the divisions of gender, generation, and ethnicity, again to blame for this type of inequality? Or are new inequalities appearing that are related to a new type of society? For

example, what does information inequality mean in the context of the evolving information society? What does unequal access to new communication networks, such as the Internet, mean for another indication of advanced contemporary societies: the network society?

5. The final cluster of questions addresses the policy issues. First of all, are there policy issues? Will the digital divide not close all by itself, as so many people have assumed lately? If something has to be done, what should be the strategy: to provide hardware, software, and services to deprived groups; to motivate people in using them, improving the technology and making it more safe, simple, and attractive, or to wage information campaigns; to educate ourselves out of the digital divide; or to design and produce better applications that really offer a surplus value to different groups of users? If policies are needed, what concrete instruments can be deployed? Who should bring them into action, and who will be responsible for the issue: governments; computer designers, producers, and service providers; information technology professionals; organizations of civil society; or individual citizens and consumers? Should a digital divide policy be the same in all parts of the world, or should it be different in, for instance, developed and developing societies?

2

A Framework for Understanding the Digital Divide

❖ A RELATIONAL VIEW OF INEQUALITY

This chapter contains the theoretical background and the backbone of the argument in the book as a whole. The conceptual distinctions and models concerned are offered as a framework for understanding the phenomenon of the digital divide, making it more appropriate for investigation. An elaborated framework for digital divide research is urgently needed, as current research suffers a lack of conceptual clarity and in-depth analysis. Even basic concepts such as access remain ill defined. The nature of most research remains descriptive: It has problems going beyond the demographics of differential new media access.

Relational and Individualistic Views of Inequality

One of the reasons for the descriptive nature of current research is the predominance of individualistic notions of inequality. Like most social scientific and economic investigations, digital divide research works on the basis of so-called methodological individualism (Wellman & Berkowitz, 1988). Differential access to information and computer technologies (ICTs) is related to individuals and their characteristics: level of income and education, employment, age, sex, and ethnicity, to mention the most important ones. This is the usual approach in survey research, which measures the properties and attitudes of individual respondents. Making multivariate analyses of several individual properties and aggregating them to produce properties of collectivities, one hopes to find background explanations. One is able to weigh the importance of these properties against each other and expect to find the most important factor correlating with unequal access. For instance, one finds the not very surprising result that income, education, and employment are strongly interrelated in their contribution to a particular level of access and the more startling result that age and gender are exceptionally important variables in describing differential access to the new digital media, as is explained in the next chapters.

These operations might produce useful data, but they do not automatically result in explanations, as they are not guided by theory or by hypotheses derived from theory. They remain on a descriptive level of reasoning. One is not able to explain, for example, what it is about age and gender that produces the differences observed. Another disadvantage of the individualistic approach to inequality is the social and political effect of simply blaming inequality of access on attributes of individuals such as a lack of motivation or the urge to spend money on things other than digital technology and the correction of inadequate digital skills.

An alternative notion of inequality uses a relational or network approach (Wellman & Berkowitz, 1988). Here the prime units of analysis are not individuals but the positions of individuals and the relationships between them. Inequality is not primarily a matter of individual attributes but of categorical differences between groups of people. This is the point of departure of the groundbreaking work *Durable Inequality* by the American sociologist Charles Tilly (1998), in which he notes: "The central argument runs like this: Large, significant inequalities in advantages among human beings correspond mainly to categorical differences such as black/white, male/female, citizen/foreigner, or Muslim/Jew rather than to individual differences in attributes, propensities, or performances" (p. 7).

The point of departure of this notion of inequality is neither the essences of individuals nor the essences of particular collectives or systems (e.g., capitalism, patriarchy) but the bonds, relationships, interactions, and transactions between people. "I claim that an account of how transactions clump into social ties, social ties concatenate into networks, and existing networks constrain solutions of organizational problems clarifies the creation, maintenance and change of categorical inequality" (Tilly, 1998, p. 21).

In looking for explanations of information and communication inequality in the use of digital technologies as a subset of social inequality in general, I adopt this relational view primarily. I hope it will produce new insight into the concrete mechanisms continually producing inequality of access. The most important categorical distinctions in this case are employers and (un)employed, management and executives, people with high and low levels of education, males and females, the old and the young, parents and children, whites and blacks, citizens and migrants. At the macrolevel of countries, we can observe the categorical inequality of developed and developing countries, sometimes indicated as countries from the North and countries from the South of the globe. The first of these pairs is the dominant category in almost every part of the world, the white-black distinction excluded. With two exceptions (the aged and parents), this also goes for digital access, as may be seen in the next chapters.

Benefits of the Relational View

A first instance of the insight offered by the relational view is an explanation of the differential appropriation of technology. Access to new technological means is a part of this. The dominant category is the first to adopt the new technology. It uses this advantage to increase power in its relationship with the subordinate category. I provide here a preliminary example of the type of explanation the relational view is able to produce. Gender differences in the appropriation of technology start very early in life. Little boys are the first to pick up technical toys and devices, passing the little girls, most often their sisters and small female neighbors or friends. These girls leave the operation to the boys, perhaps at first because the girls are less secure in handling them. Here a long process of continual reinforcement starts in which the girls "never" learn to operate the devices and the boys improve. This progresses into adulthood, where males are able to appropriate the great majority of technical and strategically important jobs and, in practice, keep females out of these jobs, whether they are conscious of this fact or not. This kind of explanation will unearth more of the actual mechanisms creating inequality than will an explanation in terms of individual attributes (females being less technical, etc.).

A second advantage of the relational view of inequality is the capacity to make better distinctions between types of inequality. Individualistic notions of inequality produce an endless number of differences that can be observed between individuals, with no particular priority among them. Even the basic distinction between *difference* and *inequality* poses problems. With the decline of social class as the most popular type of inequality in the explanation of social differentiation during the 1980s, other competing categories, such as gender and ethnicity, have come forward. Subsequently, the concept of inequality itself dissolved in the rise of postmodernist thinking, replaced by the concept of ubiquitous "difference." According to Blackburn (1999), it is crucially important to make a distinction between difference and inequality:

> The fact that everyone is different in all sorts of ways means they are not identical. Whether or not they are social equals is an empirical question, to which the answer depends on the structure of society. . . . Where differences are socially recognized, but only were recognized, they tend to form a basis for inequality. (p. 5)

The social recognition of differences and the structural aspects of society refer to the relatively permanent and systemic nature of the differentiation called inequality. In Tilly's definition, inequality is the unequal distribution of resources in society as a result of the competition of categorical pairs (noted earlier), which produces systems of social closure, exploitation, and control (Tilly, 1998, pp. 7-9). Although this competition and the resulting distributions are changing continually, the categorical pairs reproduce themselves through mechanisms of social closure, exploitation, and control (definition follows). These mechanisms are described extensively in the following chapters, with regard to information and communication inequality. In this way, inequality becomes a systematic or structural characteristic of societies. Using Tilly's terminology, it is "durable" as soon as it depends heavily on the institutionalization of categorical pairs (Tilly, 1998, p. 8).

Another advantage of the relational view is that it is not necessary to give priority to any of the pairs in advance. Their relative importance is a matter of empirical observation, producing different results for every society. Moreover, the pairs overlap with individuals. Take, for instance, a relatively poor, young, single, female, Jamaican teacher living in the United Kingdom. Her inclusion in the categories of educational workers, young people, and inhabitants of a developed country would put her on the "right" side of the digital divide, as may be observed in the next four chapters. However, being a female with relatively low income, perhaps living alone without a partner or children to share a computer or Internet connection, and being part of an ethnic minority means that she would most likely be on the "wrong" side of the divide. This example shows the complexity of this type of inequality. In this book, we will observe that labor market position, educational position, age, and sex or gender are the most important categorical inequalities determining the present digital divide but that they overlap in complicated ways and that they are not the only categories of importance. A relational view forces us to study the complicated combination of categorical inequalities.

A final benefit of the relational view of equality is that it directs our attention to relative inequality between people and their positions and resources. All too often, the metaphor of the digital divide suggests a yawning gap and the absolute exclusion of certain people. Earlier, I claimed that the simple picture of a two-tiered information society might better be replaced by the image of a continuum or a spectrum of positions across the population that is stretched when inequality increases (van Dijk, 1999, 2000). The absolute exclusion of access to digital media remains important, even in the developed countries, but the emphasis is shifting to the relative differences between people who already have access in a certain way or to a particular extent. Relative inequalities of access are becoming even more important in the information society and the network society. In chapters 7 and 8, it is argued that inequality in the information society is a matter of more or less access to information as a so-called primary good and as a positional good. In the network society, inequality is characterized by more or less access to positions in networks. In my opinion, individualistic notions of inequality are inadequate if one is to understand these relatively new kinds of inequality.

Problems of the Relational View

The main problem of this study is that the relational view is in an early stage of development. It is a minority view in contemporary social and economic science (Tilly, 1998, p. 29). A large number of operational definitions of the abstract concepts developed by this view have still to be made. However, its main disadvantage is the lack of available data. Data about relationships, ties, and networks are very scarce. Most often, I have had to work with demographic data that are recorded in the tradition of methodological individualism: individual units and their attributes cross-tabulated in data matrices of mainstream survey research. I have used them as proxies to support the argument as far as I can.

Another problem of the relational view is that it tends to disregard the characteristics of individuals, as compared to their relationships. This is unacceptable for the analysis in this book. I demonstrate that the explanation of the digital divide also requires personal categories. However, because these categories are of a more social and cultural than biological nature, they can be linked to social relations. For example, the personal categorical inequality of sex appears in this study as a particular gender relation in the appropriation of the new technology.

❖ THE CORE ARGUMENT

This book is about the causes and consequences of the digital divide. It is a detailed elaboration of the three elements of this topic: the phenomenon of the digital divide as a sequence of different kinds of access, the multitude of causes of this process, and its potential consequences. The ultimate purpose of this elaboration is to find ways to intervene in the process to solve the problem of the digital divide as it is currently defined.

The core argument of the book sets particular relationships between four states of affairs, in a process creating more or less information and communication inequality in using digital technologies:

1. A number of personal and positional categorical inequalities in society

2. The distribution of resources relevant to this type of inequality

3. A number of kinds of access to ICTs

4. A number of fields of participation in society

1 and 2 are held to be the causes, and 3 is the phenomenon to be explained, together with 4, the potential consequence of the whole

Figure 2.1   A Causal Model of the Core Argument

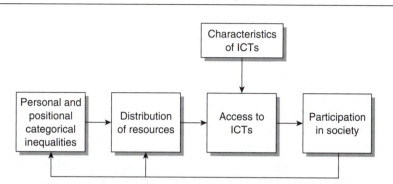

Note: ICT indicates information and communication technology.

process. Being part of a process, 4 feeds back upon 1 and 2, as more or less participation in several fields of society will change the relationships of categorical inequalities and the distribution of resources in society. Finally, a fifth state of affairs determining the type of inequality to be explained has to be added as a side factor: the special characteristics of information and communication technology. In this way, a dynamic model can be drawn that forms the core argument of the book. It can be seen as a circulation system, which will be filled with blood and have flesh added to it in the pages and chapters to follow. See Figure 2.1.

The core argument can be summarized in the following statements, which comprise the core of a potential theory of the digital divide:

1. Categorical inequalities in society produce an unequal distribution of resources.

2. An unequal distribution of resources causes unequal access to digital technologies.

3. Unequal access to digital technologies also depends on the characteristics of these technologies.

4. Unequal access to digital technologies brings about unequal participation in society.

5. Unequal participation in society reinforces categorical inequalities and unequal distributions of resources.

What is special about this argument in comparison to other descriptions and explanations of the digital divide? First, the independent factors are more conceptually elaborated, against a particular theoretical background, than they usually are in mainstream survey research on the digital divide. As noted earlier, this research sticks to the demographics, as independent variables that are all on an equal footing. In this book, a sharp distinction is made between (a) categorical inequalities, (b) the distribution of resources they produce and their direct responsibility for inequalities of access to ICTs, and (c) technological factors. What mainstream survey research calls "income" is one of the material resources in my analysis. The variable of *education* is comparable both to particular educational positions serving as a cause and to mental resources resulting from these positions. A final example is the variable of *occupation* that is so often correlated with more or less access to ICTs. In my analysis, a particular position in the division of labor in society causes a particular distribution of material resources (income, possession), social resources (relationships), cultural resources (assets and credentials), and mental resources (knowledge), concepts to be explained below. It is not occupation that directly causes unequal access to ICTs but a particular distribution of the four kinds of resources related to particular occupations.

A second characteristic of my argument is a refinement of the concept of *access*. The use of this term has caused a lot of confusion in recent years. As it has been equated with physical access all too often, calls to go "beyond access" have been made. In this book, the concept of access is elaborated as four successive kinds of access, covering "full" access, or a complete appropriation of this technology: motivational access, material or physical access, skills access, and usage access (elaboration follows).

A final and perhaps most important distinction between this argument and others is a particular elaboration of the potential consequences of unequal access to ICTs. Most often, arguments remain silent or implicit about them. Perhaps it is taken for granted that the digital divide is a problem. However, is it a problem when the old media and face-to-face communications are still able to offer the same opportunities as the new digital media? If this is not the case, for what reasons is the digital divide a problem? Are the reasons economical (fewer chances in the labor market and a smaller consumption market), educational (missed opportunities), political (lack of democracy and citizenship), security (the risk of those not connected and registered), or in some other area? All of these reasons implicitly appear in arguments about the digital divide as problems (see chapters 9 and 10).

In this book, my view on the stakes of the digital divide are made explicit. The stakes are participation in or exclusion from society in the present and future in a number of fields: the labor market, education, politics, culture, social relationships, spatial arrangements, and institutions such as citizenship and social security or health provisions. I argue that those at the "wrong" end of the digital divide will become second-class and third-class citizens, or no citizens at all. I demonstrate that it really makes a difference in these fields when people have no or limited access to the digital media. Finally, I clarify that having access only to the old media and the use of face-to-face communication, however favorable and important, puts people in an increasingly disadvantaged position.

❖ CENTRAL CONCEPTS

Categorical Inequalities

In the following chapters, I demonstrate that a number of personal and positional relational categories are responsible for unequal distributions of those resources needed for new media access. Personal relational categories are based on the physical or mental properties of individuals, such as age, sex, race, intelligence, and personality. Their significance for social inequality is that they also are social and cultural categories revealing differences of generation, gender, ethnicity, cleverness, and appeal, respectively. Positional relational categories are linked to particular positions in the division of labor, in education, in households, and inside or between nations. Inequalities based on these categories are fully social.

Not all relational categories produce unequal resources manifest in the digital divide. For instance, the personal relation Muslims-Jews, or Muslims-Christians, or any other religious categorical pair is not significant for information and communication inequality. The same goes for the positional categories of landlord-tenant and pimp-prostitute. Others are more important, such as the positions of doctor-patient and teacher-pupil. Access to digital technology might strengthen the position of patients and pupils in their relation to doctors and teachers. However, we will observe much stronger links between labor market or educational position and a particular location in the digital divide and between generation or gender position and a digital divide location. The list of most important relational categorical pairs linked to the digital divide is as follows.

Personal:

- ♦ Age or generation (young-old)
- ♦ Sex or gender (male-female)
- ♦ Race or ethnicity (white-black and many other pairs)
- ♦ Intelligence or cleverness (cognitive, emotional, social) (high-low)
- ♦ Personality (extrovert-introvert and other pairs)

Positional:

- ♦ Labor (employer-worker, employed-unemployed, management-executive)
- ♦ Household (parent-child, husband-wife)
- ♦ Nation (between: developing-developed; inside: city–rural area, citizen-migrant)
- ♦ Education (high-low, in school–finished, in school–dropout)

Resources and Mechanisms of Distribution

Relational categories do not directly create differences of access to new technologies. This only appears to be the case in mainstream survey research working on the basis of methodological individualism. Here, observed differences of access are simply correlated with individual attributes measured in variables such as age, sex, employment, and level of education. In the theoretical framework proposed in this book, (at least) three mechanisms link categorical inequalities with a particular distribution of resources. This distribution creates several kinds of unequal access (explanation follows). The mechanisms are *social exclusion, exploitation*, and *control*.

Social exclusion is a mechanism first described by Max Weber. It refers to efforts of the powerful to exclude the less powerful from particular benefits of a social relationship by keeping the relationship closed (Parkin, 1979, pp. 44-116; Weber, 1968, pp. 43-46). In the following chapters, it becomes clear that people with dominant positions in the categorical pairs I have listed are using their extended access to computers and network connections to exclude the other part of their pair from particular benefits in several fields of society. One of the supporting mechanisms is a process called "opportunity hoarding" by Charles Tilly (1998): "Members of a categorically bounded network acquire access to a resource that is valuable, renewable, subject to monopoly, supportive of network activities, and enhanced by the network's modus operandi" (p. 10). The importance of this mechanism for inequality in the network society is explained in chapter 8.

Exploitation is a mechanism specifically elaborated by Karl Marx. The concept is adopted by Tilly (1998) in a definition that sounds fully Marxian: "Powerful connected people command resources from which they draw significantly increased returns by coordinating the effort of outsiders whom they exclude from the full value added by that effort" (p. 10). In the next chapters, chapter 6 on usage access in particular, we will see that this discredited notion might be rehabilitated in the explanation of the use of ICTs as tools of exploitation in employer-worker and other relationships.

Control is the enactment of a relation of authority in several of the categorical inequalities listed here. Access to digital technologies might change the relationships of power between (for example) management and executives, males and females, parents and children, teachers and students, doctors and patients. In many cases, this will also lead to more or less unequal distributions of all kinds of resources (listed later).

The resources distributed by categories of people exerting these mechanisms are called "forms of capital" by some social scientists. Most often, these scientists refer to the work of Pierre Bourdieu and James Coleman. Bourdieu (1986) distinguishes between economic capital (property and money), social capital (connections and obligations), and cultural capital in the three forms of the embodied state (training of the mind and body), the objectified state (possession of cultural goods), and the institutionalized state (educational qualifications). Coleman (1988) makes a comparable distinction between physical capital (material forms of property), social capital (relations among persons that are characterized by obligations, expectations, trust, information channels, and norms or sanctions), and human capital (skills and knowledge). The only reason to call these tangible and intangible items *capital* is that they tend to accumulate with people, and in this way they adopt a structural character. However, these terms (forms of capital) do not have the explanatory value they suggest. They remain descriptive terms for items of unequal distribution. They are the perceivable result at a particular time of the processes (mechanisms) and categorical relations producing them. For this reason, I prefer the more neutral and descriptive term *resources*.

Making resources and mechanisms of distribution so central to my approach to the digital divide reveals much about the concept of or theoretical approach to inequality that I have chosen. This concept or approach stresses the *means* and the barriers or constraints to reaching *particular* goals, such as equal opportunities in particular fields. Contrary to Amartya Sen (1992), I am not in favor of a very general and morally grounded concept of equality as a goal that has a close relationship to the concept of freedom. From a philosophical point of view, this may be interesting, but in handling concrete types of inequality, such as the digital divide as an instance of social and information inequality, it does not show us the way. Instead, I have adopted a materialist approach of taking resources (or forms of capital) and primary and positional goods (see chapters 7 and 8) as the point of departure. The resource approach is inspired by Ronald Dworkin (1981) and the goods approach by John Rawls (1971).

The following list of resources are linked to the different kinds of access to digital technology discussed in this book:

- ◆ Temporal resources (time to spend on different activities in life)
- ◆ Material resources (income and all kinds of property, computer equipment and services excluded)
- ◆ Mental resources (knowledge, general social and technical skills, not digital skills—which will be explained)
- ◆ Social resources (social network positions and relationships)
- ◆ Cultural resources (cultural assets, such as status and all kinds of credentials)

As intermediary factors, resources should be clearly distinct from categories on the one side and kinds of access on the other. For example, having computer equipment and services should be excluded from material resources; otherwise, we would be suggesting a tautological relation with access to this technology. Further, intelligence should be kept apart from its results, the mental resources of knowledge and skills obtained. All resources should be measurable in a quantitative way in regard to individuals having more or less access to digital technologies. Resources are the perceivable results of the preceding processes listed earlier. For instance, the (unequal) distribution of mental resources is, first of all, the result of personal intelligence and educational positions stirring particular mechanisms of social exclusion and control in the transfer of information.

Successive Kinds of Access

A distinctive feature of this book is a conceptual division of the general term *access* into four specific, successive kinds of access to digital technology, computers, and Internet connections. These kinds or stages are

1. Motivational access (motivation to use digital technology)

2. Material or physical access (possession of computers and Internet connections or permission to use them and their contents)

3. Skills access (possession of digital skills: operational, informational, and strategic)

4. Usage access (number and diversity of applications, usage time)

An alternative would be to preserve the term *access* for material or physical access only, as many people do when they narrow the problematic of the digital divide to the possession of computers and Internet connections. Since the year 2000, there have been several appeals to go "beyond access" and to deal with the usage of the new technologies. I do not think this alternative is a good option, as it reinforces a narrow conception of the digital divide and because the process of appropriation of a new technology is only finished with a particular, satisfactory use of it—the actual purpose of access.

I have argued before that access problems of digital technology gradually shift from the first two kinds or stages of access listed here to the last two (van Dijk, 1999, 2000). When the problems of mental and material access have been solved, wholly or partly, the problems of unequally divided skills and usage opportunities come to the fore. I propose to define digital skills not only as (a) the skill to operate computers and network connections but also as (b) the skill to search, select, process, and apply information from a superabundance of sources and (c) the ability to strategically use this information to improve one's position in society. These are called instrumental, informational, and strategic skills, respectively.

The last stage of access is usage access. Here I make distinctions between, among others, simple and advanced applications of the new technology and applications for entertainment and for work, for schooling, and for one's career. Figure 2.2 contains a model of the four stages of access as they are described here.

Figure 2.2 should be explained as follows. The four successive stages or kinds of access are supposed to be cumulative. The first, motivation, is conditional to this. Trying to gain physical access might be successful. When this happens, appropriation of the new technology

Figure 2.2   A Cumulative and Recursive Model of Successive Kinds of
Access to Digital Technologies

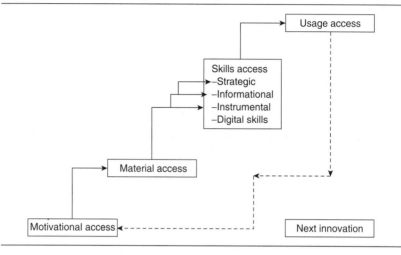

tends to lead to the development of digital skills of all kinds. Both physical access and adequate digital skills are requirements for a satisfactory use of the potential applications of the new media. Subsequently, the stages are recursive, as they return, wholly or partly, with every new technology or innovation. For example, after the diffusion of computers and narrowband Internet connections, we observe the diffusion of broadband technology. Here problems with material and usage access return: This innovation is expensive, and really new applications only started developing between 2000 and 2005. Again, people with many material and mental resources were the first to adopt broadband. However, I argue that the motivation and skills to use broadband appear to be a lesser problem for those who already have computers and narrowband connections. Which kinds or stages of access return with every new technology is partly determined by that technology's properties.

Properties of ICT (Hardware, Software, and Content)

Technological determinism is rejected in this book. The digital divide primarily is a social problem, not a technical one. This does not mean that the properties of the technology concerned are irrelevant. Some of these properties support access and others reduce it. In chapter 6, it is explained that hardware and software properties, like the current complexity and expensiveness of ICTs, are frustrating access; characteristics such as the multifunctionality and network effects of ICTs, on the other hand, are extending it. The same goes for the properties of information produced and retrieved in the new media. The formats of some kinds of information are more approachable and usable than comparable formats in the old media. Other formats lead to information overload, or the information is in a foreign language or is the kind of information that is irrelevant to many people.

Fields of Participation in Society

The main consequences emphasized in this book of more or less access to the new media are social inclusion in or exclusion from several fields of society. These consequences are subsumed under the concept of (societal) participation. The fields under consideration are the labor market, education, politics, culture, social relationships, spatial arrangements, and institutions such as citizenship and social security or health provisions. I attempt to show that people who have less access to the digital media increasingly have smaller chances of participation in these fields. In this way, they may become second- or third-class workers, students, citizens, consumers, and so on.

❖   A FRAMEWORK MODEL AND FUTURE RESEARCH

A Causal and Sequential Model of Access

These central concepts and the core argument and statements described can be concentrated in a causal and sequential conceptual model that serves as the framework for the whole book. It is a complicated model that combines the causal statements and analytic distinctions of successive kinds of access explained before (Figures 2.1 and 2.2). See Figure 2.3. This extensive model cannot be put to the test as a whole. To be able to test it in empirical research, all concepts have to be made operational in survey questions, observation categories, or experimental measures.

In the coming years, I hope to test all parts of this model, with the help of colleagues in my home country and abroad. The sequential core of the model has already been put to the test in survey research in the Netherlands, producing data for the population in 2001. Using the techniques of so-called path analysis and structural equation modeling, it appeared that a model of accumulation in which every successive kind of access was a condition to the following kind was a better fit to

Figure 2.3   A Causal and Sequential Model of Digital Technology Access
by Individuals in Contemporary Societies

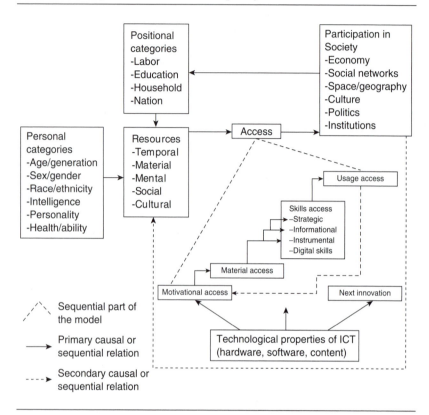

Note: ICT indicates information and communication technology.

the data of computer and Internet access than an alternative model that
considered the four kinds of access to be equally important and relatively independent of each other (de Haan & Iedema, in press).

The largest part of the causal model contained in Figure 2.3
hypothesizes that a number of personal and positional categories
explain the distribution of a number of the resources that are held to be
directly responsible for the four successive kinds of access. Most available data on the digital divide are appropriate for one or more of the
relationships and statements concerned. As has been argued before,
these data are rather fragmentary and are confined to simple demographics and single-shot studies of 1 year. In the following chapters,
I relate them using my conceptual framework and select the best
longitudinal data I can find.

The third part of the model relates the properties of ICTs to the whole process of access. To test this part of the model would require large-scale historical comparative research on the differences and similarities of the technological properties of the old and new media and their effects on media access. Do they support or impede access for all? In this book, I am only able to make a list of these factors (chapter 6).

The last and ultimately most decisive part of the model is the consequential part of it. A basic assumption in this model is that more or less access to the new media means more or less participation in several fields of society. Unfortunately, empirical data about the relationship between more or less computer or Internet access and more or less participation in these fields are very scarce. In chapter 9, I have gathered all the data and arguments I could find to describe this relationship.

Priorities of Future Research

Future research will not only be needed to test the parts of this model but to fill a large number of gaps still characterizing digital divide research. A short list of the most important lacunae contains the following issues. First, as has been argued before, digital divide research suffers from a lack of *theory*. In the past 5 to 10 years, it has remained at a descriptive level, emphasizing the demographics of income, education, age, sex, and ethnicity. The deeper social, cultural, and psychological causes behind the inequality of access have not come to the surface. The most striking fact is that the digital divide has not been discussed against the background of a general theory of social inequality, other types of inequality, or even a concept of human inequality in general. The only theoretical background that has played a role is the diffusion of innovations theory. However, in chapter 4, I argue that this theory only has a limited role to play in the explanation of the evolution of the digital divide. Its most important popular expressions, the so-called S-curve and the trickle-down principle of the adoption of innovations, pose serious problems, and they bear a determinist flavor. Now that we have reached the stage of causal model building, explicit theories are urgently required.

A second problem is the lack of *interdisciplinary research.* Following the usual demographics and the emphasis on physical access, there is a preponderance of sociological and economic research. Contributions from psychology and even from communication and education studies are relatively small (Bucy & Newhagen, 2004; Mason & Hacker,

2003). However, in this book, I hope to show that the digital divide cannot be understood without addressing issues such as attitudes toward technology, technophobia or computer anxiety, communication in new media diffusion, educational views of digital skills, and cultural analyses of daily usage patterns.

The next lacuna is a lack of *qualitative research.* Most digital divide research is based on quantitative data collection and tries to describe the large picture of the problem. Although this produces vast amounts of correlations, it does not bring forward the precise mechanisms explaining the appropriation and division of the technology concerned in everyday life. This is what I argued before suggesting the elaboration of a relational view of inequality. In this book, I also portray the big picture of the digital divide, up to the global level. However, I call repeatedly for the necessity of qualitative research, which will show how inequalities are created in particular small individual and group settings.

The fourth basic problem with digital divide research is that it is rather static, both in arguments produced and in empirical data used. There is a lack of *dynamic approach* (van Dijk & Hacker, 2003). For example, according to the trickle-down principle, present technologies such as a personal computer and an Internet connection will soon be available to all because they are getting cheaper and easier to use by the day. Such reasoning seems dynamic, but actually it is static, because one forgets that the technology is changing fast and that the people who adopted it first do not stop to obtain new technologies. As soon as the laggers have caught up, the forerunners have already moved further ahead and are using a more advanced technology. Concerning the data used in digital divide research, cross-sections in time of a single year are common, but longitudinal data are scarce. They are only beginning to appear now in regular or annual replicated survey research. It goes without saying that a model such as the framework model proposed here cannot be tested without a large number of time series data.

A final and most serious omission of current digital divide research is the lack of *conceptual elaboration and definition.* Filling this gap is the most urgent task. Unfortunately, even the most basic terms and concepts still are ill defined. The most important is the concept of access itself, of course (see Bucy & Newhagen, 2004). Others are exact definitions of the technology concerned and the way it is used. What exactly is a *computer* and an *Internet connection*? What precisely is *having access to the Internet* and what parameters delineate the phrase *having access*? What are the so-called *digital skills* and similar terms? What exactly is *Internet use*? In this book, I want to contribute to the conceptual elaborations required.

3

Motivational Access

❖ INTRODUCTION

The first phase of access, considered as a process of full appropriation of the new digital technologies, is a preliminary condition of all other phases. It is the motivation of potential users to adopt, acquire, learn, and use these technologies—computers and Internet connections in particular. The appearance of this motivation should not be taken for granted. This is often done by both uncritical admirers of the digital media and technology pushers who want people to use computers and get connected to the Internet the sooner the better, as if this would automatically solve their problems. In this chapter, we observe that our societies do not only contain information and technology have-nots but information and technology want-nots. Some people are not intense seekers of information and communication. Others do not like computers and are not attracted to the Internet. In the next section, I attempt to identify who these want-nots are. Even in developed countries, about 20% of the adult population declines to use computers. According to particular surveys, about half of those currently not connected to the Internet in these countries explicitly refuse to get connected. Lack of motivation is not limited to the reluctant; it also is present in adopters who rarely or irregularly use these new media.

In the third section, I focus on the computer and Internet dropouts and on the people who are temporarily or permanently disconnected. Here we note that user populations are continually shifting. Many people do not get access once and for all, to keep connected for the rest of their lives. They drop out for some time, or they pull out forever. Some become heavy users, others lose their interest in frequent use of the technology.

What are the reasons for this presence and absence, this rise and fall of motivation? The process appears to be composed of a complex series of backgrounds that is difficult to unravel. It varies from relatively simple lacks of interest, time, money, and skills to a difficult-to-grasp mixture of technophobia, computer anxiety, lack of self-confidence, and a particular image of the self in relationship to the technology concerned. Here, I analyze these reasons and link them to the resources and the personal or positional categories of people distinguished in the former chapter. I argue that most of these reasons are completely rational and based on proper experience. The finger should not be pointed at backward people refusing to adopt a technology that could bring them prosperity; instead, it should be directed to digital technology itself, which offers insufficient surplus value or fails otherwise, for instance in user friendliness, safety, and attractiveness. Here we might find solutions to problems of motivational access, in case people are looking for them.

❖ THE HAVE-NOTS AND THE WANT-NOTS

If we look for reasons people offer for not having computers or Internet access in surveys of computer possession and network connections, we will find a mixture of motives that indicate both a condition of deprivation and lack of motivation. Clearly, many of the have-nots also are want-nots. These two aspects are extremely difficult to separate. Some people with a lack of means rationalize their condition, indicating that they do not want or need the resource under consideration. Others really are not motivated to adopt the new technology, and they will deliberately spend their money elsewhere. To unravel the two aspects, we need to take a closer look at the motives people give for not having a computer and Internet access. A survey among 501 German offliners in 1999 revealed the following reasons for not buying a personal computer (PC).

Figure 3.1   Reasons Mentioned by German Offliners in 1999 for Not
Buying a Personal Computer (N = 501)

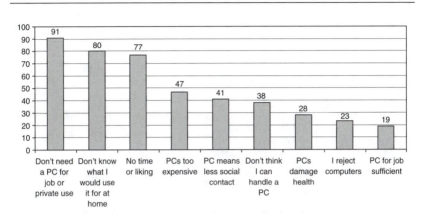

Source: ARD/ZDF-Arbeitsgruppe Multimedia (1999a).

Most contemporary surveys contain questions about motivations to get access to the Internet or to refuse such a connection. The reasons are close to the motivations for accepting or refusing computers. In the year 2000, a U.S. National Telecommunications and Information Administration (NTIA) survey showed that representatives of households who had a computer or WebTV but never accessed the Internet gave the following reasons as most important: "don't want" (31%), "too expensive" (17%), "can use it elsewhere" (10%) and "no time" (9%). Two years later, the Pew Internet and American Life Project found a list of reasons for not being online among the 42% of American nonusers that is shown in Table 3.1.

When we take a close look at the reasons supplied in Figure 3.1 and Table 3.1, we are able to summarize them as the following five basic motives:

1. No need or significant usage opportunities

2. No time or liking

3. Rejection of the medium

4. Lack of money

5. Lack of skills

Table 3.1   Reasons for Not Using the Internet, Percentages of Nonusers (United States, 2002)

	Major Reason	Minor Reason	Not a Reason
I don't want it	52	16	26
I don't need it	52	19	24
I'm worried about online pornography, credit card theft, and fraud	43	14	37
It's too expensive	30	18	42
I don't have time to use the Internet	29	17	49
The Internet is too complicated and hard to understand	27	19	43
Don't have a computer	11	n.a.	n.a.

Source: Lenhart et al. (2003).

Note: n.a. indicates not applicable. N = 910 for nonusers who have never been online. Margin of error is ±3.5% at 95% confidence.

Only the last two and the fourth are the motives of have-nots. The first three are mainly motives of people who do not want the new technology. The reasons that explain these motives make sense. In many jobs, computers and Internet connections are not required (yet). People who have left school some time ago and have no school-going children themselves do not need a computer for education. For information, communication, and entertainment they still have other options (such as radio and television, the telephone, print media, and traditional games and sports). It is no surprise that among the people saying they do not need or want the new media are a relatively large number of elderly, retired, and unemployed people; housewives; manual laborers; people from rural areas; and people with low education in general (ARD/ZDF-Arbeitsgruppe Multimedia, 1999a; Lenhart et al., 2003). The reason "no time or liking" is more complicated. Here we do not only find the categories just mentioned but also many "haves" with busy jobs or other activities but no need to use computers themselves, as well as parents with young children. Some of these people simply hate computers; others have pressing interests that do not include computers.

A number of special motives are rejections of computers and Internet access for social, moral, and safety reasons. They are the clearest indication that one should not always look first to the defects of potential users when motivational access is lacking. About 5 years ago, many potential German computer users thought that using this medium caused health problems (such as repetitive strain injury and computer or Internet addiction) and that it would be detrimental to social contacts. This opinion may now have diminished, but the problems with objectionable activities on the Internet may have increased. For 43% of American nonusers, worries about pornography, child abuse, credit card theft, and fraud on the Internet were major reasons to decline access in the year 2002. Women, parents, Americans more than 30 years old, and those with less education were the groups most likely to report concern over online content (Lenhart et al., 2003, p. 10).

Lack of money and operating skills are still very important reasons for nonusers. Thirty percent of American nonusers say that the cost of using the Internet is a major reason to refuse access, and for 18%, it is a minor reason. Twenty-nine percent agree that the complexity of Internet use is a major reason, and 19% say it is a minor reason to decline access. Among this group, people with low income and low education, women, and African Americans are dominant (Lenhart et al., 2003, p. 11).

A conspicuous result of several American and European surveys among Internet users and nonusers, reported between 1999 and 2003, is that about half of current nonusers said that they would refuse to go online in the near future. In the Pew Internet and American Life Survey of 2002, it appeared that 56% of the total 42% of American nonusers declared they would not go online (Lenhart et al., 2003, p. 16). This is 23% of the population of the United States. The categories that score above the average of 56% are females in general (61%, compared to 49% for males), seniors (62% between the ages of 50 and 64 years, and 79% for ages 65 and older), non-Hispanic Whites (62%), people with less than a high school education (70%), retired persons (76%), and people with disabilities (65%). This means that many retired, disabled, and low-educated people refuse access. The fact that a lot of (non-Hispanic) Whites also turn down access—62%, compared to only 39% of African Americans offline and 38% of Hispanics offline—testifies to the fact that this is not only a matter of deprivation but also of lack of interest.

❖ INTERMITTENT USERS, DROPOUTS, EVADERS, AND THE TRULY UNCONNECTED

One of the biggest mistakes in digital divide research is the assumption that the users of digital technology are either in or out, included or excluded. In analyzing nonusers, it soon becomes evident that many

Figure 3.2   Spectrum of Internet Access in the United States (2002)

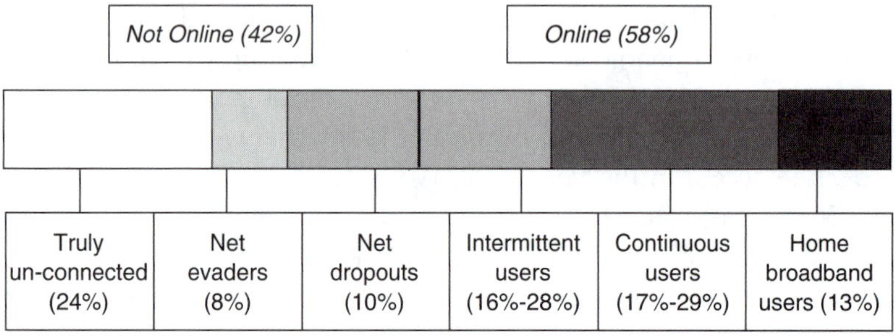

Not Online (42%)			Online (58%)		
Truly un-connected (24%)	Net evaders (8%)	Net dropouts (10%)	Intermittent users (16%-28%)	Continuous users (17%-29%)	Home broadband users (13%)

Source: Adapted from Lenhart et al. (2003).

of them are sometimes with computers and sometimes without them and that they are occasionally connected and occasionally disconnected. Rightfully so, the Pew research team has called their 2003 survey report about nonusers *The Ever-Shifting Internet Population* (Lenhart et al., 2003). Another misconception is to think that nonusers are loners. In fact, many of them use computers and the Internet via others, that is family, friends, or other sources. They refuse or cannot afford to be connected themselves, but they take advantage of the resources of others.

This does not mean that the problem of the digital divide should be downplayed. It implies that it has to be seen in a dynamic perspective. Many people assumed to be included are in fact nonusers, and many nonusers benefit from a technology they formally do not access themselves. The best way to portray the dynamic perspective required is to picture it as a *spectrum of access,* ranging from those with full access using the best available technology in a mass market in the developed countries (broadband, these days) to the truly unconnected. The truly unconnected are people who have never had any access to computers or the Internet and who often are not even aware of this technology. The Pew research team (Lenhart et al., 2003) has classified such a spectrum for the American population as shown in Figure 3.2.

Reading the 2002 statistics on American users and nonusers, one is able to conclude that there is no reason to trivialize the problem of the digital divide because so many nonusers were once users (dropouts) or refuse to get online (evaders). The same number of people are registered as online but in fact are nonusers from time to time. They are called intermittent users.

The composition of the four categories of present or potential nonusers (intermittent users, dropouts, net evaders, and the truly unconnected) can be described in the following way, using survey research data from the Pew Internet and American Life Project (Lenhart et al., 2003), the NTIA (2000), and the longitudinal 1995-2000 surveys reported by Katz and Rice (2002). Unfortunately they offer American data only, but their advantage is the amount of detail they offer for analysis.

Intermittent Users

Between 27% and 44% of American Internet users in 2002 said that they had gone offline for extended periods in the past (Lenhart et al., 2003, p. 19). The most important reasons these intermittent users gave were technical problems with a broken computer or a failing Internet connection (18%). The next most important problems were moving to another place or no longer having access to the place where they used to have access; for example, a school or a job (13%), and lack of time (12%). Finally, the whole range of reasons described earlier for nonusage in general was given (Lenhart et al., 2003, p. 23): concern about online crime, privacy, and children's safety (12%); do not need it (7%); do not like it (7%); too hard to use (4%); and too expensive (3%). Intermittent users are disproportionately young, single, students, minorities, part-time workers, novice Internet users, with a low income and low level of education (Lenhart et al., 2003, p. 23). The common denominator seems to be an insecure and mobile position in society.

Dropouts

Dropouts are people who have more or less permanently lost connection to the Internet, voluntarily or not. The number of dropouts is large in every survey among American users. It centers around 10% each time. According to Katz and Rice (2002, p. 68) approximately one fifth of all people who have ever used the Internet are or have dropped out at some time. These researchers summarize the results of four surveys between 1995 and 2000 in five main reasons to stop using the Internet: all kinds of physical access problems (22.9%), cost (15.7%), too hard or complex to use (14.9%), not interesting (12.2%), and time (7.5) (Katz & Rice, 2002, pp. 72, 75). Net dropouts tend to be single, young people less than 40 years old, parents with a lack of time, minorities

(African American), novice Internet users, and people with low levels of education and low incomes (Katz & Rice, 2002, pp. 76-78; Lenhart et al., 2003, p. 21).

In additional analyses, the Pew research team and Katz and Rice discovered a number of interesting differences between dropouts and current users. Dropouts are aware of computers and the Internet and have learned to use them via family or friends, not by themselves (Katz & Rice, 2002, p. 79). However, dropouts also say that they have hardly any people they can turn to for support when they need help (Lenhart et al., 2002, p. 22). Compared to users, they feel they have less control over their lives and they have a more negative outlook on society. These are clear indications of motivational problems. Two thirds say they will return to the Internet someday (Lenhart et al., 2003, p. 19)—primarily people with temporary physical access problems—but one third may have disconnected for ever.

Net Evaders

The most explicit motivational problems appear among the so-called net evaders. Most of them belong to the "haves," as they live in households with Internet connections, and many of them even belong to the social elite. Twenty-eight percent of net evaders have used the Internet in the past (Lenhart et al., 2003, p. 20). At least a part of this group lets other household members or employees search for information on the Internet or send and receive e-mail on their behalf. Others are proud of never using the Internet, or they state lack of time or interest as the most important seasons. The Pew research team reached the conclusion that their decision not to use the Internet was "a distinct lifestyle choice" (Lenhart et al., 2003, p. 20).

Who are these people? They appear to be more likely to be men than women, young than elderly, White than African American, rural than urban, rich than poor, and highly educated than less educated (Lenhart et al., 2003, p. 20). With the exception of the rural community type, this is the exact opposite of all other average nonusers! It appears to be a luxury problem, if it is a problem at all. However, if we dig somewhat deeper, we may observe that a large part of this group consists of parents who leave the use of the net to their children, never learning to use it themselves. Then there is the top management of organizations who order their subordinates to use the computer daily but never use it themselves. Net evasion may also be a matter of cognitive dissonance and an easy escape from embarrassment.

The Truly Unconnected

The final group to describe is the truly unconnected. In the United States, this was 24% of the population in 2002. In most other developed countries, and all developing countries, this share of the population is much bigger, as may be seen in the following chapters. This group has never used the Internet before and does not live in households with a connection. This goes for 69% of American nonusers in 2002. A large percentage of this group (31%) is composed of people who say that they know no or very few people who go online. The first distinguishing mark of the truly unconnected is their social isolation. They lack the social networks that would encourage them to go online. They have a low level of education (74% have only high school or less). They also have low incomes (43% have incomes of below $30,000 a year). They tend to be older than other nonusers (62% are more than 50 years old), and there is a clear majority of women (59%). These data are all from the same 2002 Pew survey (Lenhart et al., 2003, pp. 25-26).

These last percentages depict a part of the population that really is deprived. However, the reasons supplied for not being connected reveal a difficult-to-unravel mixture of have-not and want-not causes (see Lenhart et al., 2003, pp. 25-26). Some 54% of the unconnected say they do not need the Internet, and 53% declare they do not want it either. More than half (55%) do not think they are missing anything by not being online. They tend to have a more negative view of the Internet, and they are more worried about its consequences than other nonusers—and much more than users. However, "only" 33% find the Internet too expensive and 27% too complicated or hard to use. Instead, the Internet's lack of perceived usefulness seems to be more important for this group (Katz & Rice, 2002, pp. 91-94). "The Internet does not have appeal for low-income and low-education people" (p. 93). I discuss this statement (as far as I think it is true) in chapters 5 and 6. Here I want to raise some doubts about it, as the want-not reasons might also be a form of cognitive dissonance, "sour grapes" reasoning, and plain ignorance of the Internet.

❖ REASONS TO (NOT) GET ACCESS

Resources and Motivation

As with all other kinds of access, motivational access is primarily explained by particular resources people have or lack. The distribution of these resources depends on the positional categories people occupy and the personal categories to which they belong. These are central statements of the model described in the previous chapter. In this section, I make my first arguments for these statements, starting with motivational access.

Resources are available means that are used as a source of supply or support in accomplishing particular aims. In this case, the aims concern the decision to acquire other means first: particular digital means. Who reaches this decision?

It is obvious that those with sufficient *material* resources will have less difficulty in reaching the decision. Purchasing and maintaining a PC and an Internet connection is considered too expensive by many nonusers. People from the lowest income category in the United States (those who earn less than $30,000 per year) comprised 18% of American Internet users and 41% of nonusers in 2002 (Lenhart et al., 2003, p. 6). Having other property also is important, according to many surveys. People having many other media at their disposal, such as televisions, newspapers, mobile phones, PDAs, and audio or video equipment, are more likely to have computers and Internet connections as well. A third type of material resource required is the availability of physical access to computers and networks. This appears to be a problem in rural or remote areas and in poor neighborhoods with few public access facilities. Moreover, the most important reason for intermittent use of and dropout from the Internet (observed earlier) was a broken computer or failing connection.

An equally important resource is *time*. This factor is underestimated in most digital divide research. It is mentioned as a major reason by 29% of nonusers (see Table 3.1). For intermittent users, dropouts, and evaders, this reason is relatively more important than for the truly unconnected. For people with busy jobs, who do not regularly use computers, or who are parents of small children, this is even likely to be the most important resource that is scarce in relationship to computer use. Conversely, for adolescents, seniors, and the unemployed, a surplus of time is a prime impetus to start experimenting with computer and Internet use.

Another underrated factor is the *social* resources of potential users. This factor is not mentioned as a reason for nonusage by the users themselves, but it might be one of the most important background explanations for (the lack of) motivation. People become aware of the importance and applications of the new media via social contacts with family, friends, colleagues, teachers, neighbors and acquaintances. With them, they are able to observe the operation of computers and the Internet in practice. As we will see in chapter 5, these social contacts also are the agents who first learn and advise other users in using computers; this is far more common than users gaining computer knowledge in formal education or computer classes. On the other hand, the truly unconnected described earlier often are socially isolated, and they know very few people who work with computers or have access to the Internet. Thus having a large social network consisting of relatively many computer and Internet users is vital if a user is to cross the motivational access barrier. Several digital divide investigators have paid attention to the importance of so-called social capital for access (Katz & Rice, 2002; Lenhart et al., 2003; Warschauer, 2003b). However, the effect of social networks is not as straightforward and unconditional as these observations suggest. The Pew research team discovered that people who live in dense social networks and who belong to community groups and social clubs based on face-to-face communications are also less likely to go online (Lenhart et al., 2003, p. 41). Their physical proximity appears to satisfy their needs. The importance of social resources for access seems to be most important for people who combine diffuse and long-distance networking with proximate contacts. Both are helpful in obtaining the awareness and experience of computer use.

So far, I have not discussed the most important reasons supplied by non-users: "I don't want it," "I don't need it," and a rejection of the medium in general. These reasons may be related to a lack of particular mental and cultural resources, although they may be completely rational, as I argue later. *Mental* resources are of both a cognitive and an emotional kind. *Cognitive* resources are basic knowledge of computers and the Internet and the ability to use them. Many nonusers do not appear to be well informed about the actual characteristics of computers and the Internet (Katz & Rice, 2002; Lenhart et al., 2003). It goes without saying that they have no or very few skills to operate computers. It is no surprise that 27% of nonusers call the Internet too complicated and hard to understand and that they say this is a major reason for not using it.

Emotional resources are self-confidence and a particular self-image based in (not) using computers and the Internet. In a Dutch survey executed in 1996, many people who were not able to command a PC experienced this lack of skill as a personal shortcoming: 26% of the Dutch who were less than 50 years old and 40% of those older than 50

(Doets & Huisman, 1997). These kinds of self-concepts are rarely revealed by respondents in quantitative survey research. To unearth this type of data, one has to conduct qualitative research, as Laura Stanley did among San Diego non–computer users and new computer users in 2001 (Stanley, 2001). She discovered that a perceived ineptitude and a lack of self-confidence in using computers were important barriers for access. "Three out of four new computer users retrospectively described how the thought of learning computers provoked feelings of anxiety sufficient to all but abandon the idea [to acquire computer literacy]" (Stanley, 2001, p. 12). Here the denial of any necessity for access (don't want it, don't need it) might be a case of cognitive dissonance, an attempt to solve an attitude inconsistency.

However, on other occasions, the rejection of the new media is a consistent attitude. Here the actual answer is, "I don't like it." The negative characteristics of the new media are pronounced. They do not fit the *cultural* resources of many potential computer and Internet users. These are matters of lifestyle, interests, hobbies, affinities, and status marks. They are the most important background to the conspicuous role of age, gender, and ethnic or class minority culture in the adoption of digital technology (to be discussed). Having access and using digital technology are part of the lifestyle of most contemporary young people. These things belong to the status marks of the young. Conversely, access and use do not fit the favorite cultural resources of many older people. The same goes for (older) women.

Stanley (2001) has demonstrated that particular minority cultures, such as Latino and African American cultures in poor, working class neighborhoods, have more affinity with manual labor and face-to-face communication than with intellectual labor and computer-mediated communication. Working class males, especially those with a Hispanic or African American background, tend to think that computers are for women and girls. In the San Diego study, a 37-year-old Mexican American bus driver explained his view: "When I was in high school, my friends would tell me that computers and typing are for girls and ask me why I would want to do that. I shouldn't have listened to them. Even though that was a long time ago, it kinda stuck in my mind" (Stanley, 2001, p. 18).

In a qualitative interview study conducted in Austin in 1999, several poor community boys brought up that their friends did not find computers or the Internet socially acceptable (i.e., "cool"). Computer classes were held to be "boring," too much focused on "keyboarding," and "something girls do" (Rojas, Straubhaar, Rowchowdhury, & Okur, 2004, pp. 121-122).

All social classes and cultural groups reject computers and the Internet in general when their use contradicts the moral and cultural values of particular class or group members, parents in particular. This is often the case when the superabundance of pornography, racism, libel, and slander on the Internet and the violence in so many computer games is considered.

Positional Categories and Motivation

Now we are ready for an explanation of the distribution of these resources by both positional and personal relational categories. As a large part of motivational access is psychologically determined, personal categories have a relatively big impact here. However, particular positions on the labor market, in education, and in households also are primary and evident reasons for motivation to acquire access. Having a particular kind of job or wanting to find one, as well as attending a school requiring computer work and Internet access, are the most important reasons behind such motives. The next most important reason is having a family with school-going children. There is also the general reason of belonging to a nation in which computers and Internet connections are widely distributed and accepted and where they are becoming a necessary means by which to participate in society.

These positions determine the possession of the material and social resources described first. They affect the income and the motivation required for the purchase of computer hardware and software. They also create the social relationships with colleagues; other students; and children, parents, or partners needed for getting interested in the new technology and learning how to use it. Some of these positions also shape the time resources that are necessary for sufficient motivation. Busy jobs or training programs (without computers) and a busy family life with small children cause time resources to be scarce.

Even the distributions of the mental (cognitive) and cultural resources described here are partly a matter of particular labor, educational, household, and ethnic majority or minority positions. Computer knowledge, skills, and lifestyles are correlated with particular jobs, schools, family lives, nations as a whole, and ethnic cultures in parts of nations. The following chapters supply the data for these correlations.

Personal Categories and Motivation

With regard to the relationship between personal categories and motivational access, most studies and data highlight age, gender, and race or ethnicity. However, psychological and physical categories, such as personality, intelligence (cognitive, emotional, and social) and health, might be just as important, although there are fewer data available. The motivation to gain access is much higher for young people than it is for seniors. It is common knowledge that there is a generation gap in access to and use of digital technology, with elderly people above the age of 65 staying far behind. In general, there is a gap in the developed countries between people older than 35 to 40 years who have had no training with computers at school and who have not have the opportunity to catch up in a job that requires computer experience and those less than 35 years old who were trained at schools or in jobs.

The interesting motivational phenomenon in the relationship between the old and young age categories is that seniors and parents easily leave the appropriation and skills for use of digital technology to young people in general and to their (grand) children in particular. Young people take the initiative on many occasions in digital daily life. The same happens in gender relationships, a classic occurrence in the appropriation of technology by both sexes (Cooper & Weaver, 2003). Potential female users simply leave the attempt to get access or to finish a job perceived to be difficult to male users. Here we may observe a combination with age, labor, and education. Elderly women, women with low education or without jobs, and housewives appear to be especially less motivated to start using computers and the Internet.

If we look at the large differences of access to computers and the Internet between different racial and ethnic groups in the United States, with Asians taking the lead far above African Americans or Hispanics and even passing Anglo-Americans, we must conclude that these differences have a basis in motivation, ambition, and particular cultural propensities and preferences. Among some ethnic minorities, preferences collide with the predominant English and Anglo-Saxon nature of computer or Internet language and culture. This theme of ethnic relations is explored in chapter 6.

Personality is an underrated categorical difference in regard to motivational access. I have already mentioned the role of self-confidence and of a particular self-image (seeing oneself as someone who should or should not use computers). The self-confident will always take the lead above those who are not self-confident in the appropriation of technology. The same goes for those who see themselves as working with computers and those who cannot seen themselves this way (Stanley, 2001). Self-confidence in using computers also is called computer self-efficacy (Brosnan, 1998).

Several of the so-called Big Five personality dimensions (agreeableness, conscientiousness, neuroticism, extraversion, and openness) are known to be related to computer use, attitude, and stress (Hudiburg, 1999). Neuroticism aggravates problems experienced in approaching and using computers and extraversion alleviates them (Hudiburg, 1999). Finn and Korukonda (2004) found that agreeableness (willingness to submit) and conscientiousness mediated positive feelings about computer use. The same was observed for extraversion and openness to new experiences. In considering a relational view on the inequality of personality pairs, it would be interesting to know whether the opposite positions on the five personality dimensions influence each other in the appropriation of technology and computer access—for instance, whether extraverted, open, agreeable, conscientious, and nonneurotic people would dominate their counterparts in accessing technology. Unfortunately, there are no data with which to answer this question.

Among the less self-confident, open, agreeable, and conscientious and among the more neurotic, the phenomenon of *computer anxiety* appears (Brosnan, 1998; Chua, Chen, & Wong, 1999; Fariña, Arce, Sobral, & Carames, 1991; Maurer, 1994; Rockwell & Singleton, 2002; Rosen & Maguire, 1990). This is a feeling of discomfort, stress, or fear experienced when confronting computers. Those with high levels of computer anxiety are also less likely to use the Internet (Rockwell & Singleton, 2002).

Often, computer anxiety is not only a precursor of computer experience but also a consequence. *Computer frustration* is a matter of bad experiences with computers failing to do what people want them to do (Bessière et al., 2004). Other responses to this frustration can be aggression toward the machines used; regression (socially immature behavior); fixation on old, ineffective computer input; withdrawal; and resignation (Bessière et al., 2004, pp. 95-96).

Computer anxiety is often supposed to be a general type of *technophobia*, a fear of technology in general and a distrust in its beneficial effects. I think computer anxiety is a particular emotional consequence of a (perceived) personal inability to work with digital hardware and software, but technophobia is a particular attitude and opinion produced by a view of humanity, its artifacts, and the world. Technophobia as a rejection of the world of computers was very widespread at the beginning of the digital revolution in the 1980s and the first half of the 1990s. At the turn of the century, after the widespread diffusion of computers and the Internet hype, it started to lessen and turn into a more focused criticism of the technology, emphasizing problems such as excessive use of computers and the objectionable content of or lack of security on the Internet. However, computer anxiety remains as an access problem for elderly people, comparatively more women than men, and people with low education and disabilities in particular. The problem is surmountable for most potential users (Stanley, 2001), but it remains a real barrier for some of them.

A lack of all kinds of intelligence also is an undervalued motivational access problem. Actually, it is rather strange that this problem is undervalued, as it is common knowledge that those with technical affinity and skill are always asked by the lesser skilled to answer their questions and solve their problems. Technical skill is a case of cognitive intelligence. It increases the motivation to use computers and the Internet. The technically skilled always take the lead in the appropriation of a new technology. Emotional intelligence is important for a self-controlled and balanced use of computers and computer-mediated communication in comparison to physical human sources of information and communication. Social intelligence is required to combine the purposes and workings of computer-mediated communication and face-to-face communication in a fruitful way. However, in this case, people with both high and low emotional and social intelligence might be motivated more (than people with average intelligence) to get access to computers and networks. Those with high intelligence take advantage of the emotional and social benefits of computer use and evade the disadvantages, such as social isolation and addiction. Those with low emotional and social intelligence become heavy users as a means of social escape and immersion into computer interfaces (these are the so-called geeks, or nerds).

A last personal category to be mentioned is health. With the right adaptive technologies, disabled persons could gain great advantages from access to computers and the Internet. In fact, they have much less access than people without disabilities, and they have a lower motivation. Only 38% of American disabled persons used the Internet in 2002, and 65% of disabled nonusers in that year declared that they did not want to go online in the future (Lenhart et al., 2003, pp. 30, 17).

❖ CONCLUSIONS

In this chapter, I have argued that motivation is the initial condition of the whole process of new media access and appropriation of the technology concerned. Motivation partly explains why subsequent kinds of access are reached—or not. It influences the decisions to purchase a computer and network connection, to learn the requisite skills, and to use the interesting applications. Some people are not sufficiently motivated to attempt to obtain access. These want-nots consist of a diverse collection of intermittent users, dropouts, and net evaders. Currently, they comprise about half of the people having no access in the developed countries. The other half are the "truly unconnected," who have no choice about computer use or few opportunities to choose. The dividing line between these two groups is not sharp, and it is ever shifting.

The reasons supplied in surveys and interviews for this lack of motivation are both emotional and rational. They include no need for use or for significant usage opportunities, no time or liking, rejection of the medium, lack of money, and lack of skills. The people with a lack of motivation to gain access to computers and networks should not be accused of being backward. Instead, the finger should be pointed at the current flaws of the technology concerned: lack of user friendliness, usefulness, attractiveness, affordability, and safety. The work of Donald Norman (1988 and 1999 in particular) supplies plenty of evidence.

I have tried to explain the level of motivational access in regard to, first of all, the distributions of a large number of resources. Temporal, mental, material, social, and cultural resources may all be responsible for this motivation. In their turn, these distributions were explained by positional and personal categories. It is no surprise that personal categories appear to be dominant. This goes not only for age, sex, and race but also for the deeper mental categories of personality and intelligence of all kinds. These are responsible for the important phenomena of computer anxiety and technophobia.

The analysis in this chapter has shown that motivational access problems are complicated. In the final chapter, I argue that policy perspectives range from attempts to improve the technologies concerned and wage information campaigns to personality guidance and computer didactics.

4

Material Access

❖ INTRODUCTION

After acquiring the motivation to get access, the challenge for new users is to act on it. They may purchase a computer and Internet connection themselves, or they may use those of others. This may be done privately at work or at school, or with family and friends, or in public places at a particular access point. Public opinion, public policy, and all kinds of research are strongly preoccupied with this second type of access. Many people think the digital divide will be closed as soon as everyone has a computer and a connection to the Internet. In my opinion, the problems of the digital divide and information inequality do not disappear when this happens, as other, deeper divides appear. This is the main message of this book.

Nevertheless, having material or physical access is a necessary condition for development of the requisite skills and ability to use this technology. The importance of this condition should not be downplayed in stressing other types of access.

Fortunately, there is an overwhelming amount of statistical and survey data on differences in physical access to computers and network connections by relevant demographic categories and countries.

In this book, the evidence is examined mainly in regard to the diffusion of computers and their networks. From time to time I refer to the possession of other new media, such as mobile telephones and digital television. As they have spread more equally among people of high and low social class, we might be able to learn something from this difference.

Unfortunately however, most survey data on computer and Internet penetration or use are too unreliable and invalid for us to be able to draw definite conclusions from them. Internet statistics are notoriously unreliable because of the defective sampling, nonresponse, and bad quality of much (marketing) telephone interviewing or Web surveys. Often, these statistics lack validity because the surveyors have to cope with the novelty of the affairs to be observed, and they produce only time-sensitive data that are valid for only one year. Research would be improved by large surveys with samples that are representative or by census material and other official statistics. Further, to make statements and to test hypotheses about trends in computer or Internet penetration and use, longitudinal data or time series are required. These are rather rare, but they are beginning to appear now. From 1994 until 1999, we could use the biannual Graphics, Visualization and Usability Center (GVU) surveys, which were done on Internet users (GVU Center, Georgia Institute of Technology, 2001). Time series could be constructed from their data. However, a major problem with these surveys was that they involved (self-)selective sampling. The regular tracking surveys of the Pew Internet and American Life project; the University of California, Los Angeles (UCLA) Internet reports using U.S. data from 2000 and later; and the annual Nua, Inc., and International Data Corporation worldwide Internet access data are a major improvement in representativeness and continuity.

Census material and other official statistics are beginning to appear as well in the United States, Europe, and East Asia. Departments of the United Nations, the World Bank, the Organisation for Economic Co-operation and Development (OECD), and the International Telecommunications Union are supplying sufficiently reliable data about countries worldwide. The trends of the 1980s, the 1990s, and the beginning of the new century can be derived from them. Whenever possible, I base my conclusions on these longitudinal tracking surveys and official statistics.

Another basic problem of computer and Internet penetration research are the fuzzy ways of indicating access. Even physical access—the type of access that is easiest to observe—is defined in diverging and shifting ways. Sometimes it is defined as the (individual) possession of computer equipment and network connections; at other times, the opportunity to (collectively) use equipment or connections. Place of access is also mixed, as if there is no important difference between home access and access at work, at school, or in public places. On other occasions, access is defined in terms of use; for example, whether someone has once used the Internet or has used the Internet in the last month or week, but kind of use and place of use are ignored. In this way, statistics on computer and Internet access often are exaggerated, and real access problems are obscured.

In the following extended section, I show that almost every digital divide of material access in the period between 1985 and 2000 has grown, in all parts of the world. The only exceptions are the gender division in material access, which has decreased in most countries, and the disability gap, which remained equal. For the other divides, I demonstrate the widening of the gap: labor position (occupation and employment), educational position (level of education), household position (membership, composition, and household income), nations (developed and developing), and the personal demographics of age and race or ethnicity. However, as was promised in the first chapters of this book, I go beyond description and simple demographics and look for explanations in the distribution of resources and in positional and personal relational categorical differences.

In the trends these divides reveal, particular patterns can be perceived. The question rises as to whether these patterns are part of a particular curve of adoption. In the third section, I deal with the answers that mainstream diffusion theory would give to this question; the determinism of its models (e.g., the S-curve of adoption) and its phasing (innovators, early adopters, etc.), however, leave it open to criticism.

In section four, the future perspectives of the trends and curves described are discussed. The most popular opinion is that divides will narrow and evaporate according to the trickle-down concept, with some having the technology now and others getting it later. Those who get it first pay for the innovation, and they make adoption cheaper for those who get it last. It will become clear that perspectives are not that simple. I show that divides of elementary physical access will decrease—and, in fact, have already started to decrease in the developed countries—but that the total amount of spending for material access to digital technologies is not declining. Further, I argue that new technologies, such as broadband, arrive that reveal the old divides once again and that divides in other kinds of access (skills and usage access in particular) are deepening the material access divide.

❖ TYPES AND PLACES OF MATERIAL ACCESS

In this chapter, I make the following distinctions concerning material access. First, material access is differentiated as *physical access* and *conditional access*. Physical access is the entry to hardware, operational software, and services of computers, networks, and other digital technologies. Conditional access is the provisory entry to particular applications, programs, or contents of computers and networks. Increasingly, physical access is not enough. For particular applications, programs, and contents, not only special software and data carriers on CD or DVD are needed but also user names and passwords. The conditions are payment or a particular position, membership, or allowance. Conditional access becomes ever more important for material access. A currently popular marketing model of the computer, network, and peripheral equipment industries is to sell the equipment and connections as cheaply as possible so that the relatively expensive software, applications, and content may serve as the main sources of profit. Game computers and printers are cheap, but games and ink cartridges are expensive. So-called free Internet connections actually are e-commerce vehicles, advertising showers, and privacy sellers. On the Internet, customer relationship marketing is practiced by the "free" distribution of public domain software, freeware, and share ware with advertising, advanced services, and content with special value as the main sources of returns.

In this book, the definition of physical access to digital technologies is mainly confined, for the sake of simplicity, to possessing or having entry to PCs and Internet connections. These can be realized at the following points of access:

- ◆ Work
- ◆ School
- ◆ Public places: public institutions, such as libraries and community access centers, and commercial outlets, such as Internet cafés, hotel lobbies, and airport lounges.
- ◆ Someone else's house

♦ Home
♦ In transit: laptops, PDAs, mobile Internet

These points have been arranged according to the known diffusion of computers and networks in society. The evolution of this diffusion is a shift from work and school as the primary access points to home access. In the meantime, public places and the homes of neighbors, relatives, and friends have served as provisions for the disadvantaged. The last stage of this evolution is ubiquitous computing at work, at school, at home, and all public and mobile places. However, developing countries are still in the first stages of limited access at work and schools and the predominance of access in public places. For instance, the access points in Peru in 2001 were 83% Internet cafés (*cabinas publicas*), 18% workplaces, 17% schools, and only 11% homes. In the United States in 2001, primary access points were 43.6% at home, 19.6% at work, 11.9% at school, 5.8% at someone else's house, 5.4% at libraries, and 0.6% at community centers (NTIA, 2002).

The next important distinction regarding physical access is the type of computer and the type of network connection. It goes without saying that access to a traditional home or game computer, an old PC, or a small computer in a PDA or other handheld device is not the same as access to a powerful, advanced, multimedia machine. The same goes for a 28 or 56 KB modem dial-up link to the Internet as compared to a broadband "always on" connection via cable, satellite, or DSL.

All these details about physical and conditional access, among them access conditions, access points, and types of hardware, software, and services available for particular users make a tremendous difference to the potential applications and to the level of inequality between users. I refer to them repeatedly in the following description and analysis.

❖ WIDENING AND NARROWING PHYSICAL ACCESS GAPS

In the last 10 years, we have been overwhelmed by statistics revealing large differences of physical access to computers and the Internet among different parts of the population and among different countries. Frequently, statistics show the differences between people in relation to their income, education, employment status, occupation, (geographical) place of residence, age, sex, and race or ethnicity. Most gaps have been wide, and increasingly so, between 1985 and 2000, as can be observed in the "gap pictures" of Figure 4.1, which summarizes trend data from the United States and the Netherlands. When these pictures were drawn, the point change over time, not the expansion rate, of the categorical values was taken as the point of departure. Arguing that the digital divide is shrinking, as the lowest categorical values are expanding at a higher rate than the highest values, is misleading (Martin, 2003). This happened in, among others, the latest NTIA reports (NTIA, 2000, 2002). Here is an example of how it is not true. When a developing country increases its Internet access rate from 0.1% to 2% while a developed country climbs from 20% to 40%, the expansion rate of the developing country is 10 times as high as that of the developed country. However, it is much more telling in this case that the point change of the developed country is much larger: Many more new Internet users have been added.

To prevent misleading statistical presentations, the so-called odds ratios—that is, the chances of *both* the groups of users and nonusers gaining access—can be calculated on an equal basis. Recalculating the NTIA 2002 data to find these odds ratios, Martin showed that between 1998 and 2001, the decrease of American nonuse was largest for the richest households and that the poorest income category adopted the Internet more slowly than individuals from the richest income category (Martin, 2003, p. 5). This is the opposite of the claims made in *A Nation Online* (NTIA, 2002).

The question arises as to which factor is the most important in determining physical access. Income is mentioned most, although it strongly correlates with education, employment status, and occupation. The occasional multivariate analyses reveal that income is indeed the most important factor for physical access. For example, in a large-scale telephone survey of the Netherlands in 1998, it appeared that household income was the most important factor explaining possession of ICTs (computers, Internet connections, mobile phones, and other digital equipment), closely followed by education and with a remarkably high correlation with age and gender, all of them as separate (controlled) factors (de Haan, 2003; van Dijk & Hacker, 2003; van Dijk et al., 2000).

Most likely, income, as an explanatory factor for physical access, is more important for those living in poor countries and less important for inhabitants of rich countries. In poor, developing countries, it is a luxury to individually own expensive digital equipment. Here, physical access

Figure 4.1   Gaps of Income, Education, Employment, Age,[a] and Ethnicity[b]

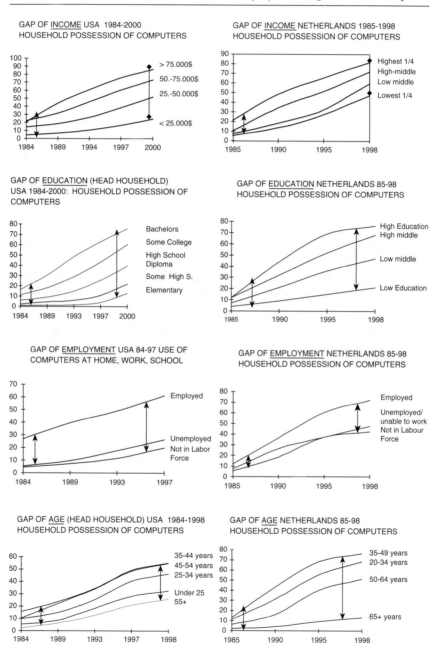

(Continued)

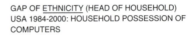

GAP OF ETHNICITY (HEAD OF HOUSEHOLD)
USA 1984-2000: HOUSEHOLD POSSESSION OF
COMPUTERS

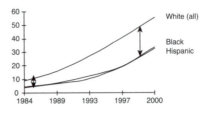

Source: U.S. information, NTIA (1999, 2000), computed from U.S. Census Bureau data; Netherlands information, van Dijk, Liset, and Rijken (2000).

a. United States, 1984 through 2000; Netherlands, 1985 through 1998.

b. United States only.

is mainly realized in public places or at work or school. Worldwide, income seems to be the most important factor explaining the possession of digital equipment (see the International Telecommunications Union [ITU] World Telecommunication Development Reports, notably ITU, 2002). In a survey conducted in 2000, income still appeared to be the most important factor in digital mobile telephone access and use in rich countries such as the United States; however, with Internet access and use, income came second after education (Katz & Rice, 2002).

Material, Mental, and Social Resources

In chapter 2, I promised to go beyond the usual shallow variables (e.g., income, education) used in explaining differences of access. The first question is, Which resources are responsible for differential material access? The next question would be, Which positional and personal relational categories are able to explain the distribution of these resources in regard to material access? Considering the resources first, one can tell from the available data that not only material resources (income and possession of other equipment) but also mental resources (technical knowledge and skill) and social resources (social networking) are decisive in obtaining material access to ICTs. The 1998 Dutch survey referred to earlier showed in a multivariate analysis that mental resources were the first factor explaining the personal possession of ICTs, material resources the second, and social resources the third (de Haan, 2003; van Dijk et al., 2000; van Dijk & Hacker, 2003). An explanation of these resources follows.

Temporal resources are important for motivational access and usage access (see the data in chapter 6) but people having busy jobs, studies, or families with children usually do have computers and Internet connections. Conversely, people with many temporal resources, the unemployed and the retired, have limited material access. However, as we saw in the previous chapter, the surplus of time these groups have motivates some of their members to purchase a computer and Internet connection. Once again, it should be explained that *material resources* consist not only of income but also of digital hardware, software, and services that belong to the individual or household, as well as the collective right or opportunity to use them at jobs or in schools. In the last two decades, these collective rights and opportunities have been among the most important stimuli for computer and Internet ownership at home. Thus material resources are an extended and cumulative pool of means that is used for all kinds of purposes. People with many material resources usually have computers and Internet connections everywhere (at work, at school, at home, and on the road). Most likely, they not only possess a relatively large number of computers and Internet connections but also fixed and mobile phones, audiovisual media, print media, and all kinds of household equipment (de Haan, 2003; van Dijk et al., 2000).

Mental resources, in this context, consist first of all of the cognitive resources needed to operate and use computers and Internet connections in a satisfactory way. When these resources are insufficient, people will not (try to or be allowed to) individually or collectively possess these technologies. Aside from these cognitive resources (skills), people will need sufficient knowledge of computers and Internet connections to purchase the hardware, software, and services they need. Most often, they obtain products that have more or other capacities than they need. Sometimes they buy the cheapest products, which can end up causing them a lot of trouble or may not offer what they want.

Having sufficient *social resources* also is vital in getting material access, both physical and conditional. Social resources include social networks of information, communication, and support. The bigger and tighter the social networks are, and the more wealthy and powerful people they contain, the more supportive they are in the acquisition of material access to all kinds of things. First, social networks at work and at school put employees and students in the position to collectively possess and use computers and their networks. In this position, they acquire from their colleagues all interest in, information about, user experience of, and support in getting access to and using these technologies. These exchanges spill over into homes and friendship networks. Social networks of (extended) families, friends, acquaintances, neighbors, and fellow community members are the second most important source of information, communication, and support in the appropriation of digital technology in daily life. They help people in getting cheap new or second-hand hardware and copies of software. They assist in getting broken hardware fixed and connected. They provide support in getting Internet access. Finally, they assist new users in learning to operate computers and to work with particular programs. Even in an individualized and sparsely populated country with high home computer access, such as the United States, more than 5% of the online population had access at someone else's house in 2001 (NTIA, 2002).

Positional Categories

Which categories explain the distribution of resources? Here the positional relational categories of labor, education, household, and nation or region are in the first place.

Position in the *labor market* (such as employment or unemployment and particular occupations) probably is the most important set of categories. These categories control physical access at work and the orientation to future work of people at schools and who are unemployed. The relationship between employer and employee and between manager and executive determines what physical and conditional access to computers and their networks is permitted. There is an enormous difference in physical access at home between the employed and the unemployed or those who are not in the labor force (any more). Here access among the employed is, roughly speaking, double as high as for those who are unemployed, retired, and unable to work, even after the turn of the century (see Figure 4.1). In fact, many of the employed have double access, as they also have a computer at work. This fact is often neglected in access statistics and their interpretation.

Who among the employed have access to computers at work is largely determined by the sector and type of work. The American laboring population of the year 2000 had 56% computer users. Managers and professionals were 80% computer users, and technical, sales, and administrative support occupations were 70% users. However, the gap in the rest of the occupations is wide: Precision production, craft, and repair occupations only reach 31%; service occupations, 25%; people in farming, forestry, and fishing, 21%; and, finally, operators, fabricators, and manual laborers are only 20% computer users.

The authors of the NTIA report *A Nation Online* hold the educational level of the people in these occupations and, to a lesser extent, their gender distribution responsible for these large differences in computer use (NTIA, 2002, p. 58). However, it seems more likely that the occupational requirements themselves are the real cause. The last-named occupations in the list I have given, from service to fishing, use all computer applications significantly less than managers, professionals, and sales or administrative support people (p. 60).

Practices at work are decisive in physical access to computers and the Internet both at work and at home. Perhaps the most important table among the many of *A Nation Online* reveals that all American disadvantaged groups (people with low income, education, ethnic minorities, and the elderly), surprisingly, have more than average access to the Internet if they use this medium at work (see Table 4.1). There still is a difference of about 20 percentage points between the average U.S. household and the groups that use the Internet at work, but the familiar gaps have disappeared for about half (originally they showed 30-40 percentage points of difference; see Table 4.1).

The second most important positional category is *education,* both current position at school and educational attainment. Regular education (primary, secondary, and tertiary) is very important for young people in the acquisition of physical access. In the developed countries, it used to be the most important position, but this has now shifted to the home, where most (pre)school-age children get access to computers for the first time. However, older generations—that is, people born in the developed countries before 1965, or even before 1970—usually have not been put in contact with computers, let alone the Internet, through school at all. In these countries, the computer just entered the classroom on a massive scale in the 1990s and the Internet only at the end of that decade. When the generations involved have had no experience with computers and Internet use on the job afterwards, their chances of physical access are small. The prime remaining stimulus then is having school-going children (discussed later). The consequence is that adult education and public provisions, special computer classes, community access centers, and the like are becoming necessary for physical access, and even more for skills access, for a large part of these generations.

Table 4.1   Internet Access of Selected Households by Use at Work, as a Percentage of U.S. Households (2001)

	Total	Someone in Household Uses Internet at Work	
		Yes	No
All households	50.5	76.8	34.8
Income less than $15,000 per year	17.7	57.2	14.8
Income $15,000-$24,999 per year	28.3	52.2	23.8
Less than high school education	18.2	54.2	14.5
Black	30.9	59.1	20.7
Hispanic	32.0	63.1	22.1
55 years old or older	33.9	71.6	25.5

Source: NTIA (2002, p. 63).

Note: Other than income, characteristics refer to reference person of household.

Regular education motivates most young people in the developed countries to get access to computers and the Internet at their school and to ask for home access to finish schoolwork. School practices lead to all kinds of collective exchanges of new ideas and applications of computer and Internet use among pupils, who have more than average motivation to use digital technology anyway because of their age. A particular position of educational attainment also stimulates physical access, primarily through ensuing jobs and secondarily through intellectual interest (cultural resources). The result is that in physical access to computers in households, gaps of education increased between 1985 and 2000, both in the United States and in the Netherlands (see Figure 4.1).

A third positional category affecting material access to ICTs is *household composition*. Families with school-going children have the highest computer ownership and use, as well as Internet connections and use; families without children and single-person households have the lowest figures in all these areas (Madden, 2003; NTIA, 2002).

The background of this distribution is (a) household size with more potential users, (b) household income with more potential earners, and (c) the presence of children needing a computer for school and for play. The presence of school-going children is perhaps the most important driver in trying to get physical access. In the Netherlands, the families of relatively poor ethnic minorities with children in secondary education had a rate of computer possession of more than 85% in 2001, far above the average of all households (70%). In all Dutch households with children in secondary education, computer possession was 97% in that year (Sociaal-Cultureel Planbureau, 2002, p. 64). A computer has become a basic necessity for these families.

A final positional category determining material access is residence in a particular *nation or part of it* (region or urban-rural location). This is a category at the macro level, up to the global scale. "Access to digital technologies is heavily contextual, depending on the structure of opportunities available within each society" (Norris, 2001, p. 33). Geographical digital access divides between countries and within countries have been impressive from the 1980s onward, and they are growing. Between 1990 and 2002, the gaps of computer and Internet access between countries of high and low income and human development have grown considerably. This is revealed by the diverging lines of the graphics portrayed in Figure 4.2, a and b. The 45 high-income countries, according to the World Bank list of 2003 (United Nations Statistics Division, 2004a), show a much steeper rise in computer ownership and number of Internet users per 100 inhabitants than the 88 medium-income and 67 low-income countries with low development. A similar picture could be drawn from the list of countries with high, medium, and low general development (according to the *Human Development Report 2003*, United Nations Development Programme [UNDP], 2003). A comparable figure could be composed showing the gap between northern and southern European countries. Computer ownership and Internet access are about twice as high in the northern European countries as they are in the Southern European countries, and in 2003 this gap was still widening, according to the Eurobarometer (Gesellschaft Sozialwissenschaftlicher Infrastruktureinrichtungen [GESIS], 2004).

The economic wealth of nations is the most important factor in explaining these gaps (Hargittai, 1999), but it is by far not the only one. Other causes, to be further discussed in chapter 10, are

- The availability and cost of digital technology in a country
- The general level of literacy and education in its population
- The language skills of its population, ability in English in particular
- Level of democracy (freedom of expression)
- The strength of policies promoting the information society in general and access in particular
- A culture that is attracted to technology, computers, and computer communication (see Norris, 2001, pp. 49-64, and Warschauwer, 2003b, pp. 52-62).

Figure 4.2   Personal Computers and Internet Users per 100 Population in
High-, Medium-, and Low-Income Countries (1990-2002)

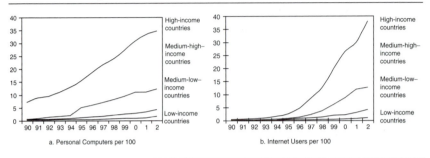

a. Personal Computers per 100   b. Internet Users per 100

Source: United Nations Statistics Division (2004b, 2004c), based on ITU estimates. Graphics
calculated and designed by author.

A broader set of indicators of development than income only is
produced by the Human Development Reports of the United Nations
(see United Nations Statistics Division, 2004b, for these indicators).
Even this broader set does not sufficiently explain the differences
between nations. For example, Greece, ranked 24 on the world list of
human development, contained only 8 PC and 13 Internet users per 100
inhabitants in 2001; Hong Kong, China (ranked 26), had 38 PC and 38
Internet users; Singapore (28) had 50 PC and 41 Internet users; and
South Korea (30) 48 PC and 52 Internet users per 100 inhabitants. Every
nation has its own collection of causes explaining physical access. The
low numbers in Greece might be a matter of culture (less attraction to
computer culture and communication in a culture that lives a great deal
outdoors and communicates primarily face to face), language (poor
English), or the high costs of technology (lack of competition). The
higher numbers in East Asia might be a matter of governmental technology promotion, attraction to computer culture, and relatively low
prices of technology.

Within nations, the divides between the regions, provinces, or states
and between city and countryside also are growing, in most cases. In the
developing countries, a trend of extremely uneven development is perceivable (Norris, 2001; UNDP, 2003; Warschauwer, 2003a). Here, material access increasingly is concentrated in a few municipal and urban
centers and the rest of the country lags far behind. This is a case of
so-called combined and uneven development: The highest social categories are linked to the globalization process by a relatively fast adoption of technology while the other categories are losing contact and
stagnating. In the developing countries, all digital divides related to

particular positional and personal categories appear to be wider and deeper than in the developed countries. The main reason seems to be higher inequality in the general distribution of resources, primarily material and mental resources (education).

Personal Categories

The most important personal relational categories explaining differences of material access are age and gender (de Haan, 2003; van Dijk et al., 2000; van Dijk & Hacker, 2003). With growing *age,* material access to computers first increases and then, after the age of 50 years, decreases, to decline very fast after the age of 65 (see Figure 4.1). Children and adolescents have relatively few personal possessions, but they take very much advantage of the household possession of computers and Internet connections and the availability of these in schools. In fact, children and adolescents appropriate the technology, to a large degree, from their parents, and they are the ones who use it most of the time. When they leave the parental home, they start their own households with few means and relatively few computers at their disposal (although they have access at school and in the workplace). After they start their own family, the number of computers and Internet connections reaches its peak, especially when children reach school age. Currently, this number drops again when the children leave the house, but this is only the case if these people, most often older than 50, have acquired no computer experience. When the present younger generations, who have computer experience, pass their 50s, they will most likely maintain material access. However, between 1985 and 1998, the gap between people older and younger than 55 in the United States and older and younger than 50 in the Netherlands has grown (see Figure 4.1). The biggest difference is with people currently older than 65. They strongly lag behind in material access, as they lack material resources (income), mental resources (technical knowledge and skill), social resources (isolation), and cultural resources (no interest, hobby, or status needs would be advanced by computers).

The only good news, from an equity and emancipation point of view, is the narrowing *gender* gap between 1985 and 2000. In the United States, physical access for both sexes was equalized by the end of the 1990s (Horrigan & Rainie, 2002b; NTIA, 2000, 2002; Rainie et al., 2000). In other developed countries, this only goes for the youngest generations, who have gained access at school (for Europe, see Eurobarometer, 1997-2003). In developing countries, the gender physical access divide is still very large (United Nations Development Programme, 2001). However, the gaps of skill and usage of digital technology between males and females have not disappeared at all. On the contrary, they tend to rise, as we may observe in chapters 5 and 6.

Girls and women mainly take advantage of the possession of computers and Internet connections in the households they are living in. In school, they will most likely be treated on an equal basis with boys and young men in regard to physical access to the scarcity of computers and Internet connections. At work, they have a better chance of working with computers than do their male colleagues. Currently the majority of computer work is done by females in the United States and some other developed countries (NTIA, 2002). In these countries, the main remaining physical access gap is for older women who live alone and have no job or other activity requiring computer work.

The third personal relational category is *race or ethnicity*. In most multiethnic societies, there is a majority ethnic or racial category and several minority categories. They differ in economic wealth, positions in the labor market, and cultural resources. One of the differences is unequal material access to the new media. Between 1984 and 2000, this "gap of ethnicity" between white Americans (of all kinds) on one side and African and Hispanic Americans on the other has grown concerning the possession of computers (see Figure 4.1, bottom). Internet access increases between 1993 and 1997 were greater for American whites and even more for Asian Americans than for Native, African, and Hispanic Americans (Bikson & Panis, 1999). Between 1997 and 2001, the gap of ethnicity in Internet access kept increasing, as Asian American access rose from 27% to 60% (+33), whites from 25% to 59% (+34), although African Americans only increased in access from 13% to 39% (+26) and Hispanics from 11% to 31% (+20) (NTIA, 2002, p. 22). A significant gap still remains in each case after controlling for income and education. The gaps are most likely caused by different cultural resources and interests. The enormous divide between new immigrants from Asia, on the one hand, and from Latin America, on the other, cannot be explained otherwise.

The only other personal category clearly related to material access is *health and (dis)ability*. Computers and the Internet could be a very important resource for people with disabilities, especially for those who have difficulty in walking, but in fact, this group is less likely than the population as a whole to use computers or the Internet. Between disabled Americans and those without disabilities, percentage point differences of 10% to 20%, depending on type of disability, in access to these media have been found in U.S. Census Bureau research from 2001 (NTIA, 2002, pp. 65-72). Two years earlier, point differences were about 20% (NTIA, 2000, p. 65). The NTIA report concluded that even when income, education, and age are accounted for, people with disabilities are less likely than those without disabilities to be Internet users (NTIA, 2002, p. 71). A peculiar fact is that Americans with walking problems have the lowest level of access. In 2003, the Pew research team observed that only 38% of disabled Americans go online, compared to 58% of all Americans (Lenhart et al., 2003). The gap of disability stayed the same size between 1999 and 2002. In the Pew study, 28% of disabled nonusers said their disability made it difficult or impossible for them to go online. A prime material access problem for people with disabilities is that the available technical and software solutions to various disabilities (vision, hearing, typing, and others) are very expensive.

❖ PROJECTIONS OF THE EVOLUTION OF THE DIGITAL DIVIDE

The divisions of material or physical access related to personal and positional categories all reveal the same pattern, except for the gender gap (decreasing) and the disability gap (remaining the same). Between 1985 and 2000, they increased, if we look at the annual point percent changes of categorical values. However, as we approach the turn of the century, some increases flatten. As one is able to see in the downward slope of the curve of the highest categories having access, they appear to reach a level of saturation. This at least goes for the curves of income and age in both the United States and the Netherlands and for education and employment in the Netherlands (see Figure 4.1). In opposition to that, the expansion rate of the lowest categories having access is higher. Thus the question arises as to whether these divides of material or physical access will disappear in the future. The answer to this question is a particular projection of the evolution of the digital divide as a physical access problem.

In making these projections, one usually departs from diffusion of innovations theory. A very popular model of diffusion theory is the S-curve of adoption of innovations. After a comparatively slow start with only innovators and early adopters accepting the innovation, adoption suddenly rises steeply upwards among a majority of early and late users. When the late majority approaches the last group to be included, the so-called laggards, saturation sets in, and the increase turns down. It is very tempting to see such S-curves in the growing gap pictures I have drawn. This certainly will be done by those who want to argue that the digital divide will "automatically" disappear by market forces alone (cheaper supply and higher demand). Their argument uses the *trickle-down principle.* It says that the adoption of new technology moves from the higher to the lower social classes of income, occupation, and education, as has happened with many types of technology and media before. It is simply a question of some having the technology now and others having it later. The first group pays for the innovation and makes the adoption cheaper for the last group.

Problems of Mainstream Diffusion Theory

Unfortunately, the diffusion of the digital technology innovations I am discussing here is not an easy and unambiguous process. Mainstream diffusion theory and the interpretations of the S-curve in public opinion and by policy makers are marked by simplicity and determinism. In fact, the diffusion of computer media, which I qualify here as heterogeneous and multifunctional, is a very complex phenomenon with few automatic elements.

There are five basic problems with mainstream diffusion theory's use of the S-curve of adoption in this context. The first is the precise *identification* of what constitutes the innovation under consideration. S-curves of adoption have become popular because they visibly describe the diffusion of a single medium that is easy to identify. This goes for media such as fixed telephones, gramophones, radios, (color) televisions, VCRs, and CD players. These media may have units different in price and quality, but their functionality remains basically the same. Contrary to this, computer media constitute a bundle of innovations, with continually changing pieces of hardware and software of which the functionality of each might be very different. PCs and computer networks serve as universal, multipurpose machines that can be programmed for almost every use. It is difficult to compare such universal machines with single-use devices such as radios, televisions, and VCRs.

If one tries to draw an S-curve for computer diffusion between 1985 and 2000, one cannot ignore the fact that the PC with limited power of 1985, which simply processed numbers and letters, is totally different from the powerful multimedia machine sold in the year 2005. The same goes for Internet connections. The old Internet, based on endless lines of commands and text, was in many ways an altogether different medium than the graphical World Wide Web that succeeded it. For the sake of simplicity, I use the general expressions *computer* and *PC* or *network connection* and *the Internet*. When it appears that the diffusion of the medium in its general expression nevertheless rises, this means that all users were getting a lot more computer and network power in 2000 than they did in 1985. However, it does not mean that all users had the same (quality of) media at their disposal in the year 2000. Concrete pieces of equipment, software, and connections used were (and are) ever more different. Most likely, this means that the gaps of physical access described in the previous section in fact are bigger, as the lower access categories also have the worst quality and the higher access categories have the best.

The second problem with mainstream diffusion theory's use of the S-curve of adoption is that it suggests a *populationwide diffusion* of mass media. We can expect this for most of the mass media mentioned earlier but not for advanced types of computer hardware and software or for network connections and services. In the developed countries, the radio and the television almost reached 100% diffusion, but after them, the telephone peaked at about 95% (see Schement & Scott, 2000). Cable TV never reached populationwide diffusion, and the VCR was challenged by DVD players before it reached 90%. It should be added that a medium such as the telephone took 70 years to reach a 95% level of diffusion, and it still has not reached that level in many poor neighborhoods in developed countries. The adoption speed of the PC is not as fast as that of the television and the VCR. The Internet is much faster, but it took advantage of existing telephone and cable infrastructures. In the 1990s, they "suddenly" appeared to be easily connectable to already widely distributed PCs.

Probably, basic forms of PCs and Internet connections will reach the household penetration level of the telephone in the future. Another possibility is that, even in the developed countries, they will stop at a level of 80% to 85%. This may be caused by skills and usage access problems (to be discussed in the following chapters). In 2002 and 2003, there were signs of a flattening Internet adoption rate in the United States and of a growing number of Internet dropouts. Immediately, doubts about the general diffusion of this medium appeared (Katz & Rice, 2002, p. 81; Lenhart et al., 2003; Madden, 2003). Later I offer reasons why I expect that basic computer and Internet adoption will continue to grow but that advanced multimedia machines, high-speed Internet connections, and their applications probably will not reach the adoption rate of the telephone in the developed countries for the next two decades at least. We do not have to mention the developing countries—here, populationwide diffusions of the old mass media are not even a realistic prospect.

The third problem of using an S-curve in the context of mainstream diffusion theory is that this theory simply draws all S-curves of media *separately*. In reality, media are combined and exchanged. This certainly goes for multimedia, realizing a process of media convergence. However, current experience shows that the old media do not disappear. They keep being used next to the new ones. In practice, old and new media are changing each other in a process called "mediamorphosis" by Fidler (1997). What is most important in the context of the digital divide is that they are used in accumulation. An increasing number of media presses on the household budget. Total expenditure for media tends to rise in the developed countries (see chapter 6). For people with small or shrinking household budgets, this means they have to choose among media. It appears that the newspaper is the first victim of this need. However, there will also be savings on the types and applications of computers and Internet connections. In this way, material access problems are increased.

The popular argument and cornerstone of the trickle-down principle, that computers and Internet connections are getting cheaper by the day, eventually enabling access for all, has to be severely qualified. In general, the new media are more expensive than the old media because they become outdated much more quickly, and new peripheral hardware and new software must always be purchased (van Dijk, 1999, p. 150). Moreover, there is a shift in expenses from hardware to software and applications that are not getting cheaper. In the evolution of the new media as a whole, interactive audiovisual services are becoming more important. However, they require more computer and network capacity and expenses for usage rights. Conditional access is on the rise, and it will take an ever-larger share of total new media expenses. Thus more computer capacity for a lower price barely solves material access problems. This argument is further developed in chapter 6.

A fourth, and perhaps the most basic, problem of mainstream diffusion theory's use of S-curves of adoption is the *determinism* of the stages and rates of diffusion proposed. Why should there be innovators, early adopters, early majorities, late majorities, and laggards with every innovation? Some innovations never reach a majority of users, at least not a majority of the population at large. It only makes sense to speak about laggards when there is a real and perceived need among all the people concerned. This may not be the case with, for instance, advanced multimedia machines. Similar doubts may be raised with the rate of diffusion and the slope of the S-curve. They are assumed to reveal a sudden upturn after some time, a period of fast diffusion, and a gradual tapering afterwards. However, the diffusion of new mass media in the developing countries does not reveal sudden S-curves but a more gradual secular trend (Norris, 2001, p. 32). Here diffusion takes much longer and is not that fast (see Norris, 2001, p. 34, Figure 2.4).

The last weakness of mainstream diffusion theory's use of the S-curve in the context of the digital divide is that it is drawn for *whole populations* and not for partial or target groups. There may be different S-curves for particular social categories of people. If this is true, it would be decisive for the interpretation and the extrapolation of the pattern revealed in the gap pictures I have drawn in this chapter. They can be interpreted as combinations of different S-curves. Pippa Norris (2001) has assumed the existence of deviating S-curves for different groups working in accumulation. However, this accumulation can result in both a normalization and a stratification of diffusion (see Figure 4.3).

Normalization and Stratification Models of Diffusion

In a normalization model, it is presupposed that the differences between groups only increase in the early stages of adoption. The leading group (A) as a whole starts the curve earlier and enters the fast upturn phase sooner. However, in the last stages, differences disappear, as the leading group enters a phase of saturation, and the following groups (B and C) reveal higher expansion rates. The presumed mechanism is falling prices attracting new users and allowing laggards to catch up. Clearly, this fits the trickle-down principle discussed earlier.

In the stratification model, it is assumed that the same stages of acceleration and saturation appear as in the normalization model, but there is (a) a different point of departure for the higher and lower social strata and (b) a different point of arrival. It is argued that higher and lower social strata have different resources to start with. This means that they start the diffusion process (long) after each other. Further, it is claimed that the higher strata reach a higher top level and start saturation later in their curve of adoption than the lower strata, which reach a lower top level and start saturation earlier.

The data, particularly the gap pictures presented in this chapter, still fit both models. However, in this book I argue that the stratification model will prove to be the best model for explaining the long-term

Figure 4.3   Combinations of S-Curves of Adoption for Different Classes
According to Normalization and Stratification Model

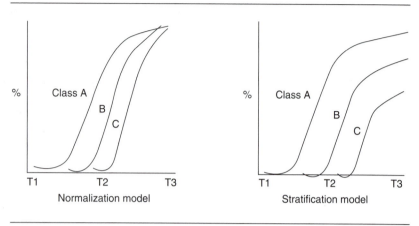

Note: T indicates time.

trend. It can already be shown that the first special assumption of the stratification model holds. The different strata analyzed in this chapter (according to the positional categories of labor, education, household, and nation and the personal categories of age, gender, [dis]ability, and race or ethnicity) clearly reveal diverging subsequent points of departure in time. The second assumption of the stratification model cannot yet be proven to be true. Only some of the higher strata have reached a stage of saturation. Moreover, this is only the case in the developed countries. None of the lower strata have reached such a stage, so we do not know yet where the top of their curve will end. However, the problems of motivational access (dropouts and evaders) discussed in the previous chapter, the problems of material access analyzed in this chapter (e.g., the limited material, mental, and social resources of the lower categories of those people with access), and the problems of skills access and usage access to be dealt with in the following chapters increase the probability that the top of the adoption curve of the lower strata will be at a lower level.

❖ CONCLUSION: THE SHIFTING DIVIDE

In this chapter, we have seen that in the period between 1985 and 2000, all divides of physical access to computers and the Internet have increased, except for the gender gap and the gap between people with and without disability. The reasons are unequal distributions of material, mental, and social resources, in their turn caused by particular characteristics of positional and personal categories. The most important positional categories appear to be labor market and educational positions, followed by contextual positions of being part of a particular type of household and nation. The most significant personal category appears to be age, followed by gender and disability.

At the turn of the century, the categories with relatively high physical access entered a phase of saturation in some developed countries and the categories with low physical access, who had started later, were still catching up. This might mean that an S-curve of adoption is appearing in these countries. In that case, we could make a projection of the evolution of the digital divide as a physical access problem. Its general pattern would be a narrowing gap at the beginning of the 21st century. However, the first problem that appears is the uncertainty of how far and how fast it will close. When there is no single S-curve behind the general trend observed but a combination of curves that are different for every category, potential future trends may diverge widely. The gap might close completely or only partially. It depends on whether one applies the normalization model or the stratification model I have described. In both cases, the physical access gap in the developed countries is narrowing. (In the developing countries, it is still widening in the first decade of this century.) When the stratification model holds, some categories of the population would reach their peak of physical access at a penetration rate of 60% to 80% in the following 15 years, and others will reach 95% or more. These different projections for the most developed countries are shown in Figure 4.4. It expresses that the physical access gap may more or less close in the years to come (2005-2020), depending on whether the normalization or stratification model holds. Further, it shows that a new, still widening gap has appeared with the innovation of broadband.

When the normalization model holds, the physical access problem for computers and Internet connections will be solved in the next 15 years. However, this will only go for the most developed countries. Another condition is that it only concerns basic access: the simplest computers and narrowband connections. For the next innovation, the introduction of broadband, the whole story starts anew. Once again, the highest social classes in terms of occupation, income, and education; family households with children; and male users are the first to

Figure 4.4   Real and Potential Future Evolution of the Material Access
Divide for PCs and Internet Connections, Narrowband and
Broadband

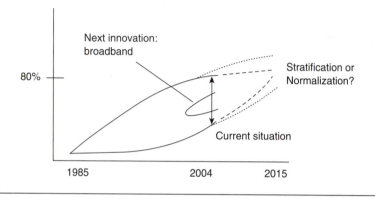

adopt this innovation (Horrigan & Rainie, 2002a; NTIA, 2000, 2002). It
should be added that the divides are less pronounced this time. This
can be explained by the fact that narrowband and broadband, less
powerful and more powerful computers are continuations. The step
from no computer and no connection to having them is bigger than the
step from one type of computer or connection to the other. Moreover,
the availability of audiovisual services in broadband communications
makes them more attractive to a larger part of the population in terms
of motivational access. Broadband connections are changing the daily
use of computers and the Internet to a considerable degree (Horrigan
& Rainie, 2002a). The "always on" facility and the availability of popular applications for everyday life are extending use. The first facility
removes an important barrier of material access for people with less
income. However, prices remain relatively high, so the material access
problem is not solved. Again, new technologies, basic and peripheral
equipment, connections, software, and services have to be purchased.
Having partly gained on the high-access categories, the low-access
categories are again running behind with every new innovation. Thus
the digital divide is continually shifting in terms of physical access.

Moreover, physical access is not equal to material access.
Conditional access is getting more important. The always-on facility is
a condition for which one has to pay. Following conditions are payments for special audiovisual services, programs, and contents marked
by intellectual property rights.

The most general conclusion of this chapter is that the material access divide is in the process of becoming *partially* solved. This is happening only for basic types of physical access in the developed countries. However, the most important shift in the whole phenomenon of the digital divide has yet to come. Divides in skills access and usage access are not disappearing; instead, they are growing. It is to these types of access that the book turns now. It will become evident why the phrase is not the *widening or narrowing* divide, but the *deepening* divide.

5

Skills Access

❖ INTRODUCTION

After having acquired the motivation to use computers and some kind of physical access to them, one has to learn to manage the hardware and software. Often new users have observed others using them before. Perhaps some limited previous experience was gained by using someone else's computer or a publicly available one. However, as soon as more or less permanent access to a computer at work, at school, or at home is obtained, specific efforts have to be made to learn to operate and use the new medium. This might be learned through practice or in some kind of formal education.

Concepts of Computer Skills

From the very beginning of the computer revolution in the 1970s, it was noticed that particular skills were needed to be able to use the new technology at all. Computers were held to be difficult and user-unfriendly machines. Only computer experts and programmers were able to deal with them in the 1960s and 1970s. In the 1980s, the shift was made to the mass of nontechnical users. In 1981, the first concept incorporating the idea that special skills were required for the use of computers was invented and published in the *Washington Post* (Warschauer, 2003b, p. 111). The term used was *computer literacy*. It was a very narrow concept of computer skills, as it only indicated basic forms of computer operation, such as turning on a computer, opening a folder, and saving a file. Similar narrow definitions of skills required for computer use have remained customary since that time.

Broader concepts of the special computer skills required appeared under the names of *information literacy, digital literacy,* and *media literacy.* The American Library Association (1989) introduced the concept of information literacy, which indicated that the possessor has the ability to recognize when information is needed and to locate, evaluate, and use it effectively. The concept of digital literacy has been used more often. Paul Gilster (1997) defined it as "the ability to understand and use information in multiple formats from a wide range of sources when it is presented via computers" (p. 1). Media literacy was an older concept, from the 1970s, invented after the discovery that not only print media required some kind of literacy but also audiovisual media. It was used to promote a critical confrontation with visual culture. Silverblatt (1995) and Potter (1998) characterized media literacy as a (large) number of analytical skills needed to process audiovisual mass media contents in a critical way.

Mark Warschauer (2003b, pp. 111-119) composed a complete update of types of literacy required in working with computers and networks. He made a list containing computer literacy, information literacy, multimedia literacy, and computer-mediated communication literacy. He defined computer literacy as basic forms of computer and network operation, information literacy as managing vast amounts of information, and multimedia literacy as the ability to understand and produce multimedia content. He added computer-mediated communication literacy as the skill to manage online communications (e-mail, chatting, videoconferencing) in an effective way that included keeping to the rules of "netiquette."

In the tradition of the concept of literacy, the Dutch Sociaal-Cultureel Planbureau (SCP) research team (van Dijk et al., 2000) has tried to extend the traditional literacy of print media with *numeracy* (handling numbers, calculating) and *informacy* (having the specific skills needed to use and understand ICTs).

Finally, the most general term came from Cees Hamelink. In the tradition of Bourdieu's forms of capital, he added *information capital* (Hamelink, 2001). It indicates four abilities: (a) the financial ability to pay for the costs of computers and networks, (b) the technical skill to deal with them, (c) the capacity to filter and evaluate information, and (d) the motivation to look for information and the capacity to use this information in society. This concept is extremely broad; the first ability clearly indicates that it means more than skills. In fact, *information capital* has become a synonym for the four types of access distinguished in this book.

Before I propose my own concepts of skills access, it might be helpful to clarify what this host of terms tries to distinguish as novel about the use of these technological media. The first thing that was new and different about computers and networks is that they were held to be difficult to operate. Particularly in the early phases of the technological development of computers, they were much more difficult to handle than radios, televisions, telephones, record players, CD players, and even videorecorders. Special technical skills seemed to be required. This aspect appears in concepts such as *computer literacy* and *computer skills*.

The second novel aspect is that more perceptual and creative skills are required than just reading and writing. Increasingly, not only text but also numbers, images, and sounds are appearing as kinds of data on multimedia computer screens. This contingency is responsible for a series of extensions of the term *literacy*.

The final innovation is the exponential growth of sources of information and the need to manage them. The presence of skills to search, select, process, and use information in the complex environment of the computer world cannot be taken for granted. These skills have to be learned. Then they will become a part of daily practice. This requirement appears in concepts such as *digital literacy, information literacy* and *information capital*, discussed earlier.

Every concept trying to incorporate the skills needed in using computers and networks will have to take into account these three new aspects. The general concept of *digital skills* is able to do this, provided that they are divided into at least three types of skills needed, in succession: operational skills, information skills, and strategic skills. My definition of *digital skills* is the collection of skills needed to operate computers and their networks, to search and select information in them, and to use them for one's own purposes. Within the digital skills succession, *operational skills* are the skills used to operate computer and network hardware and software. *Information skills* are the skills needed to search, select, and process information in computer and network sources. Finally, *strategic skills* are the capacities to use these sources as the means for specific goals and for the general goal of improving one's position in society (in the labor market, in education, in households, and in social relationships). In the following sections, these three special types of skill are elaborated in detail.

Table 5.1 offers an overview of these skills in different types of media. Reading this table, one can see that there are many similarities in the skills needed for using print, audiovisual, and computer media. They all contain a particular type of operation, perception, cognition, and creation. This would justify the use of the concept of *(multi)media literacy*. With print and audiovisual media, getting access to these media and using them is relatively easy, although creation (printing books and magazines or making audiovisual programs) is rather difficult, as it requires expensive equipment and advanced technical skills. With computer media, it seems to be the opposite. It is rather difficult to get access to them and to develop the operational skills to use them. As soon as these conditions are met, creation is relatively easy, as all means of production are available in preprogrammed formats.

Contents of this Chapter

The following three sections specifically discuss not only operational, informational, and strategic skills but also how they are distributed among the populations of developed and developing countries. I demonstrate that the differences in mastering these skills (skills access) are enormous, or at least greater than the divides in motivational and material access described in the previous chapters. Once again, I relate these gaps to the possession of resources and to particular positional and personal categories.

In the subsequent section, a popular myth is destroyed. This myth holds that computer skills are acquired or should be acquired in courses or other types of formal education, using course material, operation manuals, and help functions. Instead, acquiring computer skills most often is a question of learning through practice, by trial and error, and with the help of others who are close. Again this reveals the importance of having a particular position in society (job, school, household, social network) and the personal qualities of motivation and ability. Of course, formal education remains necessary to create a solid basis of digital skills for young people in schools and for older adults who have missed this opportunity in their school years.

Table 5.1   Kinds of Skills Required for Using Print Media, Audiovisual
Media, and Computer Media

	Operational Skills	Informational Skills	Strategic Skills
Print media	Read and write texts Understand and count numbers	Search, select, and process information from texts and numbers (e.g., statistical information)	Taking own initiative in searching, selecting, integrating, valuing, and applying information from all sources as a means to improve one's position in society
Audiovisual media	View, listen to, and make audiovisual programs	Search, select, and process information from images, sounds, and narratives	
Computer media	Operate computers and programs	Search, select, and process information from computer and network files	

Source: Table inspired by Steyaert (2000).

❖ OPERATIONAL SKILLS

The skills needed to operate computers and Internet connections always have dominated popular and policy ideas about computer skills. It appears as if mastering a computer is an end in itself and as if the whole problem of the digital divide vanishes as soon as someone is seated at a computer keyboard and is visibly using it in one way or another. Substantial aims in working with a computer and the Internet are lost.

In fact, being able to operate a computer to a certain degree is a necessary condition of using it. With many applications, only minor operational skills are needed for basic functions. On the other hand, we should not underestimate the problems many senior, disabled, low-educated people and manual workers have in performing even the simplest operations on keyboards. Working with extended keyboards is an activity that is far more complex than the operation of a remote control of a television and other equipment. A personal example: I have a brother who is a manual laborer in a floral greenhouse. He learned to use a computer at the age of 42. His first experience was that his fingers were too fat to manage the keyboard without numerous errors and that he was too slow in double-clicking. These kinds of problems are much more common than a large part of the readership of this book may think.

What is the state of affairs regarding the command of operational skills among the population at large in both developed and developing countries? To answer this question, an operational definition of these skills must be provided. The definition mentioned earlier was "skills to operate computer and network hardware and software." The most extended, concrete, and practical operational definition of the concept *operational skills* is provided by the seven modules of the European computer driving license (ECDL), extended as the international computer driving license. These modules are standardized and have to be completed with separate tests. Passing all seven tests results in achieving the computer "driver's license," which can be used for and will be accepted in job applications. The seven modules are

1. Concepts of Information Technology (IT)

2. Using the Computer and Managing Files

3. Word Processing

4. Spreadsheets

5. Databases

6. Presentation

7. Information (the Internet and the World Wide Web) and Communication (e-mail).

The numerous subcategories, skill sets, and task items of these modules can be examined at the ECDL Web site (http://www.ecdl.com/main/index.php). All the skills there are useful to command. Nevertheless, even experienced computer users will not meet the requirements of most of the skill sets tested. I have never taken a computer course myself, although I have worked with computers for more than 20 years, about 6 hours every day, and I am ready to admit that

I would certainly fail the exam for this computer driver's license. In at least three modules, I would receive an "unsatisfactory." This personal example points out one of the most important conclusions of this chapter: most digital skills are not the result of computer courses but of learning through practice in particular social user environments. However, it also shows that it is extremely difficult to determine the actual level of a person's command of operational skills.

There are very few valid and reliable estimates of the level of operational skills among populations at large. Of course, we could analyze the results of computer courses such as that of the ECDL, their number of students, dropouts, and people passing particular modules. However, they would be very (self-)selective groups to observe. The only available data for general populations are from surveys based on self-reports of skills commanded by respondents. Real tests of existing operational and informational skills for the purposes of research are very scarce. I mention some self-reports here first: two population overviews based on surveys from South Korea and the Netherlands.

These surveys asked respondents for their mastery of a number of skills closely corresponding to the ECDL and international computer driving license modules. The South Korean survey measured four items of skill: word processing, Excel, utilities such as WinZip, and information searching on the Internet (Park, 2002). The Dutch survey asked for nine skills: use of Windows, word processing, spreadsheets, presentation programs such as PowerPoint, capacity to install programs, ability to find information on the Internet, and the e-mail skills of making folders and distribution lists and sending attachments (de Haan, 2003). Although the Dutch study is more elaborate in its analysis, I present in Table 5.2 the results of the South Korean survey held in the year 2000. South Korea is perhaps the most important instance of a country in which both government and industry are making enormous efforts to provide physical access to computers and the Internet (see chapter 10). According to the data in Table 5.2, this effort does not automatically solve skills access problems.

The differences of operational digital skills among South Koreans of different sexes, ages, occupations, and education are highly significant. On average, males have higher skills than females. The age difference is the largest: South Koreans older than 50 years (actually, older than 40) have practically no operational skills. White-collar workers and college students have far more skills than blue-collar workers, farmers, and fishers. Finally, the differences between Koreans with low,

Table 5.2   Distribution of Operational Digital Skills Among South Koreans in 2000

Category	Value	No or Very Few Skills	Reasonable Skills	Good Skills
All		45.6	41.0	13.4
Gender	Male	41.3	42.3	16.3
	Female	51.8	39.2	9.0
Age	13-19	47.5	41.3	11.2
	20-29	31.3	50.4	18.3
	30-39	51.4	34.6	14.0
	40-49	63.2	30.5	6.3
	50-59	72.9	27.1	0.0
	60-64	100	0.0	0.0
Occupation	Farmer or fisher	66.7	25.0	8.3
	Self-employed	61.9	28.5	9.6
	Blue-collar	52.2	37.4	10.3
	White-collar	27.2	51.8	21.0
	Housewife	68.5	26.6	4.8
	Middle or high school student	49.2	39.8	11.0
	College student	27.8	53.3	18.9
	Unemployed	39.4	48.5	12.1
Education	Low	93.3	6.7	0.0
	Low-middle	59.7	33.2	7.1
	High middle	42.0	44.0	13.9
	High	28.1	50.0	21.9

Source: Information Culture Center (2000), quoted in Park (2002).

Note: N = 1513, index reliability Cronbach's alpha = 0.82.

middle, and high levels of education are very telling. No Koreans with low levels of education have good operational skills, and 93.3% have no or very few skills.

The Dutch survey, which measured operational skills in 1998 and 2001, produced results that are very similar to the South Korean case. The differences are a bit less extreme but nevertheless highly statistically significant (de Haan, 2003, p. 39). Here, detailed multivariate analyses were made. "After controls, women still turned out to be less skilled than men, the lower educated less skilled than the higher educated and students and working people more skilled than those responsible for the household" (de Haan, p. 37). However, the differences between age groups also are the largest in the Netherlands. The "beta" (a statistical measure of association) was .29 in 1998 and .34 in 2001. The second most important variable is income (.24 and .19 in 1998 and 2001, respectively), directly followed by education (.23 and .19), gender (.21 and .18), and labor market position (.16 and .19). The total explained variance of these variables increased from 42% in 1998 to 48% in 2001, indicating that the *relative* differences of operational skills between groups are increasing, not decreasing.

Two remarks have to be made about the validity of self-reported skills in surveys. The first is that *relative* differences concerning age and gender probably are smaller in reality. It is common knowledge that senior and female respondents are more modest in reporting the level of their skills than younger and male respondents. The second remark is that the *absolute* level of operational skills possessed will be lower in tests than in self-reports. I think that the result would be amazingly low. The actual development of digital skills is highly affected by personal experience and practice in particular settings and applications. Software and applications are very much underused. As soon as users have found their way through a particular program and reached their specific goals, they have not much intention of looking for other applications of or other ways in which to use the program. In most general tests of their abilities in using this program, they would fail.

Explanation of Operational Skill Divides

What are the resources and positional and personal categories explaining these significant divides in operational skills? Here the most important resources are mental resources (general technical skill and understanding, tenacity in learning), material resources (permanent availability of the digital hardware, software, and connections required) and social resources (social network positions and relationships). The distribution of these resources is explained by labor market and educational positions and the availability of the digital media in one's household and nation or region. Further, these divides are clarified by the personal categories of age, gender, personality, intelligence, and health or ability. I explain and underpin these statements in the following paragraphs.

Clearly, the most important variable is age (see de Haan, 2003). This can be explained by the distribution of mental, material, and social or cultural resources. It is common knowledge that children and young people have much more manual and technical skill in working with keys or buttons and visual interfaces than do older people. The speed of young people's operations is much higher. They are growing up with these skills. Moreover, most young people in the developed countries have the material resources of broadly available digital media at their disposal at schools and in households. Finally, young people have a social network of peers and friends hailing the control of digital skills as a matter of status and exchanging clues and new ideas continually. In practice, young people appropriate the available hardware and software in their households and other places. They take these material sources from older people in their environment, often teaching their elders to manage computers instead of the older people teaching them.

Unlike young people, elderly people did not grow up in the age of push-button media. People older than 35 or 40 years rarely have had any experience with computers at schools. Depending on circumstances, most people above this age in the developed countries have still been able to learn (more or less) to use extended keyboards and computer programs. However, learning is much slower for them. It gets worse about the age of 50, when many seniors start to experience physiological changes in vision and hearing abilities, cognitive functioning, and motor skills.

Younger people with these kinds of disabilities also have difficulties in mastering operational skills, of course. They have to use the special utilities for the disabled. Unfortunately, these utilities are not developed and disseminated to such an extent that they sufficiently help the disabled to compensate for their vision, hearing, or motor deficiencies and other physical shortcomings.

Gender differences in operational skills are primarily caused by elderly women. Young women are almost equal to men in mastering these skills, in particular when they have learned them at schools. Moreover, the majority of (executive) computer work in the labor market of the developed countries is performed by women. Remaining differences are caused by motivation and cultural resources; these appear when technical or operational problems have to be solved.

In regard to positional categories, positions in the labor market and in education are decisive for the acquisition of operational skills. The South Korean and Dutch data described earlier testify to this conclusion. Most adults have to (first) learn operational skills in practice on the job and at schools to carry them on at home. For people without jobs or education, self-training of operational skills at home depends on sufficient income or other material resources, such as the availability of a computer in the household. One develops these skills sooner at a home computer that is always within reach than at a community access center or other public place.

❖ INFORMATION SKILLS

Operational skills have received all the attention, but the information skills needed to apply them to reach particular goals rarely are elaborated. Perhaps they are conceived to be too abstract. Still, it has become a commonplace to say that being able to work with information is vital in an information society and that the possession of a large stock of ready knowledge is not that valuable anymore. Instead, knowledge continually has to be extracted from an overload of information. Knowledge can become obsolete within days or even within seconds; for instance, at a stock exchange.

I have defined information skills concisely as the skills used to search, select, and process information in computer and network sources. In fact, they are an extended collection of abilities that I split up here into *formal* and *substantial* information skills. Formal information skills are the abilities to understand and work with the formal characteristics of a particular medium. A book has a table of contents at the beginning; chapters, sections, and paragraphs in the middle; and references with indexes at the end. A television program has an introductory sequence; a large number of items with episodes, sequences, scenes, and shots; and an end. Computer disks, files, and programs, as well as Web sites, have a completely different order. They have file and menu structures, and sites are hyperlinked. The formal structures of computer and network media are complicated and novel. One has to learn to use them. *Substantial information skills* are the abilities to find, select, process, and evaluate information in specific sources following particular questions. Basically, they are the same in all media. However, as the contents of media may vary considerably, finding, selecting, processing, and evaluating information in them will be different too. For example, finding, selecting, and evaluating a particular fact in an encyclopedia is rather different from doing the same in a search engine on the Internet. The difference is not only a matter of the formal structure of the medium but of the nature and value of its contents.

Formal Information Skills

Some of the formal information skills of computer and network media are part of computer operation courses, such as the seventh module of the ECDL, in which students become familiar with the makeup and structure of e-mail and Web addresses and have to combine selection criteria in using a search engine, but most of them are not. This means that they have to be learned in practice, or they will not be learned. The following are the seven formal information skills.

1. Getting to know and to control the *file structure* of a computer and the Internet. The infinite subdivision of computer filing makes this operation very much different from any traditional office archive. Most people do not attain the level of abstraction and systematization needed to exploit all the opportunities of computer filing and Web sites. The file structure of the average computer user is a mess. When surfing on Web sites, many users do not even discover Back and Find buttons (Hargittai, 2003).

2. Getting to know and to control the *information structure* of the Internet in general and a Web site in particular. Many people have no understanding of the makeup of the Internet; that is, what happens when a search engine is used or a Web site is consulted. This makes it difficult to assess the results. Web sites should be designed in such a way that users can easily find what they want. When this condition is met, there still is no guarantee that users will succeed in doing this. They simply may not understand the structure offered because it is completely new to them, compared to books, libraries, encyclopedias, and so on.

3. Getting to know and to control the *hyperlink structure* of the Internet. This structure is a completely new media characteristic, with a revolutionary potential for media production and use. The center of attention in both production and use is shifting from separate items (e.g., books, articles, and programs) to networked pieces of information that can be linked in self-chosen sequences. Making these links according to clear individual criteria and priorities is a new skill that is rarely mastered by people who are not experienced information seekers like academics and journalists. Most users stop when they have found the link that seems to serve their needs. Usually, not a fraction of the opportunities of the hyperlink structure is used.

4. Getting to know and to control the layout and design of *multimedia screens*. Increasingly, these screens have become filled with

different kinds of data combined in a particular way (images, sounds, texts, and numbers). They are ordered in very complex new ways, with banners, trailers, and special frames rolling over the screen, not to mention the surprise of special pop-up screens. The speed and complexity of multimedia computer (and television) screens is not, or is only partially, digested by a majority of computer and Internet users. This is true primarily, but not only, for middle-aged and elderly people.

5. Learning to handle the *fragmented nature* of computer and network sources. Traditional information sources such as manuals, encyclopedias, standard works, and the libraries containing them offer coherent collections of knowledge, and a lot of effort is made to produce them. Computerized and Web-based information sources have a highly fragmented information structure. Users are expected to produce order and coherence themselves; for instance, when students have to complete assignments or write a paper using Internet sources. The skill to do this varies enormously. Therefore all kinds of services (e.g., portals, frequently asked questions [FAQs], thesis and paper services) are offered to average users so that they do not have to learn the skill necessary to do it themselves. Nevertheless, this kind of skill is required for special tasks and original work.

6. Learning to handle the *continually changing contents* of computer and Internet information sources. This is the skill to deal with digital information and its sources, which changes from 1 day, or perhaps 1 minute, to another. Who is able to keep up with these shifting sources? How should they be evaluated, stored, and referred to? Perhaps this skill is not even completely mastered by experienced journalists.

7. The final, but certainly not the least important formal information skill, is the ability to *read and write English*, as a clear majority of Internet sources, in particular, still use the English language although this is not the native language of a vast majority of Internet users. To a lesser extent, the same goes for computer programs and information content. According to Warschauer (2003, p. 95), about 350 million people worldwide speak English from birth, 350 million speak it as a second language, and 700 million speak it as a foreign language, the last two groups often rather poorly. Three quarters of the world population knows almost no English.

In a limited way, the first three of these formal information skills are learned in computer and Internet classes. However, the last four are never learned there. They are other skills learned before (such as English skills) or they are (more or less) learned in practice by those who strongly lean on existing intellectual skills.

Substantial Information Skills

Existing intellectual skills are even more vital to substantial information skills. In fact, these skills are more or less learned, as far as formal education is concerned, in regular classes of language, history, mathematics, geography, social studies, and art. Here one should be able to learn the skills of the selection, abstraction, generalization, and evaluation of information in general. They are required for the following list of six substantial information skills:

1. Learning to *search information*. This skill is summarized by Warschauer (2003b) in the following steps:
   a. Develop good search questions
   b. Determine the most likely places to seek relevant information
   c. Select the most appropriate search tool
   d. Formulate appropriate search queries
   e. Rapidly evaluate the result of a search query (reliability, authorship, current nature of the source)
   f. Save and archive located information
   g. Cite or refer to located information. (p. 113)

These search skills are most often not even sufficiently mastered by university students, let alone the population at large (data follow).

2. Learning to *select information* continually (not only in search operations). The growing overload of information requires ceaseless selection. One has to keep up a strict discipline not to drown in a sea of information. It is easy to download information and to pile up an endless amount of digital files. It is far more difficult to refrain from doing this and develop an attitude of being focused on an explicit information need.

3. Learning to *edit information oneself.* In the old media of the press and broadcasting, editors and publishers serve as gatekeepers, selectors, processors, and editors of information in an attempt to protect the reliability, validity, and usability of information for readers, viewers, listeners, and other consumers. In the new media, especially on the

Internet, enormous amounts of unedited "raw" material presenting themselves as information are appearing. It is left to the users to do the editing job. Moreover, in using computers and the Internet, the consumers of information are able to become producers of information themselves. However, this editing and producing job is simply too much for the average user. Thus all kinds of professional editors appear on the Internet in the role of portals, electronic papers and magazines, special information services, and sites for special expertise and advice. According to Hargittai (2003), most users heavily rely on these sites to present them with information instead of developing sophisticated search strategies themselves. In this way, the skills of those who are themselves able to search, produce, and edit information on computers or the Internet are running further ahead of the skills of those who are not.

4. Being able to apply a *quality assessment of information sources* in computer files and on the Internet. As authorized or competent editors and publishers are not a majority on the Internet, users have to make quality assessments themselves. They have to evaluate the validity, reliability, and usefulness of sources themselves. The speed of Internet use forces them to do this very fast. The sites passed while surfing and found as the result of a search operation open themselves immediately as a string of sources and pieces of information. Estimating the validity of sources means being able to judge their authority and credentials. For example, everybody can offer themselves as doctors or medical experts on the Internet. Assessing the reliability of a source means being able to estimate whether it is biased in a particular direction, whether it is inaccurate or outdated, whether its information is controlled, and even whether it is committing fraud. Everybody is selling all kinds of things on the Internet. In general, the origins of and the dividing lines between types of information, such as controlled news items and propaganda or advertisement, that used to be clearly visible, are getting lost in this medium (van Dijk, 1999). Finally, estimating the usefulness of sources means being able to assess whether they really give an answer to one's questions and whether the answer is appropriate to one's purposes. Again, the urge to catch the eye among the overload of sources on the Internet is enormous.

5. Being able to *combine information from an increasing number of media, channels, and individual sources.* In the present multimedia environment, with an increasing number of old and new media working in

parallel and linked to each other, users need the skill to estimate the value of, for instance, a news program on television, the editorial quality of a newspaper, the news items of a particular Web portal, and a posting in a newsgroup on the Net. As has been discussed before, information sources increasingly are fragmented in the new media environment. Combining them in a number of coherent views and conclusions is not easy. Actually, this would require the skills of a professional journalist.

6.   Being able *to derive associations and to generalize from specific pieces of information.* As the possession of ready knowledge is becoming less important, continually developing new knowledge from endless pieces of information becomes a vital skill in the information society. To begin with, this means being able to distinguish between important and unimportant pieces of information. After that, one should be capable of making connections between separate pieces of information—this means making associations. Third, the ability to distinguish the particular from the general is required. Finally, one should be competent in producing valid generalizations from the abundance of pieces of information. This presupposes the strong mental skill of abstraction.

These six substantial information skills certainly are not specific to the use of computers and their networks. They also are needed for print media and audiovisual media and, where print media are concerned, they are learned in several traditional courses and subjects at schools, such as in language courses, history, and art, in which pupils learn to distinguish main and side issues in reading. Perhaps it is even better to learn them first in these courses. In these traditional courses, the learning process is not distracted by technical problems and the need to master operational skills. However, in computer and network media, they acquire special importance, for the reasons mentioned.

Clearly, the substantial information skills required are intellectual skills. They are increasingly so when following the series from one to six just given. One is tempted to say that the first skills noted are those best mastered by professional journalists and the last by academic researchers. Even so, average users of the new media should command them to a certain extent as well, as they are necessary for proper use (valid, reliable, and useful). What is the state of affairs concerning both formal and substantial information skills among the populations at large?

Information Skill Divides

Unfortunately, generalizable data from surveys and tests of these skills are very scarce. Most data are from experiments and tests on user groups of Web sites and search engines. Eszter Hargittai (2002, 2003) conducted experiments and tests with American user groups charged with tasks of finding particular information. In one experiment, a demographically diverse group of 54 subjects (although people with higher education were overrepresented) was charged with five Internet tasks, from finding a music file and downloading a tax form to discovering a Web site that compared different presidential candidates' views on abortion. Only half of the group was able to complete all tasks. Music files were found by almost everyone (51 of the total of 54), but the time needed varied from 5 seconds to 7.83 minutes. However, only 33 out of 54 subjects succeeded in finding a Web site comparing candidates' views. The time required ranged from 27 seconds to 13.53 minutes (Hargittai, 2002).

No significant gender differences were found in this investigation, although age and education proved to be highly significant. Subjects older than 30 years completed many fewer tasks than subjects in their late teens and 20s. Moreover, they needed much more time. Those between 30 and 50 years old used twice as much time and those between 50 and 80, three times as much. People with a graduate degree completed more tasks and were much faster than people with no college degree. The same applied to people with 3 to 7 years' experience on the Internet compared to people with fewer than 3 years' experience.

In another test of a random sample of 100 Internet users, Hargittai (2003) found that only one subject ever used the Find button on a Web site and that many users were not even aware of the Back button. Silverstein, Henzinger, Marais, and Moricz (1999) and Spink, Jansen, Wolfram, and Saracevic (2002) observed the amazingly primitive use of search engines. Analyzing almost a billion queries on the AltaVista search engine, Silverstein et al. discovered that 85% of users only viewed the first page of results. Spink et al. found approximately the same with the use of the Excite search engine from 1997 to 2001. Also, the amount of pages looked at decreased in these years. Increasingly, search engines show the most popular and commercially viable sites first; they may be adequate for many users, but it is not at all certain that they are the best options. Even more important is these researchers' conclusion that the large majority of users only makes simple queries and does not use any advanced search options.

One has to consider that these facts and categorical differences are found with the most basic of formal information skills. Imagine what the facts and differences will be when the distribution of more advanced substantial information skills is finally investigated. It is a safe prediction that the differences will be more spectacular and much larger. These skills are extremely unequally divided between people with high and low education, intellectual and manual jobs, and long and short media experience.

❖ STRATEGIC SKILLS

I argue here that deficiencies and differences between categories of users are even more pronounced with strategic skills, defined as the capacities to use computer and network sources as the means for particular goals and for the general goal of improving one's position in society. Searching, processing, and using information can be the means to reach a particular goal by one's own initiative. This is goal-oriented behavior in the contexts of business, employment, educational careers, politics, social relationships, and leisure activities. However, not all computer and Internet use is particularly goal directed. As with all media, their use may be a matter of daily routine or habit, or they may only be used because teachers, parents, or managers are demanding it. Explicit and conscious goal orientation in the use of computers and networks is a matter of having adequate resources in general and motivation and position in particular. This orientation is found more at the highest levels of business organizations and educational careers than at the lowest. It is more widespread among people with a large social network than with a small one. Finally, it is to be observed more with all kinds of people who are heavily engaged with cultural and political activities than with people exhibiting a relatively passive lifestyle.

Goal-oriented behavior and strategic skills for using computers and networks are vital in the information and network society (this is argued in chapters 7 and 8). In this society, an increasing number of activities is affected by purposive searching, processing, and use of information and by attaining or retaining positions in all kinds of relationships. Those able to search, process, use, attain, and retain will have a considerable advantage in social competition and educational or job careers.

Strategic Skill Divides

Strategic skills for working with computers and the Internet are not learned in school or on the job in explicit ways. They are incorporated into the daily practices of education, work, and leisure time. This is the main reason why there are scarcely any data about the distribution of these skills among the population. We are only able to observe how some people get better chances to learn them on the job and at school than others. For example, using data from a National Assessment of Educational Progress in mathematics in the United States in 1996, Wenglinsky (1998) found that eighth-grade pupils from disadvantaged groups used computers in the classroom significantly more for remedial drills and practices; pupils from advantaged groups used them more often for applications and simulations promoting higher order thinking. "In eighth grade, minority (Black or Hispanic), poor and urban students are more likely to find themselves learning lower-order skills than their White, non-poor and suburban counterparts; disadvantaged students are also less likely to find themselves learning higher-order skills" (Wenglinsky, 1998, pp. 23-24). In a comparative investigation of Hawaiian schools, Warschauer (2003b, p. 132) concluded that "the elite school used technology to help prepare scholars, whereas the poorer school used technology to help prepare people for the workforce."

Wenglinsky's and Warschauer's conclusions are extremely important. They show that the acquisition of information and strategic skills is not only a matter of personal but also of positional categorical inequalities and that these inequalities tend to become institutionalized in school practices.

Strategic skills are not only defined by the substantial and practical *goals* attained but also by a proper and effective use of *means*, in this case a computer or Internet connection. For most users, these media still are opaque machines or worlds. They do not know their composition, the way they are designed, or the way they are working. This means that they cannot help themselves when things go wrong or when they are maltreated by others in the computer world. I am referring to problems of security and privacy in particular. It is evident that those who know how to protect their connections and personal data, because they know how the technology and the organizations offering it work, will feel more free to use these connections and data and accomplish more. This is not only a matter of operational skills but also of technical, organizational, and political know-how. This means that the most experienced users in the computer world, from hackers to system operators, information officers, and managers of government and business organizations, probably have the best chances of developing strategic skills. It also means that all other users will acquire a level of strategic skill that ranges from fairly high to extremely low, depending on their knowledge of the contexts they are working in.

❖ WHY PRACTICE IS MORE IMPORTANT THAN FORMAL EDUCATION

The context in which people are working is the breeding ground of all digital skills. Accompanying the (wrong) idea that digital skills are equal to operational skills and that they always are difficult to master is the fallacy that they primarily are learned, or should be learned, in computer courses or classes. The second source of learning, in particular for individuals, is supposed to be operating manuals, help files, and help desks. Anyone trying to remember how she or he has gathered digital skills in the past knows that on most occasions these assumptions are wrong. The data of two surveys in the Netherlands, one among pupils of secondary schools and the other among the general Dutch population, reveal a more familiar picture (see Table 5.3). First, it shows that computer courses and books are not the most important sources for learning computer skills. From other data in the secondary school survey, it appeared that 40% of Dutch computer users in 1998 had followed no computer course at all. Most popular were courses in word processing (42%), specialist programs (32%), Windows (28%), and spreadsheets (22%). Other courses, such as those for the Internet (7%) and e-mail (6%), received minor attention.

Compared to this, the do-it-yourself approach is a much more important source of learning. Most computer and Internet users learn by trial and error, young people even more than seniors.

The second most important source of learning is people close to the user. For children and adolescents, this means parents (fathers in particular), friends, brothers or sisters, and teachers at school. It is striking that the first are more important than the last. When new users are in their 20s, 30s, and 40s, the most important sources after self-tries are becoming first, tertiary education (for those 18-34 years old) and, subsequently (for those 35 and older), colleagues at work and friends, acquaintances, or neighbors.

With people older than 50, an important shift occurs. Formal education loses its significance: Relationships with colleagues, friends,

Table 5.3   Important Sources for Learning Computer Skills for People of Different Ages in the Netherlands (2001) (%)

"I learned a lot from. . . ."	Pupils in Secondary School (15-17 years old)	Ages 18-34	Ages 35-49	Ages ≥ 50
Self-try	92	92	87	64
Computer courses	19	32	46	48
Computer books	26	41	46	51
Secondary education		25	1	0
Tertiary education		56	17	6
Colleagues		54	56	43
Friends, acquaintances, neighbors		52	41	24
Parents		20	1	0
Children		3	18	29
Teacher (primary school)	34			
Teacher (secondary school)	46			
Father	51			
Mother	20			
Brother or sister	42			
Friends	49			

Sources: van Dijk et al. (2000) and de Haan and Huysmans (2002).

acquaintances, and neighbors are diminishing and external help is getting more significant. Increasingly, people older than 50 have to rely on computer courses, computer books, and the help of their children (see Table 5.3). This is one of the reasons why it would be utterly wrong to draw the conclusion that, as practice is more important than courses, the digital divide problem can be solved without computer courses. I return to this later.

Learning by doing and learning from people who are close are cases of learning in *communities of practice* (Brown & Duguid, 2000; Lave & Wenger, 1993). People do not only learn by transmission or discovery but also by acting as members of particular social and cultural contexts that can be called communities. They simultaneously work or entertain, communicate and learn here. Communities of practice are at home, in neighborhoods, at schools, at workplaces, and in all kinds of clubs and associations. In all these settings—even in formal educational settings—informal learning is happening. "It occurs informally or incidentally as learners and experts observe, imitate, experiment, model, appropriate, and provide and receive feedback" (Warschauer, 2003, p. 121). In this relational view on learning (and inequality, when conditions differ), people learn from each other by question and answer and by observation and imitation. The experts can be both mentors (teachers, instructors, parents) and peers. They can work both offline and in online learning communities.

❖ CONCLUSIONS

In this chapter, I have shown that the inequalities of skills access are even bigger than the differences of material or physical access observed in the former chapter. Regarding skills access in its own right, I stressed that the series of three types of digital skills distinguished— operational, information, and strategic skills—exposes an increasing level of inequality. Few data are available about the command of information and strategic skills possessed by different parts of the population in developed and developing countries. However, all indications point in the direction of extreme unequal divisions of these skills, which are so important for the information and network society (see chapters 7 and 8). This type of inequality is one of the main reasons to call this book *The Deepening Divide*.

This type of inequality rests more on the distribution of mental than of material resources. Increasingly, the inequality is in intellectual skills. Those having a high level of traditional literacy also possess a high level of "informacy," or digital skills. For these skills, literacy appears to be more important than "numeracy," the capacity to deal with numbers and to calculate with computers (van Dijk et al., 2000). The second most important type of resources for digital skills is social and cultural resources. In this chapter, it was emphasized that the social context of computer and Internet users is a decisive factor in the opportunities they have for learning digital skills. They learn more from practice than from formal computer education and guidance.

Both positional and personal categorical inequalities are responsible for the unequal distributions of these resources. The positional categories of having a particular education and employment define the social contexts that enable computer and Internet users to learn digital skills in practice. The personal categories of age and intelligence appear to be the strongest individual determinants of digital skills, followed by sex or gender.

The importance of practice does not rule out the absolute necessity of formal education for particular purposes. Operational skills will remain incomplete when they are only learned by trial and error. For users to learn better information and strategic skills, school subjects and didactics will have to change considerably, as is argued in chapter 10. Finally, adult education regarding digital skills requires formal education in computer classes, community technology centers, computer books, help desks, or online learning communities. However, the extent and diversity of daily computer and Internet usage are decisive in learning the broadest set of digital skills. It is to this kind of access that we turn now.

6

Usage Access

❖ INTRODUCTION

Now we have reached the last stage in the process of full appropriation of the digital media. This is the final destination, the ultimate goal of trying to obtain access. The goal is to use these media for a particular purpose of information, communication, transaction, or entertainment. These words read as if this is a natural process, but it is not. The types of access I have discussed—motivational, material and skills access—are necessary preconditions or steps to reaching the final type, *usage access*. However, they are not sufficient conditions. A user may be motivated to use computers and the Internet, have access to them physically, and command the digital skills necessary to use them but nevertheless have no need, occasion, obligation, time, or effort to actually use them. Usage data indicate that many skillful users only use their computers and Internet connections once or twice a week. Usage access has its own grounds, although the resources and positional or personal categories concerned overlap with those determining the other types of access.

A recent survey in the Netherlands revealed that there is a more than .80 correlation between digital skills and usage time, as well as diversity of use (de Haan & Iedema, in press). This correlation might be explained by resources, positions, and personal characteristics affecting both skills and usage. Candidates for explanation might be a particular job or school training, a certain level of education, age, gender, culture, and the time and opportunity to practice computer use.

In this chapter, I focus on the potential causes of the large differences found in computer and Internet use. In a survey of (a) actual use, (b) usage time, (c) usage diversity, (d) broadband use, and (e) creative use, it can be observed that, generally speaking, usage gaps are bigger than physical access and skills gaps. Finally, I explain the rise of usage gaps with the so-called Matthew effect, which has its basis in current societal and technological tendencies of differentiation. This effect generally means that the rich are getting richer. In this case, it means that those already having the most resources and best positions in society also take the most advantage of every new resource, such as the possession and use of new technology. The name is derived from an expression in the Gospel of Matthew: "For to everyone who has, more shall be given" (Matt. 25:29, New American).

First I describe the properties of the technology concerned; that is, the hardware, software, and content of the new media. These properties are factors in the causal and phase model of access that serves as the backbone of this book (see Figure 2.3). Some of these properties support usage access; others impede it.

Properties of ICT (Hardware and Software)

The two distinguishing characteristics of the new digital media, or ICTs, are *interactivity* and *integration* (van Dijk, 1999). All old media either are not interactive (radio, television) or not integrated, as they are based on the single communication mode of sound, text, images, or numerical data (such as the traditional telephone, for sound). Perhaps they lack both characteristics, like print media do. Interactivity, in regard to media, means a sequence of actions and reactions by a medium and a user. A medium can be more or less interactive, depending on the availability and level of two-way communications, synchronicity, user control, and user understanding it offers (van Dijk, 1999, 2001). Interactivity has contradictory effects on media access. On the one hand, it makes media use more attractive, stimulating, immediate, involving, and participatory; on the other hand, it makes use more demanding, as it requires many cognitive resources (Bucy, 2004). Further, media can be more or less integrated to the degree that they combine sound, speech, or text with (moving) images or numerical data and become multimedia. Here the same kind of paradox appears. Integration supports mental access by richness of stimuli; on the other hand, more mental capabilities are required to process them.

The combination of interactivity and multimedia integration offers so many opportunities for the users of digital media that they become powerful tools in everyday life for all kinds of activities and for everybody. In particular, they enable the replacement or completion of offline activities by online activities (van Dijk, 1999). Some groups use these tools more than others, as will be seen later.

Old and new media can also be compared in regard to the communication capacities they possess (van Dijk, 1999). The capacity of particular importance in this context is *selectivity*. Senders and receivers in human-computer interaction and in computer-mediated communication are allowed to be much more selective in choosing options from menus, applications, and addresses than in the old media. This is a technological characteristic that enables the inequality of use of the new media.

There are five other technological characteristics either supporting or impeding usage access. The digital new media are complex and expensive; they produce so-called network effects, and they are multifaceted and multifunctional. I deal here with each of these characteristics in turn.

Complexity

The usage complexity of the digital media has been substantially reduced since their mass introduction in the 1980s. In those days, endless lines of code had to be entered to start and use a particular application. Operating the hardware of computers and their peripherals and connecting them to a network via modems and leased lines was a hell of a job, requiring technical expertise. The introduction of graphical interfaces, the invention of the World Wide Web, and the simplification of connections to the Internet were giant steps forward in the reduction of the complexity of the technology concerned.

However, 20 years later, the situation is still far from satisfactory. Even now, the computer as a technical device is making its presence felt too much between users and the things they are trying to achieve (Norman, 1999). It still is far more difficult to operate a computer or to have an Internet session than to operate a radio, a television, a telephone, a stereo, or even a video recorder or camera. It is even more difficult for the illiterate and the disabled. Complete and functional illiterates comprise 10% to 20% of the population of the developed countries. Just like the disabled, they have extra handicaps. They discover that digital or computer literacy is more demanding than traditional literacy. Moreover, the usability of particular computer hardware and software leaves a lot to be desired. The smaller a device with computer functionality becomes, the more problems it poses (advanced cellular phones, palmtops, and other handheld equipment). Even extended keyboards are redesigned continually. Software and Web sites are very different in the usability and the clarity of the information structures they offer. It goes without saying that these problems of user-friendliness impede usage access, in particular for people with low digital skills.

Expense

Information and communication technology are relatively new and advanced types of technology, with high production costs that make them expensive. However, the prices of the components of hardware and of software have dropped considerably since the 1980s. Many observers think that computers and Internet connections have become so cheap that price is no longer a problem in access. This is a huge mistake, as I argued in chapter 4. When developing countries are considered, this would even be a ridiculous view. In these countries, only a small elite of rich people can afford private computers and Internet connections. The large majority of the population has to rely on community access centers, Internet cafés, and a small number of equipped school classes and workplaces. In the developed countries, computers and Internet connections have become or are becoming regular household commodities. However, this does not mean that costs are no longer an impediment for material and usage access in these countries.

The first argument in support of this conclusion is that the total expenses of households or individual consumers for media and communications is not declining but, on the contrary, tends to rise if we look at the statistical data supplied by institutions such as the OECD (see the biennial Communication Outlooks, available from http://oecdpublications .gfi-nb.com/) and the UNDP (see the annual Development Reports, available at http://hdr.undp.org/reports/default.cfm). Also, within the media and communications budget expenses for computers, their peripherals and network connections are rising. The reasons for this increase are fivefold:

1. Computers and connections require a large number of peripherals, both hardware and software, that increases with the number of applications and with the rise of multimedia. Some of these peripherals are getting cheaper (for example, printers), but their accessories (such as ink and paper) are getting more expensive.

2. Computer hardware and software become outdated much faster than those of older media: The hardware has to be exchanged about every 5 years, and new software updates are offered almost every year.

3. Computer hardware is swiftly getting cheaper in terms of price-performance ratio, but the prices and licensing of software are barely declining.

4. Computer applications are shifting from processing and exchanging texts, images, and numerical data to working with audiovisual technologies; however, these require more computer capacity, more bandwidth, and more payment for conditional access and intellectual property rights.

5. Finally, the rise of the number of applications and the usage time required or needed by the average user is the most important reason, of course.

In any case, the availability of more computer capacity for a lower price does not solve physical and usage access problems, as I argued in chapter 4 concerning physical access and argue later in this chapter in regard to usage access.

Network Effects

Undoubtedly, the availability of e-mail is the main trigger application for people achieving Internet access. This application becomes more valuable when a growing number of people are connected. This is a prime effect of all networks: After a network has acquired a "critical mass" of connections, access to it becomes ever more attractive and rewarding (Markus, 1990). When the network grows, people even feel forced to get connected if they are not to be excluded from social life. Subsequently, many governments feel obliged to support universal access to the network in one way or another.

The more applications the network offers, the more important it will become for those connected and the more it will attract new users. The rise in the number of users produces an increase in market and business opportunities on the network and a decrease in the prices of connections and services—attracting more new users. This is happening with the Internet at the beginning of the first decade of the 21st century in developed countries.

A similar network effect will appear with the diffusion of broadband networks. The transition to broadband for Internet use substantially changes the daily use of this medium (Horrigan & Rainie, 2002a). Internet applications become part of everyday social life. Usage access is no longer impeded by the costs of connection time and the extended wait when turning on the computer and connecting to the Internet. The "always on" option and the space available for audiovisual applications increase daily use and connections to others on the network. This will force others to purchase broadband as soon as it is available and they have the means to do so.

Clearly, network effects support usage access for all people willing and able to get connected.

Multiple Facets

In this book I often use the phrase "computers and Internet connections" for the sake of simplicity. Actually this is much too simple. Computers and Internet connections show extremely different faces in the market of available technology. First, computers with very high and very low capacity are available. They range from advanced, powerful, multimedia machines to simple computers with small disks and low speed, perhaps because they are old or they are network computers without their own disks and capacities. They range from large desktop computers connected to powerful servers to small mobile laptops, palmtop or pocket PCs, and other handheld devices, usually with much less power and fewer usage options. When all these kinds of computers are connected to networks, they can achieve capacities ranging from 28 KB to more than 100 MB per second. Finally, these computers and networks can be accessed from home, workplaces, or schools; from public places; or in transit, using mobile computing and telecommunications. These points of access are the most important conditions in shaping the daily faces and opportunities of computer and Internet access. They determine the ease and comfort of working with them and the number and kind of available applications.

Being multifaceted, computers and Internet connections support access as they increase usage options. However, this characteristic also increases the chances of inequality of physical and usage access, as the available applications are unequally divided among people.

Multiple Functions

The same conclusion can be drawn when we discuss the last characteristic of the digital new media. They are the most multifunctional information and communication technology in history. The functions of information, communication, transaction (business, finance, and shopping), work, education, and entertainment are described in this chapter. I demonstrate that computers and Internet connections offer all these functions in both simple and complex forms. The only competitor in fulfilling all these functions is the telephone. Using this medium, one also is able to inform, to communicate, to order things, to trade or negotiate, and to entertain by chatting or by calling a sex line. The telephone is frequently used at work but rarely in education. One of the reasons is that the plain old telephone has far fewer information and communication capacities than the computer and the Internet. It is not a multimedium; it only transmits speech and sound and, in some cases, a limited amount of text. Primarily moving images are lacking. Unlike the computer, the telephone has a very limited storage and forwarding capacity; simple answering devices and voice-mail functions are all that can be used with most phones. The amount and level of software that can be programmed into a telephone is far less than the software a computer can store itself or receive from the Internet. As soon as the differences between the telephone and the computer start to disappear (because digital and mobile phones offer more options for word processing and sending moving images), telephones will in fact become (mobile) computers.

For these reasons, the computer and the Internet are superior to the telephone in all advanced information, communication, transaction, and entertainment tasks. I argue that, if only for these technical reasons, computers and the Internet are more multifunctional than all media before them and that they offer both very simple and very advanced applications. This may be the basis for divides in usage access. On the other hand, the multiple functions of computers and the Internet offer something for everyone, and this may support usage access.

Properties of ICT (Content)

The technological properties of ICT that affect usage access are not only those of hardware and software. While people work with this technology, they are confronted with all kinds of content. Some of these properties support usage access; others impede usage with certain categories of people. The properties to be discussed in this section are approachability, usability, information overload, reflection of culture and language, relevant information, and conditional access.

Approachability

As soon as one has installed a computer and an Internet connection, it becomes easier to type some lines in the word processing application, to play a CD, to enter a word in the field of a search engine, and to send everybody around the world an e-mail. New media content can be very approachable in its production and use. It can be as simple as using a typewriter or a CD player. Typing a term in a search engine seems to be easier than using a card index in a library. Sending an e-mail to someone living in Japan might be more straightforward than trying to get connected to that person by telephone. If you want to hear a particular song played on the radio, it might be much easier to find it on the Internet than in a record shop. The approachability of the new media for these simple applications of typing plain text, sending e-mails, searching for particular terms, playing CDs, and downloading music files has considerably supported the usage access to these media for all sections of populations able to read and write.

Approachability has been mixed up with accessibility. However, this is not justified. You will be able to approach the president of the United States directly by e-mail, but chances are small that you will get access to him. It is easy to enter a search engine, but it is a lot more difficult to find what you want among the thousands of hits you get in return. The skills of the average user of a search engine are surprisingly low, as was explained in the former chapter. Some contents of a CD or DVD appear to be inaccessible on your specific player. When you send someone a letter using a word processor, it happens that the other cannot read it because an awkward program is used. These chances are greater with particular images, drawings, photos, or videos. However, hardware and software is not addressed in this section; it is about the approachability of *content*. In many ways, content is more approachable in the new digital media (or will be as soon as the technical problems of admission and conversion have been solved) than in the old print and audiovisual media in libraries, video stores, and record shops.

Usability

The problems are accessibility and usability. Concerning them, things have considerably improved since the 1980s, when complex and extended command lines of text and codes had to be entered to reach a particular file or address or to execute an operation. The coming of the World Wide Web and graphical computer interfaces probably has done more to expand usage access than all other technical improvements together.

However, there is still a lot to be achieved. This goes not only for the usability of software but also for the contents it offers. Web sites used to be simple electronic translations or conversions of printed documents, with the only difference that their parts were connected by hyperlinks. The information structures of Web sites and their opportunities for navigation and for interactivity with the hosts and their electronic messages are at an early stage of development. Many users get lost in consulting a Web site. The feedback to hosts by users trying to change or inform about contents offered could be much better. Considering search engines, we have seen that users most frequently retrieve only the first pages of results. The same goes for other applications, as a mere fraction of the application is used in most software programs. Help functions are rarely used. People learn by trial and error, as we saw in the previous chapter. The result of this state of affairs is that usage access in terms of usability still is a big problem for many computer and Internet users, principally for users with few digital skills of every kind.

Information Overload

Another mounting problem is the extent of contents offered in the digital media. This is simply too large for the average user. Having access to these contents is no problem, of course, but the selection of relevant information and addresses of information and communication partners is. Evidently, the problem is biggest for people with few information and strategic skills. Managing the information overload in the new media is a skill so unequally distributed that it is directly responsible for unequal usage access in terms of content. The solutions offered, such as installing all kinds of information agents and consulting portals instead of separate Web sites, are ambiguous in their effects.

On the one hand, they help people with lesser skills to manage the overload and reach the contents they are looking for. On the other hand, they confine these people to the most popular contents and the ones they are familiar with. Meanwhile, people with many information and strategic skills keep looking for better information sources (in terms of substantial quality and usefulness) to improve their knowledge and their position in society.

Culture and Language

The contents offered in any medium reflect the culture and language used by their developers and designers. Computers and the Internet started as a technology made by young, male, highly educated, English-speaking technophiles from developed, primarily Anglo-Saxon countries. The hardware instructions, software, and contents they produced mirrored their preferences, ways of thinking, use of language, and other cultural habits. It is no surprise that, at least at the start of this new media development, their creations were not attractive to old people, women, technophobes, people who were not well educated, most ethnic minorities, and, in general, people who did not speak English. The cultural characteristics of new media content have been barriers for motivational, skills, and usage access from the very beginning. Here again, the situation has improved but is still far from satisfactory.

All in all, the massive overload of digital content created for computers and the Internet "does not necessarily meet the needs of diverse communities around the world" (Warschauer, 2003b, p. 81). For them, useful content can be scarce or even absent. A fact mentioned in the previous chapter is that three quarters of the world's population knows almost no English. Still, the majority of Web pages and software languages were English until fairly recently. By the time this book was published, the majority of Web pages in the world were no longer in English. Other languages, such as Chinese, Japanese, German, French, and Spanish, are on the rise. The predominance of English has been not only a *barrier* for the global diffusion of the digital media; this language also has *promoted* worldwide circulation because it served as the lingua franca of the computer world, enabling communication between most developers, designers, producers, and users.

(Lack of) Relevant Information

Within countries, people also may have problems finding the information and the communication facilities they want in their own culture and according to their own needs. This applies first of all to people such as "low-income and underserved Americans," as they are called by the California-based advocacy group and think tank The Children's Partnership (2002). This group produced a number of reports stressing the need to improve online content creation and evaluation in the interest of deprived Americans who have physical access. The first report, by Lazarus and Mora (2000), stressed the lack of practical information for people with low incomes, the shortage of local information, the literacy barriers (for people with a low level of literacy), the language barrier (English), and the lack of cultural diversity for ethnic minorities in online content at that time. According to this report, the following kinds of information and application were very scarce on American Web sites in 2000:

- ◆ *Practical local information:* Local listings of jobs and housing, job training programs, low-cost child care, public programs for families, public benefits news, tax filing support, immigration assistance, information on local clinics, low-cost insurance resources
- ◆ *Cultural local information:* Community information, special sites for ethnic and local cultural information, interests, and activities
- ◆ *Information at a basic literacy level:* Information not only composed and compiled for children but also for adults (e.g., learning materials with multimedia components, literacy programs and high school degree programs, homework assistance)
- ◆ *Multilingual content:* Information in minority languages produced by minorities themselves, with familiar cultural figures and examples

Three years later the situation was only slightly improved (Lazarus & Roberts, 2003).

Conditional Access

It is a matter of fact that most content is still free on the Internet in its initial stages of development. Additionally, there is a lot of public domain software, freeware, and shareware to be downloaded from the Internet. Free content and free applications have both produced a strong boost in the usage access of this mew medium. For most Internet users, free access is perceived to be some kind of right, to the great despair of the content and software industries, who copyright their products. However, this "right to use" perception is going to change

(Lessig, 1999, 2001; van Dijk, 1999). New laws of intellectual property right protection, such as the *Digital Millennium Copyright Act* in the United States, have been adopted that try to safeguard not only content but also the technical means invented to protect works with copyright. These means will become increasingly effective (backed by legal protection) and realize access that is conditional on payment for the big majority of users. The exception will be a small minority of hackers, crackers, and Internet experts. In this way, really valuable content and communication facilities will have to be paid for.

However, the market for intellectual content will not return to its pre-Internet condition. To retain its copyrights, industry will be forced to introduce new business models based on a cheap pay-per-view basis (such as legal downloading of music files) or a free supply of initial applications with later or advanced applications that have to be paid for. Both methods (effective technical and legal protection and new business models) will once again threaten usage access for all—this time in a rather deceptive way, as users will have partial access or even free access, paid for by advertising, but may not want, or will not be able to pay for, the complete or advanced application.

❖   A SURVEY OF COMPUTER AND INTERNET USE

Surveys describing the use of computers and the Internet are strongly focused and, in a particular way, biased toward household applications. This is the result of using the traditional way of approaching samples of populations: telephone interviews and mailed questionnaires. The overwhelming share of data on computer and Internet use is about their usage at home, with a bias in favor of leisure applications. Another bias gives a false impression of total usage time of computers and the Internet. For people using a computer on the job or in their own business, the total average usage time of computers and the Internet at work often exceeds usage time at home. We should not forget that the diffusion of computers and the Internet started at offices or other workplaces and in educational contexts. It then spread to the home, which is now the most important place of access in terms of availability of equipment and connections for everyone during the majority of the day. However, even at home, computer applications that concern the job, business, or school remain among the most important. Thus when we try to estimate potential divides of usage access at home in terms of usage time and diversity, we should not forget that these divides come on top of divides to be observed at work and at schools.

In this section, I first analyze usage access in terms of the actual use of computers and the Internet. Subsequently, usage time and diversity are the focus of attention. Finally, I discuss the transition to broadband and the distribution of more or less creative use, such as contributions of content to the Web.

Actual Use

The data about the actual use of computers and the Internet are somewhat different from the data indicating material or physical access described in chapter 4. Material or physical access generally is measured by questions like "Do you have access to a computer (the Internet)?" or "Have you ever used a computer (the Internet)?" The first question asks about potential use and the second about particular use in the past that does not have to be significant at all (for instance, one-time use) or that might have been a long time ago. The figures on and divides of the actual use of computers and the Internet mostly are sharper and bigger than those of physical access. Someone may have physical access in a household but never or rarely use the medium, as it is used by the spouse or children. A child may have physical access at school, but he or she also may be forced to share the available computers with (too) many other children. Computers may be accessible at work, but the particular job or task does not require use of them. In the year 2001, at the time a number of physical access divides started to close in some developed countries (see chapter 4), the divides of the actual use of computers among the personal and social categories of Americans that are regularly investigated were still wide and both statistically and substantially significant. This applies to gaps of age, education, employment status, and income. The American gender gap in terms of usage was not closed in 2001, as opposed to the physical access gap (chapter 4; also, see Table 6.1). In the United States, the level of diffusion of computers and access to the Internet is among the highest of all countries. My impression is that, in most other countries, usage gaps are wider, but currently I cannot prove this, as the available international statistics are difficult to compare.

Usage Time

The precise daily usage time of computers and the Internet is a more valid indicator of usage than the declaration of respondents that

Table 6.1   American Computer Use by Demographics (%)

Use of a Computer at Work, at School, at Home, or Elsewhere			
	Yes	No	n
Sex			Significance = 0.000
Male	70.2	29.8	1958
Female	64.9	35.1	2139
Age			Significance = 0.000
18-24	82.0	18.0	521
25-34	85.4	14.6	725
35-44	79.5	20.5	855
45-54	75.2	24.8	741
55-64	55.1	44.9	481
65+	23.0	77.0	674
Education			Significance = 0.000
Less than high school	35.2	64.8	559
High school graduate	57.1	42.9	1504
Some college	79.0	21.0	975
College and more	89.5	10.5	1032
Labor market position			Significance = 0.000
Student	91.7	8.3	24
Employed full-time	81.8	18.2	2109
Employed part-time	76.3	23.7	507
Not employed for pay	62.6	37.4	553
Disabled	31.3	68.7	67
Retired	28.8	71.2	768
Income			Significance = 0.000
Less than $20,000	42.7	57.3	635
$20,000 to $39,999	64.9	35.1	991
$40,000 to $74,999	83.3	16.7	924
$75,000 and up	92.4	7.6	681

Source: Data are from Pew Internet and American Life Project (2002).

Note: Data are for the United States in 2001.

they use these media at some time or place. However, the time diary data required are scarce. One exception is the regular time diary studies in the Netherlands. Table 6.2 reveals detailed information about the usage time of all categories of people in the Netherlands from 1985 to 2000, based on these studies.

The most important conclusion to be derived from this table is that most gaps of usage access to computers at home have widened in this

Table 6.2   Weekly hours of Computer and Internet Use as Main Activity
of Leisure Time (Netherlands)

	Computer Use				Computer Use 2000	
	1985	1990	1995	2000	Internet	Other
Subjects ≥ 12 years	0.1	0.5	0.9	1.8	0.5	1.3
Sex						
Male	0.3	0.8	1.5	2.5	0.7	1.8
Female	0.0	0.1	0.4	1.0	0.3	0.7
Age						
12-19	0.4	0.8	1.9	3.4	0.7	2.7
20-34	0.1	0.5	1.3	1.6	0.6	1.0
35-49	0.1	0.5	0.8	2.0	0.6	1.4
50-64	0.1	0.5	0.5	1.7	0.5	1.2
≥ 65	0.0	0.1	0.3	0.6	0.1	0.5
Household position						
Living with parents	0.3	0.7	2.0	2.7	0.6	2.1
Living alone	0.1	0.5	0.9	1.5	0.5	1.1
With partner, without children	0.1	0.3	0.7	1.4	0.5	1.0
Parent with child(ren)	0.1	0.5	0.6	1.8	0.5	1.3
Educational level						
Low	0.1	0.2	0.7	1.4	0.3	1.1
Medium	0.3	0.5	0.9	2.1	0.6	1.5
High	0.1	1.1	1.4	1.9	0.7	1.2
Labor market position						
Student	0.4	0.9	2.2	3.4	0.7	2.6
Working	0.1	0.6	0.9	1.7	0.6	1.2
Housewife, -husband	0.0	0.1	0.3	1.1	0.3	0.8
Unemployed, unable to work	0.2	0.8	1.3	3.0	1.1	1.9
Retired	0.0	0.2	0.6	0.7	0.1	0.6

Source: Sociaal en Cultureel Planbureau (2001, p. 91).

time span, if we focus on exact usage time. Again, this also goes for gaps that have closed or are closing in terms of physical access, such as the gender gap. The usage time for males in the year 2000 was 2.5 times longer than that of females. However, we should not immediately draw the conclusion that the gender usage gap in general is increasing, as it is known that in developed (Western) countries, women at work are using computers and the Internet more and longer than men. (The types of applications they are using casts another light on usage; this issue is dealt with later.) Neither should we conclude that the Dutch unemployed and those unable to work are catching up with the sharp increase in computer usage time in 2000. Clearly, they have no usage time at work. For comparable reasons, students use computers and the Internet most often at home because they are more available for them at home than at school.

According to the UCLA Internet reports (UCLA Center for Communication Policy, 2000, 2003), the total average of weekly hours online in the United States grew from 9.4 in 2000 to 11.1 in 2002. The number of times users connect to the Internet from home is larger than that number at work, but the sessions at work are longer, particularly when the job requires computer work (Horrigan & Rainie, 2002b). The biggest differences in usage time are caused by online experience that is known to be related primarily to employment and school-going status and second, to educational level and income. The average number of hours that Americans used the Internet per week in 2002 was 15.8 if they had been using computers for 6 or more years; for newcomers (with 1 year or less of computer experience) it was 5.5 hours. Evidently, there are more people with high education, high income, and full-time employment and more males and young people among the long-time and experienced users; their counterparts comprise a larger part of the newcomers (Horrigan & Rainie, 2002b).

Usage Diversity

As I have argued, computers and the Internet are the most multi-functional media in history. There are several ways to classify their use functions. The most popular way is the distinction between information, communication, transaction, and entertainment. I have to extend this distinction, as these functions are used in the rather different usage contexts of work, business, education, and leisure time, and a function such as transaction can refer to the very different activities of electronic shopping, banking, voting, and making reservations. The classification I propose should start with main functions because operations such as information retrieval and communication also are used as help functions in other activities. Moreover, the classification should be applicable to both computer and Internet use. Table 6.3 contains my overview of computer and Internet use diversity, which fits the data and arguments

I present later. The personal computer and the Internet primarily are media of information processing or retrieval and communication (writing, reading, and exchanging messages). Initially, they were used at work, in education, and in business, but in the last 10 years, they have expanded to the areas of shopping and entertainment.

Regarding PC applications, I have presented older data from the United States and the Netherlands in previous publications (van Dijk, 2000, 2004; van Dijk & Hacker, 2003). These data indicated that people with high education and income tend to use databases, spreadsheets, bookkeeping, and presentation applications significantly more than people with low education and income, who favor simple consultations, games, and other entertainment.

A comparable distribution is to be observed with the applications of the Internet. The most condensed summary of data I could find is published by Howard, Rainie, and Jones (2001, Table 2). They also analyzed raw data from the Pew Internet and American Life Project collected in the year 2000 for a representative study of the American population. Howard et al. found that using e-mail and browsing just for fun were the most popular Internet applications in the United States in the year 2000. More generally, it appeared that the Internet primarily was an information and communication medium in that year. In other categories, such as shopping and entertainment, users were also primarily looking for information.

Howard et al. (2001) also discovered important differences in Internet use by gender, education, and race. As far as I know, the educational and gender differences are not specific to the United States. However, the racial differences may be specific for this country. Female Americans used most Internet applications significantly less than males. They used applications of communication and particular information more than those of business, shopping, and entertainment. Compared to males, they used e-mail more, sought more health information, and played slightly more games.

Regarding educational differences, people with a high level of education used more e-mail and more information, education, work, business, and shopping applications than people with less than a bachelor's degree. However, they used significantly fewer entertainment applications. This is a revealing fact that will be used later.

The racial differences observed by Howard et al. (2001) clearly refer to social and cultural ethnic differences, not biological ones. Asian Americans sought much more for government information than

Table 6.3   Most Important PC and Internet Applications According to
Their Primary Functions (2004)

Primary Function	PC Application	Internet Application
Information	Consultation (encyclopedia, etc.)	Search engine News Political and government information Information about religion Health and medical information Information about housing Travel information Weather information
Communication	Word processing	E-mail Instant messages Phone calls via the Internet Participation in online groups, support groups Dating Create content (Web site, etc.) Share files
Work	Databases Presentation Graphics and drawing	Job research Job information Job search
Education	Courses	Class or college online
Business and finance	Spreadsheets Bookkeeping	Information about stocks and funds Bank online Online auction Online stock exchange
Shopping		Information about products and service Buy a product Make reservations
Entertainment	Games Audiovisual programs	Information about hobby or leisure activities Information about movies and books Sports information Download music or films Watch video and audio clips Visit adult Web site Participate in chat rooms Play games Gambling

did white Americans. African Americans looked more for religious information and for the weather. However, white Americans used e-mail much more than did Hispanics and African Americans. Generally, Hispanics and African Americans used fewer business and shopping applications than white Americans. However, Asians employed them more than whites. Finally, Hispanics and African Americans used more entertainment applications, on average, than whites, and Asians used fewer.

Broadband Use

The actual usage, the usage time, and the range of applications of computers and the Internet are considerably extended in broadband connections. New usage patterns appear, and a new lifestyle has even developed, according to surveys by the Pew Internet and American Life Project (Horrigan & Rainie, 2002b) and the UCLA Center for Communication Policy (2003). Gradually the use of computers and the Internet has become embedded in everyday life. With the "always on" feature of broadband, people do not have to worry about the cost of connection time anymore. The result is that the connection is used even for insignificant questions and communications. The second most important feature of broadband is greater bandwidth, of course. This not only saves waiting time in operations but also enables a large number of new applications requiring video streams.

People with broadband connections take much more advantage of the opportunities of the new media. However, worldwide, less than 10% of Internet users were connected this way in 2003. South Korea had the lead in that year, with 21 subscribers to broadband per 100 inhabitants (most often, there is more than one user per subscription) and 93.9% of all its Internet users. Hong Kong was second, with 15 per 100 and 42.5% of Internet users. Japan was 10th, with 7.1 subscribers per 100 inhabitants and 30.8% of Internet users, and the United States was 11th, with 6.9 subscribers and 18.3% of Internet users (International Telecommunication Union [ITU], 2003). The definition of *broadband* adopted in the ITU report was the potential exchange of 256 KB in two directions. The costs of broadband connections for subscribers appear to be very different worldwide. Causes of differential broadband access other than cost are the availability of suitable infrastructures in a country (cable and fixed telephone lines realize 99% of broadband connections) and government or business policies promoting this technology.

With the introduction of broadband, old physical or material access problems are reappearing. This is a case of a "next innovation," depicted with a feedback line to former phases of access in Figure 2.3. As in the first 10 to 15 years of narrowband Internet connectivity, the first adopters are male, white, suburban, middle-aged persons with high education and income who have been online for many years (Horrigan & Rainie, 2002a). The main physical access problem is not only cost but also geographical reach: Even in developed countries, broadband simply is not available in many remote regions.

With the adoption of broadband, users substantially increase the amount of time they spend connected and the number and diversity of Internet applications they use. The usage of some of the applications (for information seeking and entertainment) in Table 6.3 is twice as high as their usage by narrowband or dial-up users. For other applications, it is two to three times as high (work and education) or even three to five times (information producing, business, shopping, downloading, and streaming media productions), according to the Pew Internet and American Life Project (Horrigan & Rainie, 2002a). The UCLA *Internet Report* for 2003 (UCLA Center for Communication Policy, 2003) measured exact usage time, revealing that communication, professional work, and downloading of music increased the most. E-mailing went from 3.0 hours per week to 4.8 hours and instant messaging from 1.3 to 3.3 hours. Professional work stepped up from 1.3 to 3.4 hours. Simple browsing swelled from 2.1 to 3.3 hours and downloading of music (undoubtedly accompanied by other tasks) from 0.7 to 2.3 hours (p. 25). The conclusion of the Pew report was that there has been a shift to information producing, instead of only information seeking, using the Internet for the job and for education (telecommuting included), and that there is a swing to downloading audiovisuals. Use of all (other) kinds of entertainment and transactions was also strengthened. In general, a broadband lifestyle of connecting to the Internet several times a day and for long periods of time is appearing. User attitudes seem to be more active and productive, increasing communication, job tasks or educational tasks, and all kinds of transactions.

The Pew 2002 broadband report (Horrigan & Rainie, 2002a) even detects the rise of a *broadband elite*. This is a group of about a quarter of all broadband users, who do ten or more online activities on a typical day. Every day, half of this group uses almost all the applications listed in Table 6.3. With these people, instant messaging is substituting for e-mail. They are busy doing job research and seeking product information. Another characteristic of the broadband elite is that they are information downloaders *and* producers, posting content to the Web, sharing files, and storing information online. Demographically, "members of the broadband elite tend to be technophile males at both ends of the age distribution," 18 to 24 years old and more than 45 (Rainie et al., 2000, p. 16). The broadband elite lives in households packed with equipment, among them three computers or more, on average. At first sight, these people appear to be the same as the early adopters of computers and the Internet in the 1980s and early 1990s, but there is one important difference. The broadband elite also consists of older (45+ years) professional workers in high positions in society. The first early adopters were relatively marginal young technophiles and academics.

It is difficult to underestimate the importance of a broadband connection to equal access to the opportunities of the information and network society, as is explained in the following chapters. According to the Pew broadband report discussed here, it appears from their multivariate analyses that "the availability of a broadband connection is the *largest single factor* that explains the intensity of an online American's Internet use" (Horrigan & Rainie, 2002a, p. 14). According to this report, this is even more important than online experience and the demographics of age, gender, income, education, and employment.

Creative Usage

Broadband users also are considerably more active in creating online content themselves than are dial-up users (Madden, 2003). The difference between a relatively active or creative and a relatively passive and consuming type of usage of the Internet is a much-neglected aspect of the digital divide. Here the differences between social categories of users are the most pronounced, particularly as they concern content creation requiring intellectual skills. Despite its image of being interactive, most Internet usage, apart from e-mailing, is relatively passive and consuming. Creative usage means that users create content for the Web themselves. The most important examples are helping to build a Web site; creating an online diary (a "weblog," or "blog," or a live journal); and posting contributions on an online bulletin board, newsgroup, or community.

About 20% of online Americans said they had created content for the Internet in 2002 (Lenhart et al., 2003, pp. 72-73). In a 2003 survey, this number was raised to 44%, as more popular activities, such as sharing music and video files and posting photographs to Web sites, were added (Lenhart, Fallows, & Horrigan, 2004). Twenty percent of American users were sharing music and video files in 2003. The most frequent other activities were posting photographs to Web sites (21%), posting written material on sites (17%), maintaining a Web site (13%), and posting comments to an online newsgroup (10%). However, significantly more highly educated, high-income, young, broadband-using, experienced Internet users had done these things than had their counterparts. Among the content creators, 46% were college graduates or more (as compared to 26% of all Americans); 25% were high school graduates or had not graduated from high school. See the Pew reports (Lenhart et al., 2003; Lenhart et al., 2004) for other demographics.

❖ EXPLANATIONS OF DIFFERENTIAL USAGE ACCESS

We move now to the causes of the different uses, amounts of usage time, and applications described. For this purpose, I want to return to the causal model in Figure 2.3. What are the most important resources related to usage access? What positional and personal categories explain both these resources and usage access? Once someone has acquired physical access and is able to work with the new technology (skills access), it is to be expected that material resources will become less important. This appeared to be the case in the multivariate analysis of the Dutch 1998 survey of access to ICT discussed in chapter 4. The importance of income and material resources in the determination of physical access largely disappears with skills and usage (van Dijk et al., 2000). Instead, cognitive (mental) resources and the personal characteristics of age and gender came forward. These characteristics call attention to social and cultural resources. With usage access, all familiar social and cultural differences in society appear in the form of differential use of computers and networks.

Resources and Usage Access

First, let us consider the resources. Perhaps the most important resources related to usage access are temporal resources. This relation is obscured by the fact that most surveys measure household use. Instead, they should add all usage at work, in educational settings, and in public places or the home of someone else. All the hours spent with computers and the Internet at work, at school, at home, and elsewhere have to be counted. Then it will become clear that people working with the new digital media daily, both at work or school and at home, have much greater usage access than those working with them at home only. For people with a full-time job or training, leisure time and household activity time are scarce goods. This is not the case for the unemployed, people disabled for work, the retired, and people caring for the household. This explains the relatively high household usage time of the unemployed, disabled, and retired (younger than 65) in recent years, as shown in Table 6.2.

Usage time at work or at school is distributed, controlled, and often monitored by management and by teachers. Employees and pupils do not have the freedom to use computers and the Internet as long as they wish and for every application. The actual appropriation of computers and the Internet (usage access) is determined by a particular relation of power between management and employees and between teachers and students. At home, the actual appropriation in terms of usage access is a matter of relationships of power and interest (motivational access) in using the new technology between partners, between parents and children, and between young and old and male and female children. Here, particular relationships of gender, parenthood, and age or generation are realized. All these small-scale relationships of power and interest are obscured by the summarizing data of survey research.

Material resources are less important for usage access than for physical access. Still, they keep playing their role after a physical connection is acquired. The steep rise in usage time and number of applications that appears after the transition to broadband testifies to the fact that the high costs of connection time are a major barrier for dial-up users of the Internet. For offline computers, the relatively high costs of computer and printer accessories, which grow with increasing uses and applications (software, paper, ink, blank and prerecorded CDs), are a problem for low-income users. Finally, with the expansion of the Internet and the audiovisual services of broadband connections, the costs of conditional access (pay services) are growing.

Mental resources are less important for usage access than they are for motivational and skills access. In spite of that, they remain a foundation for actual use, length of usage time, and range and difficulty of applications used. The most familiar indication of the presence of mental resources is the level of education. Table 6.1 shows that only 35% of

Americans with high school or less actually use computers, although 89% of Americans with college and more are using them. Computer and Internet usage time also is much longer among people with high than with low levels of education (see Table 6.2; UCLA Center for Communication Policy, 2000, 2001, 2003; and the annual online activities tracking surveys of the Pew Internet and American Life Project, available at http://www.pewinternet.org/data.asp). Additionally, Howard et al. (2001) have shown that Americans with a bachelor's degree or higher use significantly more applications for information, e-mail communication, work, education, business, and shopping, but Americans with less than a bachelor's degree use more entertainment applications and instant message or chatroom communication. These differences are not only explained by differential skills and by the greater or less experience of long-time versus new computer and Internet users; they also are related to the special knowledge and understanding needed to use advanced applications for information seeking and producing, job research, higher education, and business or finance (e.g., stocks, insurance, mortgages).

However, the differences might be even better explained by differences of social and cultural resources. Here the core concept of understanding is interest in or motivation to develop these resources. The motivation for development differs with gender and racial or ethnic background. This was already noted in the description of actual use, usage time, and diversity. For example, the observation that females are using e-mail more and longer than males (Table 6.4; Boneva & Kraut, 2002; Howard et al., 2001) but like chatting less reflects particular gender preferences in electronic communication. The same goes for information: Searching for health information is very popular among (at least American) women, but getting the news or political information and checking sport scores are quite unpopular. Finally, the use of electronic business and shopping appears to be gendered (see Table 6.4). These applications are significantly less used by (American) females. This even goes for shopping (Howard et al., 2001). Perhaps the physical mode is preferred, as compared to the virtual mode.

A comparable commentary can be made on the racial or ethnic divisions appearing in the data (Howard et al., 2001). The fact that Hispanic and African Americans use e-mail significantly less than white Americans might reflect a preference for face-to-face conversation. The observation that African Americans seek more religious information, check more sport scores, play more online games, and take more part in chatrooms than do white Americans might reflect their propensity for

Table 6.4   Percentages of U.S. Internet Users Conducting Specific Activities (2002)

Internet Activities	Some High School or Less	High School Graduate	Some College	College Graduate or Higher	Male	Female
Information						
Used search engine	76.3	79.5	81.5	88.2, n.s.	53.1	45.0
Searched with specific question	65.0	73.8	81.3	83.5	77.1	78.0, n.s.
Got news	57.5	55.0	61.0	73.3	66.1	57.8
Sought news about politics	25.0	24.9	39.0	43.6	36.8	31.1, n.s.
Sought information from local government site	21.3	36.6	53.9	57.8	48.7	44.0, n.s.
Sought religious or spiritual information	18.8	18.1	31.5	32.2	23.1	28.3, n.s.
Sought health information	37.5	55.0	58.8	71.2	49.2	68.5
Communication						
Used e-mail	74.1	81.6	91.4	97.5	83.6	92.2
Sought information on person or sought to meet person	30.9	21.8	26.6	19.5	28.7	18.8
Sought online personal and medical support	28.8	37.4	46.8	53.4	34.5	52.1
Created online content	3.7	13.8	8.6	15.3	11.9	11.2, n.s.
Participated in online group	10.0	10.6	8.2	13.1	11.7	9.1, n.s.
Work						
Did work online	22.2	27.7	32.0	54.2	37.7	33.5, n.s.
Education						
Did research for school or training	35.0	38.8	50.9	57.6	43.9	49.9, n.s.
Business						
Got financial information	19.8	29.9	37.5	41.5	40.4	28.9
Bank online	10.0	15.6	23.2	31.8	24.0	19.4, n.s.
Bought or sold stocks, bonds, shares	6.3	6.9	8.2	10.2	10.8	5.4
Shopping						
Bought a product	38.8	47.8	52.8	60.2	53.3	49.9, n.s.

(Continued)

Table 6.4 (Continued)

Internet Activities	Some High School or Less	High School Graduate	Some College	College Graduate or Higher	Male	Female
Entertainment						
Online just for fun or to pass time	88.2	71.6	63.0	54.0	71.4	61.1
Checked sport scores	35.0	44.1	39.3	41.0, n.s.	55.7	27.8
Sought information about a hobby	73.4	77.5	79.6	74.6, n.s.	38.6	24.9

Source: Data are from Pew Internet and American Life Project (2002).

Note: All differences significant (Pearson chi-square) below the 0.01 level except those indicated n.s. (not significant).

a culture of religion, sport, and play. Hispanic and African Americans also use significantly fewer business and shopping applications. However, this difference seems to be caused by fewer material resources (income and employment). In contrast to these data, Asian Americans use more business and shopping applications than do white Americans. They buy stocks and bonds twice to three times as much. They are considerably more interested in political information and use the Internet less as an entertainment medium than do whites, African Americans, and Hispanics. Perhaps these differences reflect a culture of economic and political ambition and career mindedness.

The motivation to develop the social and cultural resources needed to get access to particular new media or Internet applications also differs among people expressing specific lifestyles. In the 2002 German ARD/ZDF Online Study (van Eimeren et al., 2002), a general media user typology was applied to compare the German online population with the general population of the country. The results showed that people with a solitary or retired and home-loving lifestyle used the Internet far less than the average (see Figure 6.1). To a lesser degree, this also was the case for people who embraced the classical culture and people who had a sociable and active lifestyle. The first group preferred classical music, books, and museums and the second group, social meetings and physical community life. In contrast to these groups, people with achievement- and experience-focused lifestyles and a preference for new cultural expressions used the Internet significantly more than the average population. This applied even more to the "young and wild" dynamic lifestyle of that part of German youth

Figure 6.1   Distribution of Media User Types Among Germans Online and
                  Population at Large in 2002 (%)

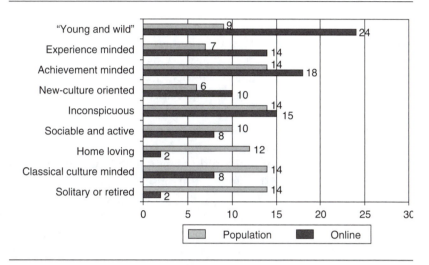

Source: van Eimeren, Gerhard, and Frees (2002).

that frequently uses and explores all kinds of new digital media in
every environment (van Eimeren et al., 2002).

Positional Categories and Usage Access

The distribution of all these resources is determined by the positional and personal categorical inequalities I turn to now. As a general
rule, it can be maintained that the positional categories mainly affect the
temporal and material resources, and personal categories primarily
shape the social and cultural resources of new media usage access.
Mental resources are influenced by both positional and personal categories; in particular, educational position and personal age, intelligence,
health, and personality.

Specific positions in the division of labor on the job determine the
usage time and the nature and number of applications used by particular categories of employees. As we have seen in describing usage time
and discussing the "broadband elite," some categories use computers
and the Internet during the entire working day. Others do this during
only part of their labor time or once in a while. Others, again, never use
a computer or the Internet at work. Regarding the use of applications

on the job, a gap appears between those working all day with the same applications of, for instance, databases and spreadsheets (administrators) or word processing (secretaries) and those who use a variety of applications for information, communication, business, and finance (managers). This distribution of time and applications at work is continued and reinforced at home when working people telecommute or work on projects begun in the office (overtime). Together they create the level of computer and Internet experience that appears to be such an important intermediate variable in explaining usage and usage applications (Horrigan & Rainie, 2002b).

Specific types and levels of education (school or special course) also determine amount of usage and the nature and number of applications. Computers and the Internet are used significantly more in higher education than in secondary school. General usage also depends on the resources, utilities, and wealth of a particular school. The number of computers, Internet connections, software applications, and knowledgeable teachers is extremely different among schools in all parts of the world. Computer applications are very dissimilar in different types of education that prepare students for various occupations. In the previous chapter, I called attention to the difference between remedial drills and advanced intellectual tasks. All these differences are continued and reinforced through increasing experience by students at home doing homework and pursuing personal interests (hobbies).

Household composition and relationships not only affect the purchase of computers and Internet connections but also their actual use, usage time, and variety of use. The larger the household and the more (school-going) children it has, the more computers and Internet connections actually are used, the longer users use the computers, and the more different applications are used. This is not only a matter of adding individuals but of a mutual exchange of ideas, interests, and experiences among members of the household. Children draw their parents' and siblings' attention to particular applications and help to master them. Parents teach young children to take their first steps in the computer world. After some time, a single home computer does not fulfill all household members' needs anymore. Sometimes competition arises among individual members wanting to use the same computer. A second and third computer is purchased when this is allowed by the household budget. The importance of household relationships for skills and usage access is underestimated in current research.

Being an inhabitant of a particular nation or region determines not only physical access but also usage access and experience. In the developed countries, actual usage and hours of daily use are rising much faster than in developing countries. The reasons are not only the rapid diffusion of computer technology in workplaces and at schools but also the predominance of home computers and home Internet connections. The restricted use of the scarce computers at work and in schools in developing countries and their people's strong dependence on computers and Internet connections in crowded public places, Internet cafés, and other such venues clearly limit usage time and applications. Unfortunately, there are very few statistics about the international distribution of actual usage, usage time, and applications for computers and the Internet.

The same disparities concerning usage arise between different regions in both developed and developing countries. Even in the leading nation for information and communication technology, the United States, large regional gaps in terms of Internet usage have appeared (Donnermeyer & Hollifield, 2003; Fox, 2003; Madden, 2003). For instance, inhabitants of the Atlantic and Pacific seaboards use the Internet much more than inhabitants of the South, the Southeast, and the industrial Midwest. On the coast, people search more for specific and advanced information and they shop more online than do users in the interior. People in the South, Southeast, and industrial Midwest focus on communicating with family and friends, surfing for fun, and looking for relatively general and simple information about the news and about health (Madden, 2003). Most likely, the transition to broadband will exacerbate regional gaps of physical access and use, as many remote and rural regions do not have the infrastructure required.

Personal Categories and Usage Access

As I have claimed several times before, the personal category inequalities of age, gender, and, to a lesser extent, race or ethnicity come forward in the explanation of unequal usage access. Age has been a prominent category from the very beginning of the rise of the new digital media. The innovators, the early adopters, and a very large part of the early majority using the new technology were mainly young people less than 35 years old. From the end of the 1990s onward, the usage distribution in the developed countries shifted to middle-aged people (35 to 55 years). This shift is partly due to the so-called cohort effect: The younger generation becomes middle aged. Young seniors (55 to 65) also were able to catch up considerably. However, older seniors (65+) kept lagging very far behind. For the younger generations, computer and

Internet use has become a normal daily affair at work, at school, and in leisure time. They have grown up with them. The older generations had to make a special effort to learn to use computers and the Internet.

Currently, most computer and Internet applications are more evenly spread among the generations. However (at least for Americans), applications such as instant messaging, taking part in chatrooms, going online just for fun, and using the Internet for school and training are much more popular for people under than over 30 (Horrigan & Rainie, 2002b). On the other hand, searching for health and travel information and making travel reservations were less popular for young Americans. For American seniors 65 years old and older, e-mailing family and friends, checking the news, and searching for health information were the only really popular Internet applications (Horrigan & Rainie, 2002b).

Although physical access is equalizing, or has equalized, among both sexes in the developed countries, actual use, usage time, and diversity clearly have not done so (see Tables 6.2 and 6.4; Howard et al., 2001). Use is very much gendered. Women use computers more at work than do their male colleagues, but they do so with a far more limited number and level of applications. Most applications are used for administrative and secretarial work and for purposes of teaching, health care, and selling (retail): word processing (including e-mail), billing, filing, and filling out databases and spreadsheets. Male employees use computer and Internet applications more for purposes of searching and creating information in the context of their job or for business and finance. Other gender differences in using computer and Internet applications have been discussed.

The influence of the personal categories of intelligence (cognitive, social, and emotional), personality, and health or ability in the actual use, usage time, and usage diversity of computers and the Internet is most likely felt in several different ways, yet there are no data to prove this. The only phenomena that have been investigated are computer anxiety, communication apprehension in computer network use, computer frustration, and technophobia (see chapter 3). According to a longitudinal U.S. survey by Rockwell and Singleton (2002), people with high levels of computer anxiety were less likely to use the Internet at all, and those with high levels of communication apprehension were less inclined to use Internet services that involved interpersonal communication. Technophobia is a phenomenon that mainly affects new Internet users and nonusers. It affects up to 30.3% of new users and 10.8% of experienced users in the United States, according to self-reports of respondents in the 2003 UCLA Internet report (UCLA Center for Communication Policy, 2003, p. 24).

❖ THE "MATTHEW EFFECT" AND THE RISE OF USAGE GAPS

With all the types of access to the digital media and their social consequences discussed in this book, it appears that those who already have a large amount of resources at their disposal benefit first and most from the capacities and opportunities of these media. This phenomenon has been called the "Matthew effect" by the sociologist Robert Merton (1968), according to the Gospel of Matthew: "For to everyone who has, more shall be given" (Matt. 25:29, New American). A popular version of this might be "The rich get richer." If we want to turn these popular and biblical expressions into a more precise statement, the Matthew effect could be framed as follows: Those who already have a head start in possessing particular resources benefit more from a new resource than those who are behind and already have some disadvantage. In the case of new media access, the existing possessions are the material, mental, temporal, social, and cultural resources discussed in this book, and the new resource is the potential value of having and using computers and networks.

A Matthew effect was clearly demonstrated in chapter 4, in which it was seen that most gaps of physical access appear to have widened, until very recently, in developed countries. In all cases, the category with the most resources at its disposal—the social class with high income, high education, high-level occupations, and full employment; the ethnic majority in a country; and the generation with the highest learning potential (the younger generation)—was the first to take advantage of the new technology. In this way, this category increased its advantage compared to the categories with lesser resources. The same was observed with regard to rich and poor nations and regions worldwide. At the start of the 21st century, the effect in terms of physical access starts to weaken in some developed countries, as the best resource categories are getting saturated. However, with every new innovation (e.g., current broadband diffusion), the process seems to start anew.

Regarding skills access, I also claimed that people of high social class, especially those with high levels of education, males, and young people were the first and the best in developing digital skills. This appeared to be the case for information and strategic digital skills in particular, which are primarily and almost exclusively mastered by people who already have a very high level of ability in using the old media.

Finally, there is usage access. Here the Matthew effect has the strongest and most lasting impact. Usage is the ultimate goal of the whole process of appropriation of the new media, of course. Here all inequalities in earlier types of access come together. Subsequently, they are mixed with all existing economic, social, cultural, and political inequalities in society. Inequalities of motivational, material, and skills access might partly disappear, as we have seen in previous chapters. Gradually, more segments of the population are convinced that they should participate in the information society and get access to computers and networks. Concerning physical access to new media that have been in existence longer, the higher social categories are getting saturated and the lower social categories are catching up. With the right educational policies, digital skills can be better disseminated among populations. However, inequalities of usage access will not disappear that easily, if they ever do. Instead, they may grow.

This conjecture is the hypothesis of the rising *usage gap* I have discussed in several previous publications (van Dijk, 1997, 1999, 2000, 2004; van Dijk & Hacker, 2003). It is similar to the classic *knowledge gap* hypothesis (Tichenor, Donohue, & Olien, 1970). Clearly, the knowledge gap thesis is based on the Matthew effect too: "As the diffusion of mass media information into a social system increases, segments of the population with a higher socio-economic status tend to acquire this information at a faster rate than the lower status segments" (Tichenor et al., 1970, p. 159). However, the knowledge gap is only about the differential diffusion and development of knowledge or information. The usage gap is broader, as it is about unequal practices and applications; that is, action or behavior in particular contexts. This includes knowledge and information.

Although the evidence in favor of the thesis of the knowledge gap has not been conclusive (Gaziano, 1983), it might get another chance in the broader context of the differential practices and applications characterizing the information or network society. In the following two chapters, I explain why. In this chapter, I first clarify which current tendencies combine to produce usage gaps in the appropriation of information and communication technology. Finally, I provide data indicating the rise of such gaps.

Causes and Characteristics of Usage Gaps

Several tendencies come together to produce the probability of usage gaps in contemporary society (van Dijk, 2000):

♦ Social and cultural differentiation and individualization in (post)modern society
♦ Rising social-economic inequalities of income, employment, and property worldwide
♦ Commercialization (privatization and liberalization) of formerly public information and communication facilities that increase conditional access

These societal tendencies, further described in chapter 10, increase the unequal distribution of resources and the positional and personal inequalities related to digital media usage. These tendencies and their results merge with the characteristics of ICT, as discussed in earlier sections.

♦ Complexity: Some advanced applications are difficult for average users to use; others are relatively simple.
♦ Expense: Some applications require special hardware, software, and conditional access; others are "free"—that is, available after the purchase of the basic technology (computer and connection).
♦ Multiple functions: The same basic and extended computer technology can be used for very different, simple, and advanced applications.
♦ Biased content: The software and information services offered favor particular social and cultural interests, languages, cultures, and multimedia literacy skills over others.

Together, these tendencies and characteristics increase the probability that the usage of the new media will diverge among different categories, sections, and classes of the population and produce more or less structural usage gaps. Such gaps also have been observed by other investigators. I have referred to data from the United States and the Netherlands in previous publications (van Dijk, 2000, 2004; van Dijk & Hacker, 2003). These data indicated that people with high levels of education and income tend to use the applications of databases, spreadsheets, bookkeeping, and presentations significantly more than people with low levels of education and income, who favor simple consultations, games, and other entertainment. Han Park (2002) replicated these statistics for South Korea, revealing the same distribution between Koreans with high and low levels of education. Using the same Pew Internet and American Life Project 2000 data as Howard et al. (2001), Cho, de Zúñiga, Rojas, and Shah (2003) claimed that U.S. Internet users who are young and have high socioeconomic status used this medium in a very specific goal-oriented way; that is, to strategically satisfy their motivations and gratifications of connection, learning, and acquisition (products and services). In contrast, those U.S. users who were older and had low socioeconomic status employed the Internet in various general and superficial ways, primarily to satisfy consumptive needs and the gratifications of connection.

A 2000 survey in Switzerland referred to by Bonfadelli (2002) indicated that Swiss people with high levels of education use many more applications for information, communication, and services than fellow Swiss with low levels of education; the latter favor entertainment applications (see Table 6.5).

The recurrent Pew Internet and American Life Tracking surveys provide more detailed information about Internet activities by U.S. users. When we look at education and gender differences, which indicate the most important background categories of usage next to age and race or ethnicity, as discussed in the previous section, we find conspicuous gaps. See Table 6.4 for the year 2002. It shows that Americans with higher levels of education use almost every application of information, communication, education, work, business, and shopping significantly more than do Americans with lower levels of education. Instead, the latter use the Internet more just for fun, although they are equal to the former in use of the Internet for hobby and sport information. Other data reveal that Americans with low levels of education also use the Internet a great deal more for playing games, chatting, gambling, and downloading music (Howard et al., 2001). In Table 6.4, clear gender differences are expressed. U.S. males use more applications for information (except when it comes to searching for health information), business, shopping, and entertainment than do U.S. females. Women use more applications of communication: e-mail, personal support, and medical support.

In my opinion, these are the first signs of usage gaps, in terms of applications, that will not narrow but widen with the further diffusion of the new media in society. Computer and Internet use increasingly reflects differences and inequalities in society and reinforces them

Table 6.5   Types of Applications Used on the Internet by Level of
Education in Switzerland(%)

Type of Application	Total	Low Education	Middle Education	High Education
Communication	92	90	92	94
Information	59	53	58	64
Services (transactions, downloading)	41	31	41	45
Entertainment	42	72	42	35

Source: Bonfadelli (2002).

Note: Data are for Switzerland in 2000. Specific applications include e-mail (communication); search engines, transport schedules, online newspapers archives and information, continuing education (information); electronic shopping and banking, booking voyages, downloading software and music (services); and gaming and chatting (entertainment).

because they are tools and because they are affected by all of the societal and technological tendencies discussed earlier. Unfortunately, I am not able to prove that usage gaps are *growing*, as we have no sufficient time series data available. Data such as the regular Pew Internet use tracking data can help, but what is needed are not only data about people who have ever used a particular application but about the time(s) of usage of applications. One-time use of applications will grow quickly among the "lowest" categories, and with the "highest" categories, it is approaching peak levels.

A more structural usage gap appears when some segments of the population systematically and permanently use and benefit from advanced computer and Internet applications for information, communication, work, business, and education, and others only use the basic or simple applications for information, communication, and shopping and enjoy more applications for entertainment.

❖ CONCLUSIONS

In this chapter, I clarified why motivational, material, and skills access are necessary but not sufficient conditions of usage. Usage also was explained in its own right. In doing this, I revealed that material and mental resources are less important for usage access than are temporal, social, and cultural resources, lifestyles included. As I explained the distribution of these resources, it became clear that the positional categories of labor, education, household, and nation were mainly responsible for temporal and material resources of usage. Compared to them, the personal categories of age, sex, race, intelligence, personality, and health or ability primarily accounted for the social and cultural resources of new media usage.

Increasingly, all familiar social and cultural differences in society are reflected in computer and Internet use. This is the first reason why the inequalities of use described in this chapter are larger, on average, than the inequalities we have come across with motivational, material, and even skills access. According to my cumulative model, inequalities of use build on the other inequalities. The second reason for the larger differences is the fact that the digital media function as tools and trend amplifiers (van Dijk, 1999). We have seen that ICTs (hardware, software, and content) have properties that both extend and reduce access. In the case of reduction of access, chances are increased that existing social disparities are pronounced and amplified. In the case of extension of access, opportunities arise for the creation of policies that can diminish these disparities. A third reason discussed in this chapter rests on the claim that computers and the Internet are the most multifunctional media in history, permeating all spheres of life and offering all kinds of applications for every interest.

In considering these three reasons, it is no surprise that we can observe the first signs of a usage gap between people of high social position, income, and education using the advanced computer and Internet applications for information, communication, work, business, or education and people of low social position, income, and education using more simple applications for information, communication, shopping, and entertainment. The objection could be made that this is not a new phenomenon. Haven't the social classes always used the media in different ways? Wasn't the knowledge gap thesis invented to show that people take advantage of the old mass media in different ways? These objections would be correct except that they underestimate the (growing) importance of the digital media for every kind of activity in contemporary society. Downplaying the importance of a usage gap in these media is a more serious error when the changing social contexts are ignored. The advanced high-tech societies are rapidly evolving into information and network societies. Here, differences of new media use in information, communication, and transaction for purposes of work, education, social life, and decision making are becoming crucial aspects of all positions and relationships in society. It is to the consequences of the special characteristics of the information and network society that we turn now.

7

Inequality in the Information Society

In this book, the topic of inequality of access to ICTs is treated in the context of the nascent information and network society. These are two typical classifications of contemporary high-technological societies of special interest to the topic of the book. They indicate very general, long-term evolutionary processes in contemporary societies. They are not concrete societal forms with precise historical beginnings and ends. To use a vivid expression, one might say that the information society did not start in 1751 with the appearance of the first part of the *Encyclopédie* of Diderot and d'Alembert and the network society did not appear with the installation of the first telegraph line by Samuel Morse in 1844. In the 19th century, after the industrial revolution, the modernizing Western societies gradually became information societies (Beniger, 1986). In the 20th century, their social structure, modes of organization, and communication infrastructure, together typified mass society's progressive change into network society (Castells, 1996; Mulgan, 1991; van Dijk, 1999, 2001).

r authors dealing with the problem of rising information inequality do not accept fashionable concepts such as the information or network society to frame their arguments. Authors working in the Marxist tradition, such as Herbert Schiller, Robert McChesney, and Frank Webster, argue that increasing use of information, computers, and networks marks just another phase of capitalism. Schiller (1996) claimed that inequality of access and impoverished content of information were only deepening the already pervasive social crisis in America. McChesney (1999) answered the question of whether the Internet will "set us free" by denial, emphasizing that corporate control of the new "rich media" will bring "poor democracy." Frank Webster (1995, 2001) is still looking in vain for the qualitatively new properties of the so-called information society. This means that I must first explain what exactly is new about the information society that warrants such a special classification. In the subsequent sections, I discuss two kinds of (nonmaterial) goods that are vital for (in)equality in the information society just defined. These are information as a *primary good* and as a *positional good.* I argue that the distribution of these goods determines productivity and power in present and future developed societies.

❖ WHAT IS AN INFORMATION SOCIETY?

My point of departure is that many classifications, such as capitalist and (post)modern society, remain valid as before. When we add the characteristics of the information and network society, these traditional classifications may even gain explanatory value. For example, it is a matter of fact that almost every contemporary society is capitalist and is based on a more or less free market economy. This may be the direct cause of inequality in material access and of those problems with the affordability of information services that we have observed in previous chapters. When present-day societies are postmodern, high modern, or late modern (whatever you like), this means that they have a high level of differentiation and of inequality in general. It also helps to explain the usage diversity and usage gaps described in chapter 6. Further, democratic societies and welfare states offer their citizens (the right to) particular public services of information and communication. As high-tech societies, they are characterized by a high level of complexity and by compulsory education that automatically highlight differences of skill. Finally, a more or less ecologically sustainable society determines the nature and number of media and technologies that are acceptable. Is ICT a relatively clean technology, or does it primarily add to environmental problems?

All these alternative characterizations of the context of inequality of access to the new media have some relevance to the topic of this book. However, the context of developing information and network societies has the most direct relationship. The concept of the *information society* is a *substantial* characterization of societies in which information increasingly is the primary means and product of all processes. The concept of the *network society* is a *formal* characterization emphasizing a particular social (infra)structure and organization of contemporary society. In general, developed societies possess more of the character of an information and network society than do developing societies. Most often, the latter are rural and (pre)industrial societies, and they might be called mass societies instead of network societies (van Dijk, 1999).

With good reason, the concept of the information society is controversial (Dordick & Wang, 1993, Webster, 1995, 2001). Webster (2001) concludes that all the definitions of this concept that he could find refer to a greater *quantity* of information, information products, information occupations, communication means, and the like, but none of these definitions identifies the *qualitatively* new (system) character of this type of society. According to Kumar (1995), increasing use of information "has not produced a radical shift in the way industrial societies are organized, or in the direction in which they have been moving. The imperatives of profit, power and control seem as predominant now as they have ever been in the history of capitalist industrialism" (p. 154).

Manuel Castells (1996) also rejects the concept of the information society, as all societies in the past have been based on information. Instead, he proposes the concept of the "informational society": "a specific form of social organization in which information generation, processing and transmission become the fundamental sources of productivity and power" (p. 21). However, this designation does not differ from many contemporary definitions of the information society.

In this book, *information* is defined as the interpretation of data and other signals by humans and animals with some kind of consciousness. Data are numerical, alphanumerical, or use other notational signs that serve as the raw material for information. *Knowledge* is information of more lasting importance, as it contains facts (recordable descriptions of reality) and established relations of cause and effect that explain how things work and how we can use them. In the information society, knowledge, information, and data are continually growing, and growing faster; that is, data are expanding more intensively than information, and information, again, is expanding more intensively than knowledge (Pool, Inose, Takasaki, & Hunwitz, 1984).

This situation has progressed to such an extreme that computer systems are barely able to process the data and human minds the information and knowledge. However, quantitative development is insufficient to define an information society. The qualitative leap made by the information society in what is typically a long-term evolutionary process means that *the information intensity of all activities has become so high* that it is leading to

- ◆ An organization of society based on science, rationality, and reflexivity
- ◆ An economy with all values and sectors, even the agrarian and industrial sectors, increasingly characterized by information production
- ◆ A labor market with a majority of functions largely or completely based on tasks of information processing requiring knowledge and higher education (hence the alternative term *knowledge society)*
- ◆ A culture dominated by media and information products with their signs, symbols, and meanings

It is the intensity of information processing in these spheres that is causing their qualitative transformation. The "imperatives of profit, power and control" (Kumar, 1995) are working differently both in form (network structure) and in substance (information). I do not have sufficient space here to deal with these transformations, but I hope it will be adequate to state that the common denominator of the change produced by the increasing information intensity of all activities is the *semiautonomous character of information processing.* Most activities in contemporary society are dedicated to *means*—in this case, means of processing and producing information, activities distancing themselves from their ultimate aims in society and gathering their own momentum and reason to exist. Castells has claimed that information has become an independent source of productivity and power. However, this claim should be qualified, as there is no complete autonomy of information production and processing. The ultimate goals of information production and

processing—to support the production, distribution, and consump.
of all goods and services in the economy; to assist in the governance
and management of increasingly complex societies and organizations;
and to fill a culture with an enormous extension of signs and symbols
attached to forms and carried by an explosion of media use and
experience—these ultimate goals still are their basic reasons for existence and extension.

It therefore remains the best option to relate the information
society to other classifications of contemporary society: first of all, a
capitalist society with a more or less free-market economy; a civil society with more or less democratic politics; and a postmodern or high-
modern culture with more or less diverse artifacts, media, and
experiences. Other necessary classifications related to the information
society refer to the technological and organizational means of contemporary society, such as the high-tech society and the network society.

INFORMATION AS A PRIMARY GOOD

Relating the information society to other classifications explains the
semiautonomous character of information production in every sphere
of society. Let us start with the economy, in which information as an
independent source of productivity and power has become a so-called
primary good (see Rawls, 1971, and Sen, 1985). Primary goods are
goods that are so essential for the survival and self-respect of individuals that they can not be exchanged for other goods. Rights, freedoms,
life chances, and a particular basic level of income are the most familiar
examples of mainly nonmaterial primary goods. According to Rawls
and Sen, people have equal rights to these goods in principle.
In particular societies, this is realized to a certain degree. Examples of
more material primary goods, often necessary to realize the nonmaterial goods, are basic education, elementary health care, and minimum
social benefits. The primary good of information is a nonmaterial good,
although it is able to materialize in the shape of an information product. As a nonmaterial primary good, information has an extremely
important special quality. One is able to exchange this good without
losing it: Suppliers transmit information to receivers without losing
the good themselves. This quality has an equalizing effect on the use
of information, as may be observed in the context of new media use
regarding the extensive practice of copying digital information sources

and exchanging them on networks, ignoring intellectual property rights.

Thus the first characteristic of primary goods is that they cannot (really) be exchanged for other goods, as they are essential for survival, and they are not lost in transfer. A second basic characteristic is their potential, and not always actual, consumption—the chance of being consumed. This certainly applies to information because the psychological meaning of this concept is the interpretation of available signs and data by the mental system of an individual. Signs and data do not have to become information. This characteristic makes the activity of information more unequal, as people have different mental qualities and intellectual skills. However, the first characteristic implies that everyone should have a particular minimum of information.

A third characteristic of primary goods is that their value completely depends on the quality of the good and on its personal use by consumers (Sen, 1976). This clearly applies to information, as it is a specific interpretation of data or signals from the environment or the body by persons according to their own goals. However, to inform is not only an individual but also a collective activity. It is a social affair as well, first of all in the act of communication. Thus the value of information as a primary good also depends on its social appropriation. As people live in different social environments, this third characteristic also implies greater inequality in the production and use of information.

In the information society, the first characteristic of information as a primary good—its necessity for survival—attains special importance. The basic level of information required is higher than in other types of society, and that level is continually rising. Moreover, the relative differences between people who have more or less of this primary good are getting more important. Information has acquired a semiautonomous character, as was explained in the previous section. It has become a special source of productivity and power.

This brings us to the core of inequality in the information society. The first problem is that the basic level of information required is not guaranteed. A large part of the world, even in the developed countries, does not possess the necessary, continually changing, and increasing *absolute* level of information: (functional) illiterates, information want-nots, and people who cannot afford or cannot receive particular information. The second problem is that the *relative* differences between all important social categories are increasing. As we saw in chapter 5, information and strategic skills, in particular, are very unevenly divided among the populations of both developed and developing societies, considerably more than are the possession of computer hardware or software and operational skills. These differences tend to grow larger because of the continually growing information overload and the arrival of ever more advanced information systems, search systems, and decision support systems. A summary of digital skills discussed in chapter 5 produces the following list of information skills:

- The ability to make associations and to transfer information into knowledge
- The ability to make generalizations and abstractions (beyond the stage of factual knowledge)
- The ability to make selections and to exercise discipline in dealing with the growing supply of information
- The ability to estimate the quality of information
- The ability to use different information channels in parallel and to choose among them

The following strategic skills can also be listed:

- The development of a "hunger" for information and an attitude that information needed can be actively searched for
- Insight about opportunities to apply information in one's own situation and the willingness to learn the skills required
- The ability to create a social network of information users with whom to work
- The ability to not only search and process information for one's own individual purposes but also to share information with others who are relevant in the situation concerned

In stressing these absolute and relative inequalities of information and skill, we should not forget that the most basic reason for calling information a primary good is that every human being needs a minimum of information to live in a particular society. The minimum depends on the level of development in that society. Every human being has the right to this particular minimum level in that society. In most societies, one even has a duty (to inform). This is the meaning of information that is passed on in compulsory education and the sense of the demand that everyone is supposed to know the law. In return for these obligations, the government cares for primary and secondary education and provides a number of public, freely accessible information services that provide information about the rules of society.

❖ INFORMATION AS A POSITIONAL GOOD

It is a great paradox that, despite the information overload in contemporary society, there still is a scarcity of information in many situations. The solution of this apparent contradiction is that the possession and control of specific information offers considerable strategic advantage in these situations. Here, information appears to be a positional good (Hirsch, 1976). These are goods that, by definition, are scarce. Their appeal to consumers depends on the extent to which others use, need, or desire the same good. Well-known examples are parking lots, nice views, empty beaches, personal favors or services, and foreknowledge or insider's knowledge at the stock exchange. One is only able to acquire these goods when one occupies a particular position. In the next chapter, it is argued that increasingly this position will be in a social and media network.

A good illustration is the information needed for buying and selling stocks on the Internet. This medium has improved the position of small private investors in their relationship to banks and investment funds. They are no longer completely dependent on their monopolies of information and transaction. However, at the same time, professional investors keep their relative lead by using considerably more advanced applications of ICT in exchanging stocks. They apply and improve their skills in using these complex applications and benefit from all kinds of information and contact through other, more traditional sources of face-to-face communication or print media that are scarce and only available to them. The elite of these investors, closely linked to the leadership of the companies and funds concerned, have even more foreknowledge and insider's knowledge than they used to have in the past. They use all sources and are able to extract the most strategically useful information from them.

In previous chapters I noted how important not only personal but also positional categories of having a particular job, business, education, household membership, and nationality are for the distribution of resources and for the types of access to the new media that were discussed. These positions determine the actual opportunities (a) to develop the motivation to get access, (b) to acquire physical access,

(c) to develop skills, and (d) to use information technology often and for a diversity of reasons. The people in the favored positions use this technology to strengthen these same positions. Therefore it is no surprise that the use of information and communication, with the support of their technology (ICT), is polarizing positions in several spheres of society (van Dijk, 1999).

The clearest case of polarization is to be found in the labor process. Here, generally speaking, the complexity and autonomy of labor in the information society is increasing with the increase in the use of ICTs, according to empirical research in the Netherlands (Steijn, 2001). The more one uses ICT on the job, the higher the complexity and autonomy of the job (with the exception of data entry and the like) (p. 105). Of course, the relation also works the other way round. Complexity is increasing, as working with this technology often requires relatively high intelligence and a high level of abstraction. Regarding autonomy, the relation is not direct, but indirect, as it is dependent on the type of organization of labor. Taylorist organizations offer far less autonomy, complexity, and opportunities to learn in using ICTs than so-called sociotechnical and team organizations, and these organizations, in their turn, offer less than do professional organizations (Steijn, 2001, pp. 106-108). (Taylorism refers to a labor organization with greatly divided tasks: Executive tasks and management tasks are first separated, and these are subsequently divided "endlessly.")

When considering individual positions, one also is able to observe a polarization of the consequences of ICT for the different types of labor.

> With regard to autonomy on the job, it is primarily managers and professionals who produce a high score; service personnel and semiprofessionals show a relatively low score. Concerning complexity, the scores of (chiefly) managers, professionals, and semi-professionals are high, and the scores of commercial and service personnel and manual laborers are low. (Steijn, 2001, p. 108, my translation)

We can draw two conclusions from this summary of findings. The first conclusion is that not having access to ICTs on the job, or using them less, provides fewer opportunities for enlarging the quality of labor (complexity, autonomy, acquisition of skills) for the employees concerned. The second conclusion is that having access to ICTs on the job and using them more extensively can have very divergent consequences for users' labor position and content, depending on the type of labor organization and labor function. Entering data all day and working with spreadsheets and databases is a kind of ICT labor that is completely different from working with advanced search systems and decision support systems, designing programs, or programming software.

❖ INFORMATION AS A SOURCE OF SKILLS

The potential, instead of actual, consumption of information turns this good into a special source of skills. The differential interpretation of available signs and data by the mental systems of individuals enables more variation between individuals than, for example, physical strength, dexterity, and speaking ability. The spread of cognitive, social, and emotional intelligence and, even more, of the knowledge base of individuals is extremely wide. Moreover, this spread is multiplied by the skillful use of information and communication technology. There is an inherent bias of information and communication technology toward a differential appropriation of skills. It is an intellectual technology that appeals to the capacities of the mental systems of individuals, all kinds of intelligence and knowledge, capacities that are very unequally divided. As was explained in the previous chapter, it also is a relatively complex technology and a technology that is multishaped and multifunctional.

This characteristic of information and this bias of ICT is likely to lead to greater inequality than will be seen in the appropriation of other primary products and older technologies. On the labor market, successful appropriation of ICT—that is, all kinds of access in succession—creates a "skills premium." Investigators Nahuis and de Groot (2003) of the Centraal Plan Bureau (Netherlands Bureau of Economic Policy Analysis) have examined the extent to which the generally acknowledged increase of income inequality in the developed countries in the last two decades can be ascribed to rising skill premiums. They show that average income inequality clearly rose in Western countries between the early 1980s and 1995. The only countries revealing a decrease were Spain and Denmark. The average increase of income inequality in this time span was 1% per year in the United States, 1.6% in the United Kingdom, 1.8% in Italy, and 3.2% in Austria (Nahuis & de Groot, 2003, p. 12).

Nahuis and de Groot (2003) show that, together with a steady and regular general increase in the supply of skill in the Western countries after World War II, the demand for skill rose even more, albeit with ups and downs. In general, the difference between the supply and demand of skills is the basis for a rising or declining premium on skills. This premium is measured as the relative wage of workers with two different types of schooling. The data presented by Nahuis and de Groot (2003, p. 21) reveal that there was an acceleration in the increase of the demand for skills in the 1980s after a relative decline in the 1970s. In the 1980s and 1990s, the skills premium of income expanded in conjunction with different levels of education completed; for example, high school and college in the United States. This skills premium did not always grow; for example, in the 1940s and 1970s, it fell in the United States. The candidate most likely to produce the acceleration in the 1980s was information and communication technology (Nahuis & de Groot, 2003, p. 29). There has been a greater acceleration of skill upgrading in more computer-intensive sectors (Autor, Katz, & Krueger, 1998). Others also found a positive correlation of skill upgrading with computer usage, computer investment, and research and development (R&D) intensity (Berman & Griliches, 1994; Machin & Van Reenen, 1998).

There are different extrapolations of this acceleration in the demand for skills related to ICT. The first is that it is only temporary, as this kind of acceleration happens more often with the implementation of a technology that is still immature (Bartel & Sicherman, 1999). High skills are needed to develop the technology. When it is implemented, relative deskilling occurs. A second projection is that ICT is inherently biased towards higher skills. An argument in favor of this view is the quality of ICT of being an intellectual technology (as discussed earlier). A third possibility is that polarization occurs, as was explained earlier. Some ICT jobs might require higher skills than before; others may be deskilled, as their labor consists of routine computer operations permanently on the brink of extinction when complete automation arrives.

Nahuis and de Groot (2003) expect that

> the demand for skill will continue to grow and that the supply of skill can no longer accommodate this in the near future due to the simple fact that talent is limited by nature and that the cost of increasing the supply of skills further increases exponentially. This will unavoidably lead to large increases in inequality; a "bad" that can in principle be countered by policy. (p. 8)

Whatever interpretation and extrapolation of the current situation is right, the chances are high that information is and will be a special source of (differential) skill that produces greater inequality. However, this is not a matter of natural necessity. Educational policies and income or wage policies of governments, businesses, trade unions, and civil institutions can counter this trend, as is explained in the last chapter.

❖ CONCLUSIONS

In the information society, the information intensity of all activities has become so high that this is leading to new forms and substances in the organization of society, the economy, the labor market, and culture. The basis of these changes is the semiautonomous character of information processing in these activities. Accordingly, many observers of contemporary society have been able to claim that information has become an independent source of productivity and power. I qualified this claim, arguing that the ultimate aim of these activities, such as making profit, holding and pursuing power, and exerting control, is there to stay. Therefore our societies may still be called capitalist, (un)democratic, developed or developing, (post)modern, and so on. However, the semiautonomous character of information processing has particular consequences, among others, that of social (in)equality.

First, information has become one of the most important primary goods in society. This means that a particular minimum of it is necessary to participate in it. With the rising complexity of society, this minimum is increasing. Moreover, all relative differences above this minimum are leading to more or less participation, productivity, power, self-respect, and identity for different groups in society. These differences are a substantial basis for inequality in contemporary society. Information in its own right is "innocent"; it has characteristics that can both extend and reduce the chances of (in)equality. Equality is extended by the fact that information can be exchanged without being lost. However, equality is also reduced because information means the potential appropriation of data, and some people have better mental capacity for this than others. Equality also is diminished by differential collective appropriation by groups or classes to which people belong, as they have different material, social, and cultural resources. The equality-reducing characteristics of information are likely to result in increasing relative differences of information processed and skills to be developed. As I pointed out in chapter 5, information and strategic skills are extremely unequally divided in contemporary societies.

Second, information also is a positional good. This means that despite the phenomenon of rising information overload, information can be scarce in particular circumstances. Some positions in society create better opportunities than others for the gathering, processing, and use of valuable information. The use of information and information technology may even have polarizing effects in several fields of society, primary among them the labor process. Existing positions and their information opportunities enable people to gain all kinds of resources and obtain (even) better positions. This is emphasized in the next chapter.

Finally, information is a special source of skills. I have claimed that information and ICTs possess an inherent bias toward a differential appropriation of skills. Both information and its technology appeal to the unequal mental capacities of individuals. In the labor market, differential skills may lead to rising skill premiums. This is probably one of the reasons for the increase of income inequality in large parts of the world since the 1980s. Information technology and digital skills may play a role in current income polarization, as they lead to higher and more valuable skills for some employees and lower and less valuable skills for others.

8

Inequality in
the Network Society

❖ ❖ ❖

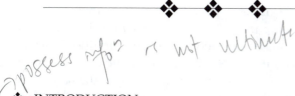

❖ INTRODUCTION

Information is not power. The familiar expression that *information is power* should be qualified. Information is a necessary, but not a sufficient, condition for the possession of power. Otherwise, those people gathering, processing, and diffusing information all day and in the highest quantities, such as scientists, teachers, and journalists, would be the most powerful people in society. Clearly, they are not. The other necessary condition is to possess a specific (powerful) position in society.

Certain positions in social and media networks increasingly establish a person's power in society (van Dijk, 1999). In social networks, one finds "stars" or "centers" as well as people who are isolated or hold peripheral positions. In media networks, there are people who design, fill, and control broadcasting, telecommunication, and computer networks and people who, more or less, only use them. Finally, one finds people who have no connection to networks such as the computer networks that are the focus of this book.

Networks have a structure that combines decentralization and centralization, connecting a number of terminals in an organized way. In this chapter, I explain that networks have a number of properties that extend and reduce the equality of exchange of information at these terminals. After defining the network society as a concept to be added to the information society, I list these properties. The largest part of this chapter then follows: This contains an analysis of the extension and reduction of (in)equality by social and media networks, computer networks in particular, in the most important fields of society.

❖ WHAT IS A NETWORK SOCIETY?

The concept *network society* is not a synonym for the concept *information society*; it is an addition to it. My assertion is that both concepts are inextricably connected (van Dijk, 1999). In the concept *information society*, the changing *substance* of activities and processes in contemporary developed societies is emphasized. In the concept *network society*, attention shifts to the changing organizational *forms* and (infra)structures of these societies. Castells (1996, 1998, 2001) defines the network society as an informational society, with networks serving as the basic structure of organization, pervading all spheres of this society. He considers networks a superior organizational form, as they combine precise task performance with great flexibility, coordinated decision making with decentralized execution, and global communication with individualized expression (Castells, 2001, p. 2). I define the network society as an information society with a "nervous system" of social and media networks shaping its primary modes of organization and most important structures (van Dijk, 1999, 2001a). An important difference between these two definitions is that with Castells, networks already are the basic units of contemporary informational societies (see Castells, 1996), while with my definition (van Dijk, 1999), the basic units still are individuals, groups, and organizations, albeit increasingly linked by networks. I consider that social and media networks are the social counterpart of individualization—the individual seen as the basic unit of contemporary modern societies. From the perspective of technology, media networks are an essential infrastructure of these societies. It must be stressed that society and technology are intertwined and that in this case, this applies to social and media networks.

❖ NETWORKS AND SOCIAL (IN)EQUALITY

As a social and organizational form and structure, networks have a number of properties that are liable to increase or decrease social equality. I deal first here with the properties that support social equality between people, then move to the properties that tend to reduce it.

Connectivity

Networks are made to connect more people and at larger distances than to connect people in dense communities, organizations, groups, families, and neighborhoods close to each other. This allows a wider dispersion of information, contacts, goods, services, and resources in general. It also enables a full exchange of them. The best example is the Internet, of course. This network can be portrayed as the biggest library in history, increasingly encompassing all others, and it is immediately available to all people connected to it. The use of the e-mail facility offers instant access to all others connected, as almost everyone uses this facility. The Internet brings new opportunities for individual citizens and consumers to directly reach institutions and officials and to interact with them to a certain extent. Using it for e-commerce, consumers are able to make price comparisons and to unite with other consumers to enforce lower prices. The Internet also presents the cheapest means of production for starting one's own business ever invented in modern history. A final example is the opportunity of distance education, which is now available to the most remote regions of the world. These capacities of the Internet to empower users have been widely acclaimed in the past 15 years, especially during the days of the Internet hype (see de Kerckhove, 1998, and Shapiro, 1999).

Flat Structure

A second property of networks that has been hailed a lot recently is their character of being more "flat" in structure and organization than traditional modes of organization. A popular view is that networks have no center and that all those connected are more equal within the network because this is the nature of networks. Networks have been recognized as a third mode of organization next to, or in between, hierarchies and markets (see Powell, 1990). Hierarchies are characterized as based on authority, formality, and bureaucracy, making people dependent and subordinate, and markets are founded on contracts and often work on the basis of unequal property and exchange, making some people rich and others poor. Networks, however, are typified as based on agreements in reciprocal and complementary relationships, with mutual advantages and dependencies. This structure is supposed to have a strong equalizing effect on actors in the network. As a matter of fact, the use of communication networks such as the Internet and mobile telephone systems is able to undermine authority, as all national governments, security officers, and established businesses know. Users of these networks are able to bypass leaderships, authorities, and institutions at large and organize their own activities. However, this does not mean that leadership, authority, and unequal positions, relations, and resources have no role to play in networks.

With this statement, we arrive at network properties that reduce social equality. In the popular literature on networks, these properties receive minor attention. However, in the context of the topic of this book, they may well be just as important as the properties that extend equality.

Selection and Competition

Networks are created through the selection of relationships by units; that is, individuals, groups, organizations, or other kinds of units. Often, the units select relationships with other units at greater distances than proximate units or groups. The aim is to extend the environment to find new contacts, sources of information, resources, jobs, and the like or to extend a particular division of labor; for example, in the making of a network organization. In traditional, less advanced modes of organization, relationships are a given, and usually they are proximate. People become members of these bounded groups, tribes, communities, or other organizations by birth, ascription, or application for a more or less permanent position, such as a job. Conversely, networks are created by particular actors choosing others to become part of the network. As a result, people or organizations are included or excluded. This is true for the participants of social networks and for those who are or are not connected to media networks.

Being included in a network gives no guarantee of permanent participation. Continually, actors are assessed for their contribution to the network. When these actors are individuals, they have to stand firm to survive in the network. Weak actors are under continuous threat of being removed or marginalized. This is rather different from traditional social communities and organizations, in which the weak are carried along by the strong in some kind of solidarity. In these traditional organizational forms, the weak remain visible (in the more abstract, diffuse form of a network, they might become invisible), and they have their own role to play, even if it is only the role of the village idiot. Therefore, the network society tends to be a harsh, individualized type of society, as compared to the relatively united traditional and mass societies (van Dijk, 1999). Social networks and the network society are competitive by nature. When media (networks) are used to create and maintain social relations, access and lasting connectivity become conditions posing additional problems. They are the main theme of this book.

Variation and Differentiation

A second property of networks is variation, leading to the differentiation of positions inside the network. The combination of variation and selection might serve as an analogy to evolution biology, as the combination is used to explain the superior organizational mode of networks (van Dijk, 2001b). Actors in networks try to vary their contacts, relationships, and information sources to acquire better opportunities of selection for survival. Everyone engaged in personal networking will recognize this idea: One has to break out of one's own small circle of people to obtain experiences and contacts outside, even when they are very superficial. Granovetter (1973) called this idea "the strength of weak ties." Relatively few actors maintain these weak ties. Most often they are the so-called bridges or connectors to other networks or other parts of the primary network. They hold important strategic positions. Some users depend on the creation and maintenance of strong ties in parts of the primary network. Actors also differ on the number and quality of strong ties. In fact, most networks are not flat or equalized social structures at all. It was not long before classical network analysis discovered that networks contain cores and stars—"spiders in the net"—as well as cliques, isolates, and other roles indicating differentiation and clustering within the network.

At the end of the 1990s, mathematicians caused a breakthrough in network theory and analysis when they moved into the field of social science (Barabási & Albert, 1999; Watts & Strogatz, 1998; see Barabási, 2002, and Buchanan, 2002, for summaries of this breakthrough). They calculated how the famous thesis of "six degrees of separation" of every actor in large-scale (inter)national networks (Milgram, 1967) could be explained. Further, they showed what happens when random networks connecting everyone to everybody change into scale-free networks. These networks have no inherent scale for the number of links. This means that not all actors are linked or that they are not connected in the same way and with the same intensity. These networks are highly clustered, with large hubs attracting many links and with connectors linking actors and clusters far apart, although most actors maintain only a few links. Buchanan (2002) calls the random networks "egalitarian" and the scale-free networks "aristocratic" (p. 119). Here appears the "the rich get richer" phenomenon that is supposed to be valid for all networks in nature, including the economy and the larger society (Barabási, 2002, pp. 79-92; Buchanan, 2002, pp. 106-120, 192-195). This phenomenon occurs with the growth of a (scale-free) network and with the preferential attachment of the actors concerned. This means that the best connected and most central actors or hubs in all these networks tend to attract more and more links.

The "the rich get richer" phenomenon is extremely important in the context of this book, as this is the process that tends to increase inequality in the network society. It is equal to the Matthew effect discussed in chapter 6. However, the supposed universal tendency of the rich to get richer should be applied to social and communication science in a detailed exposition of the precise social, economic, cultural, and mental mechanisms driving it. These are a matter of network growth and of preferential attachment of particular actors to others. What draws them to people who are already popular and well connected? Barabási and Buchanan primarily give examples of large Web sites, such as portals, increasingly drawing links to them while millions of small personal or business Web sites lag behind, linking only a few others. In this chapter, I give examples of this phenomenon and describe the mechanisms of preferential attachment for networks in several fields of society.

Unequal Distribution of Positions and Positional Goods

Thus the positions of actors in scale-free networks are not equal. Some actors occupy positions with many and strong links, and others have positions with only a few links, which might be weak. They may be stars in the network and participants in a hub, cluster, or clique, or they may be marginal or isolated in some part of the network. It may be true that networks are more horizontally and less hierarchically organized than the classical vertically integrated bureaucracy. The links and lines of communication between actors are shorter. However, this does not mean that the average position in a network is less differentiated or that power is less concentrated and centralized than in a classical bureaucracy. Positions and power are just linked in a different way. In the modern organization, a new mode of control appears that has been called *infocracy*, a mode of control replacing bureaucracy with the aid of information and communication technology (van Dijk, 1999; Zuurmond, 1994). This mode rests on the superior organization principle of networks: an intelligent combination of the centralization of authority and decision making and the decentralization of execution, using links of information and communication. This new mode of control by central managers and their databases and servers can be combined with a particular degree of local autonomy and freedom of choice or movement at terminals close to consumers and citizens.

The larger and more extended the network becomes, the more positions are spread across central and peripheral spaces and places. They are divided among the hubs (the proverbial "spiders in the net") and the terminal fringes of the network. Consequently, all existing categorical inequalities in our society concerning employers and employees, managers and executive personnel, males and females, majorities and minorities, citizens and migrants, and others are reproduced in unequal network positions and relations.

With unequal positions comes an unequal distribution of positional goods, as discussed in the previous chapter. The appropriation of these goods determines who is first in the acquisition of particular facilities and gains in networks. They control the potential speed and mobility of actors in networks (discussion follows). Tilly (1999) has called this special mechanism of social inequality *opportunity hoarding* (gathering chances). In the previous chapter, the example of buying and selling stocks on the Internet and on closed, protected networks was mentioned. Another, more familiar example is the mounting practice of direct electronic orders and booking of voyages, performances, and other services with limited capacity. When these services are provided in a fair way, the principle of "first come, first served" applies. Understanding this principle and practice will convince many potential

Internet users to obtain access. A connection is a necessary condition. Unfortunately, it does not guarantee success. A position inside or close to the distributing center that offers accompanying contacts and inside information and the command of particular strategic skills strongly increases the chances of obtaining the services that are in demand.

Differential Mobility and Speed

Networks are better able to transcend place and time than are other modes of organization. They tend to have a wider geographical reach than traditional organizations, communities, or other assemblies. With the help of media (networks), they transcend both place and time as they link units globally for 24 hours a day. However, because not all people are connected to networks and because those connected are linked in different ways and intensities, the capacity of people to transcend place and time in networks varies. The mobility of actors inside and outside of the network and the speed with which they can conduct activities is increasingly different.

This is the most important reason why Manuel Castells (1996, 1998) anticipates the growth of inequality in the network society. According to him, networks are characterized by a "space of flows" that overwhelms and pervades the traditional "space of places." "Networks of capital, labor, information and markets linked up, through technology, valuable functions, people and localities around the world, while switching off from their networks those populations and territories deprived of value and interest for the dynamics of global capitalism" (Castells, 1998, p. 337).

This means that these people are geographically and physically excluded from networks or that they are only able to attain a marginal position inside networks. The excluded and the marginal are doing local and mainly physical or executive work, fixed to particular places. They depend on local circumstances, and they are not able to benefit from the place- and time-transcending gains of networks.

❖ NETWORKS AT WORK

Now I turn to the most important applications—fields of networks in society—to examine whether they support (in)equality. Work still is the primary field. In general, having *work* is becoming more and more important for *net*work building and for social participation in an individualizing society. A comparatively large part of contacts in social and in media networks is derived from relationships formed on the job. Moreover, in previous chapters I demonstrated that the physical access to, skills for, and usage of ICTs are derived primarily from labor relationships. Most people who have left school obtain these kinds of access because they have a particular job, function, or occupation. Purchasing and using a computer and Internet connection at home also are activities initially inspired by the job (for young people without a job, the initial inspiration is education and leisure time). On the job, digital skills are learned first of all in daily labor practice and with the help of colleagues, not primarily in courses, as we saw in chapter 5. One becomes familiar with the world of information technology with ease and with the help of coworkers, who exchange pieces of hardware and software and help to solve minor technical problems.

These general facts indicate the equalizing effects of participating in networks on the job. However, networks also are part of the division of labor within organizations. They not only link jobs within and between organizations, they also tend to bound and rank them. They reflect particular task divisions and relations of authority (van Dijk, 1999). The typology of networks (stimulating centralized versus distributed processing) and the topology of networks (the centralized star network versus the decentralized ring, bus, and mesh networks) determine potential divisions of labor and relations of authority. Tasks, functions, and competencies are strictly allocated to particular groups of employees. In principle, they could be more freely exchanged in jobs at the terminals of computer networks than in traditional communication channels of organizations. The technology allows employees (businesses) to do this. In practice, and for most jobs, tasks, functions, and competencies are firmly divided for reasons of security, fine tuning, control, and job or cost savings.

The result is a polarizing effect in task division and in job content or competency (van Dijk, 1999, pp. 96-98). Some occupations enjoy task broadening and enrichment through use of advanced applications of computer networks on the job. Others experience unprecedented task division and even impoverishment through the use of simple applications. If this is the situation, it is probably the case that tasks have been standardized in programs that assign them to specific functions more strictly than before. Computer access registration and permanent surveillance of the use of applications controls whether this really happens.

The more computer networks are used to perform organizational tasks, the more the relations between employers and employees and between managers and the executive workforce are shaped by these networks. This also concerns relations of hiring and subordination. At first glance, it seems somewhat farfetched to take into consideration Charles Tilly's (1999) theory of durable inequality to explain these relations. However, from the four mechanisms of the origin and repro-duction of categorical inequality (exploitation, opportunity hoarding, emulation, and adaptation), at least two are clearly applicable, although Tilly does not refer to information and communication tech-nology or digital media at all: These are exploitation and opportunity hoarding.

According to Tilly (1999), *exploitation* occurs when "some well-connected group of actors controls a valuable, labor-demanding resource from which they can extract returns only by harnessing the effort of others, whom they exclude from the full value added by that effort" (pp. 86-87). The computer network is such a resource when it is the increasingly important means of production of a company or other organization. Again, this network as a resource helps to produce opposing effects in regard to (in)equality. On the one hand, it supports equality. Publicly available computer networks such as the Internet offer a relatively accessible and cheap infrastructure to start one's own company and to become one's own boss. Also, working within the computer networks of others might provide the opportunity to benefit from the autonomy and complexity of particular tasks assigned and to be able to leave (or at least threaten to leave) the company at any time to start one's own company when one's superior does not give suffi-cient material and immaterial rewards. This enlarges the space for negotiation of the labor contract and reduces opportunities for exploitation.

On the other hand, the use of computer networks on the job may increase exploitation, especially in other jobs. In Taylorist and bureau-cratic labor organizations and in all executive jobs that use computers and networks, exploitation may increase. ICTs have a large registration and control potential. More than ever before, employers are able to register, to control, and to settle payments for the performance of exec-utive employees in the minutest detail and from one moment to the next. The quality of the tasks concerned may be reduced to such a low level that they become interchangeable among individual workers—until the time comes when they can be automated completely.

The second mechanism of categorical inequality Tilly (1999) explains is *opportunity hoarding*. This is defined as follows: "When members of a categorically bounded network acquire access to a resource that is valuable, renewable, subject to monopoly, supportive of network activities, and enhanced by the network's modus operandi, network members regularly hoard their access to the resource, creating beliefs and practices that sustain their control" (p. 91).

Opportunity hoarding is a consequence of the Matthew effect or "the rich get richer" phenomenon in the use of networks discussed earlier. It appears in all fields where networks are used. In computer networks at work, it first of all means that it makes a difference whether employees have or do not have access to the organizational computer network. Having access means more opportunities to extend all kinds of resources and to make a career. Second, it means that those employees who have access to the most advanced applications (of design, decision making, management, research, and communication) are gathering more opportunities to extend their experience, capacities, competencies, and strategic relationships. Fewer opportunities are available to (and obtained by) employees who only use simple applications for executive or more or less repetitive tasks of data entry or maintenance, of billing for and selling goods and services, and of providing information to customers.

❖ NETWORKS IN EDUCATION

Education is the second driving force in getting access to digital media and in creating social and media networks. Even parents with low income and of ethnic minority background have aggressively purchased computers and Internet connections for their children in the developed countries. In the Netherlands, 85% to 92% of ethnic minority, low-income households with school-going children had a PC in 2001, and 49% to 66% had an Internet connection in that year (de Haan & Huysmans, 2002, pp. 64, 67).

A remarkable current fact is that getting access to the digital media and creating social and media networks such as the Internet do not primarily happen at schools but at home and in contacts with fellow pupils outside schools (de Haan & Huysmans, 2002). The main cause is that schools are investing all their efforts in training students in operational skills. However, even for this purpose, current school facilities and teacher skills are less adequate than the facilities and skills the pupils are using and developing at home. There, they have computers of their own, and they take a lot of time to master operational skills and use all kinds of applications with ease and with the help of parents, brothers, sisters, and friends. A conspicuous result is that the traditional relationship of categorical inequality between teachers and pupils is reversed. On many occasions, pupils have more skills than their (much older) teachers, and they teach their teachers all the tricks. Clearly, teachers play a minor role in the training of operational skills and the practical use of applications (see chapter 5, Table 5.3). They do not manage to train students in information skills, except in the old print media. This situation has to change when the digital media evolve from *aids* that have to be learned by mastering operational skills to *means of learning* themselves, such as currently available books, lessons, and assignments. Then the emphasis will have to shift from operational to information and strategic skills. The role of teachers in transmission and coaching will be indispensable again. Some kind of relationship of dependence will be recovered, although pupils will continue to work relatively independently.

This long introduction to the subject of the importance of formal education at schools compared to households for all types of access to computers and networks does not reveal whether these digital media reduce or support inequality when they are used for educational purposes. Again, the conclusion will be that they do both. On the one hand, computer networks such as the Internet disperse educational opportunities, sources, and contents across the globe and inside nations on a scale never experienced before. Distant education and sources of information on the Internet are available worldwide and in the most remote regions. In this way, the information elites in developing countries and regions, who have the skills to use these sources, obtain sources of up-to-date information and educational opportunities they would not have been able to dream of only 10 years ago. The Internet offers more than a badly equipped library with old books, a collection of newspapers and journals published weeks or months ago, and limited information exchange with experts or teachers in the developed countries and regions through letters or extremely expensive telephone conversations, let alone organized conferences, meetings, or teachers' visits.

On the other hand, all present experience shows that educational institutions of the highest level and with the best staff and equipment are benefiting much more from the new opportunities than are institutions of a lower level and with fewer resources. Developing software and educational contents is very costly, and the higher level institutions are only developing these resources for themselves or to sell to others. Most educational environments, sites of distant education, and educational software at universities and colleges in the developed countries are only available for their own students. When lectures, programs, and other sources are freely available on the Internet, users are rarely provided with any guidance in their use.

This brings me to a very important conclusion concerning the accessibility of digital educational sources. Most often, the lack of availability of hardware and software is not the most important problem. The most important problem is the whole social and cultural context of education or training. The human factor of stimulating teachers and fellow students and the social factor of supporting and motivating family and community environments are decisive elements in all types of education, including digital education (Warschauwer, 2003b).

❖ NETWORKS IN SOCIAL LIFE

According to recent research and understanding, the use of the Internet does not lead to social isolation and loneliness because face-to-face communication is reduced but to a reinforcement of existing social contacts and relationships and to more arrangements for meetings (Wellman, 2000, 2001). This is particularly true for nearby contacts and relationships. The Internet thus does not lessen the importance of physical proximity (Chen, Boase, & Wellman, 2002); however, the greatest gains are made in the acquisition of new contacts and relationships and the maintenance of existing ones at larger distances.

These trends work in different ways for the higher and lower social classes in their acquisition of "social capital." This term refers to social resources that support the obtainment of economic and cultural capital. In their study *Capitalizing on the Net*, Quan-Haase and Wellman (2002) define *social capital* in terms of social contact, civic engagement, and a sense of community. The data they discuss suggest that frequent use of the Internet helps to increase social capital in that it supplements and reinforces (a) *existing* resources of social contacts and civilian or community activities and (b) a sense of belonging to the *online* community. However, this works out in such a way that the Internet provides tools with which those who are already involved may increase their engagement: "The Internet provides a new sphere for those already civically involved to pursue their interests in an additional way" (Quan-Haase & Wellman, 2002, p. 318). This seems like another instance of the Matthew effect.

Compared to those people who have access to computers and the Internet and are involved in all kinds of social and community activities, people who do not have access and are less involved are truly disadvantaged. They are not only missing information, strategic information in particular, but also particular social contacts and relations required to inform and stimulate them. This lack of information and contacts tends to become greater in old age and under conditions of loneliness, sickness, and disability.

The Matthew effect and the lack of information and contacts appear even stronger in long distance relationships. This kind of relationship is much more common among the higher than the lower social classes. This relates to the differences of speed and mobility discussed earlier. Not for nothing did Granovetter (1973) call the utilization of long-distance contacts and relationships "the strength of weak ties": These relationships may be less intensive, but often they do bring new and strategic information or contacts inside networks. The lower social classes depend on strong ties in physically bounded networks and communities. Of course, these ties also can be supported by the use of digital media. In geographically bounded communities, they are used to maintain relationships, to settle affairs, and to make appointments. Increasingly, activities such as babysitting, organizing parties, preventing burglary, borrowing cars, and setting up assistance with moving are arranged using e-mail in the neighborhoods of countries with high Internet access. However, they rarely lead to really new and unexpected types of contact and information.

The last reason to be mentioned here regarding why the support of social life with the help of digital media works out differently for the different social classes is the growing role of the individual as the primary network actor. I have argued that the socially strong have fewer problems with this shift than do the socially weak. As an individual, you have to be strong in a network society. Social support is not a given; it must be obtained with human effort and adequate resources. Clearly, the phenomenon of network individualization, as discussed earlier, offers a strategic advance to the higher social classes.

❖ NETWORKS IN HOUSEHOLDS

In the household, the numerous links in the social and media networks of individual household members and inmates come together. Increasingly, this is the most important location of ICT access and use beyond the workplace and school. The most important categorical inequalities in the household are between adult partners, between parents and children, and between older and younger children. The relations between all these categories within families are getting looser because of network individualization. Increasingly, husbands and wives, parents and children are engaged with their own relationships, contacts, and activities outside the family. Face-to-face contacts within families have dropped considerably in the Western world during the past decades. For instance, in the Netherlands, these contacts were cut by 40% between 1975 and 2000 (SCP, 2001). The individual (mobile) telephone; the Internet (e-mail); and individual PCs, televisions, radios, and audio or video sets in separate rooms are the most important tools facilitating this type of modern living and networking.

Very generally speaking, the use of computers and the Internet gives more power to male partners and children in their relationships with female partners and parents, respectively. Most often, the initiative to purchase these media comes from the male partner and school-age children. They are the ones who develop the skills required and use these media most frequently. Male partners and children maintain many relationships with people outside the household, and they use all kinds of applications without their female partners and parents knowing it or being able to follow what happens.

In contrast to this, the telephone has become the old medium of emancipation par excellence in the 20th century. Women are using this medium about twice as much as males do, according to a large number of statistics in many countries. Most likely, e-mail and mobile digital telephones will become the comparable media of emancipation of the 21st century. E-mail use by females is growing at a much more intensive rate than that of males (see recent Pew Internet and American Life Project surveys for the United States: Madden, 2003; Rainie et al., 2000). Women are taking more advantage than men are of e-mail to communicate with family and friends and to develop personal relationships (Boneva & Kraut, 2002). However, it remains to be seen whether this will also apply to other more businesslike and more recreational applications of the Internet.

When all social and media trends are considered together, it appears uncertain whether computers and the Internet will extend or reduce the inequality of positions and resources in the household. As argued before, at this moment in history, male, young, and highly educated members of households are benefiting the most from using digital technology. However, with the general diffusion of the digital media in society, this may change, as is already happening with e-mail and other Internet use among women and senior family members. The chances are smaller that the Matthew effect appears in households; it is more likely to occur in other fields of society. The reason for this is evident: Household members form a single social and economic unit; they have a close relationship and a daily exchange of resources.

❖ CONCLUSIONS

More and more, having a particular position in social and media networks defines one's position in society. Having no access to these networks means absolute exclusion. Obtaining a more or less central position inside networks entails relative exclusion; that is, benefiting more or less from resources exchanged and participating more or less in decisions made. The structure of social and media networks has properties that are capable of both extending and reducing equality. They support equality through extended connectivity and a relatively flat distribution of control. However, they reduce it through highly selective membership practices and requirements of participation. One must stand firm as an individual in a network. The solidarity of traditional communities, workplaces, schools, and neighborhoods is lost. Moreover, selection entails differentiation. Large, organized ("scale-free") networks reveal the phenomenon of "the rich getting richer." It is no coincidence that we have observed instances of the Matthew effect in the evolution of networks in several fields of society.

It is an open question as to whether the rise of networks in society will increase or reduce inequality. This depends on the choices that are made regarding organization principles in networks. Such choices are made in regard to the typology and topology of computer networks, too (van Dijk, 1999). However, it is certain that physical access to these networks is the first vital condition. Subsequently, social skills are needed more and more to acquire and maintain positions in social networks. Both social and digital skills are required to obtain and keep these positions in media networks. Network competencies, the skills for using computer networks in e-mail, instant messaging, browsing, the use of search engines, and the creation of (personal) Web content are getting ever more important (see Jääskeläinen & Savolainen, 2003; Savolainen, 2002).

9

The Stakes

Participation or Exclusion

❖ INTRODUCTION

After four chapters with a detailed exposition of the factors involved in four successive types of access and two chapters describing the meaning of these factors in the context of the nascent information and network society, we are ready to deal with the effects of having more or less access to the new digital media. What are the stakes here? Is access to these media really necessary for life in contemporary society and the society of the future? Are the old media and other means of information and communication no longer sufficient? I postulate that the answers to these questions are not obvious. The basic motive behind the analysis and solutions proposed here is not a simple technological or economic drive. It is not the wish to provide everybody with a computer and a network connection as quickly as possible for the benefit of economic and social progress or the improvement of the quality of human life, a desire many people had in the years of the rise of the computer and the Internet hype. Digital technology is neither good nor bad; in many ways, it has an ambiguous character.

The Potential Stakes

What are the stakes? What are the main motivations in current society to suggest that the digital divide is a problem and that access to the digital media is a necessity? In this chapter, I describe the most important ones and then explain the most decisive motivation behind this book, which is elaborated in the rest of the chapter and serves as a basis for the policy perspectives in the following chapter.

The most widespread motivation for access to the digital media as a necessity is *technological progress*. It is assumed that computers and the Internet are epoch-defining technologies, just like the steam engine, electricity, the automobile, and earlier mass media. Everybody should be able to get accustomed to them and learn to use them to keep up to date. They are held to provide radically new socioeconomic, political, and cultural opportunities for all people in society. According to David Gunkel (2003) "technological determinism figures prominently in the rhetoric of computers and the Internet" (p. 510) and in the issue of the digital divide. This is true not only for the speakers and ideologues; the feeling is deep-seated in public opinion. A prime motive for the elderly and people with low levels of education, as well as for others without access, to buy a computer and connect to the Internet is the desire to keep up to date and not to be excluded from society in the present and the future (see chapter 3). Computers and the Internet are considered to be part of an inevitable technological development.

The second most important motivation to support access for many people is *economic competition*. This motivation drives governments, employers, and (potential) employees. Governments think information and communication technology is the crucial innovation of the current and future wave of economic development. Northern America, Europe, and East Asia fight for leadership in this latest wave of development. Developing countries are attempting to catch up and to capture a place on the world market that will stimulate access to the new technologies for at least a part of their populations. Employers believe they must innovate and increase the effectiveness and efficiency of their businesses by adopting ICTs, or they will lose in competition. Employees, the unemployed, and students want to improve their position on the labor market by becoming familiar with computers and the Internet.

However, it is important to acknowledge that these economic motivations do not necessarily imply that all of the people should have access. In the capitalist economy, access needs are determined by the state and extent of the market—the market of production, exchange, consumption, and labor. A small, rich market might be equal to a large and poor market. When the market of information and communication products or labor is small or stagnating compared to competing markets, there is no (current) economic need to achieve access for all. Access for a relatively small elite of intellectual laborers might be deemed to be sufficient for the time being. A country such as India has hundreds of thousands of software programmers and millions of professional computer users. Here, the choice is either to gradually extend the labor market for these elite computer workers or to make a strong effort to provide access to all Indians.

The third motivation to supply access for all is the ethical imperative of distributive justice: the *equal distribution of resources and opportunities or life chances*. As it is assumed that the digital media offer all kinds of valuable new opportunities in several spheres of life, these chances should be available for everyone. This normative starting point is filled in according to the political position one supports. The most interventionist position favors an equal distribution of resources. This is a classical socialist, social-democratic, or Christian-democratic position that is more popular in Europe than in the United States. In the so-called developmental states of East Asia and in some developing countries with sufficient resources of investment at their disposal, distribution is also attempted when a technological infrastructure is provided with government money. Generally, this situation implies that the government or other societal institutions (help to) distribute hardware, software, and services with a particular bias toward groups that are lagging behind. It might also mean the organization of a variety of public access facilities and computer classes for digital illiterates.

A less interventionist position is the equal distribution of opportunities. This position is increasingly popular in the Western World. It is to be found with liberals from moderate to radical. Obtaining access is held to be one's individual responsibility. Society only has to safeguard the chances of a free market and basic educational provisions (free and compulsory education). According to this view, a free market will lead to the lowest possible prices for hardware, software, and services. Free basic education for all children will enable them to develop all kinds of skills, including digital skills. Equal chances might result in allowing some people earlier access than others, but access for these others will follow, due to the "trickle down" mechanism of the diffusion of media that occurred many times before.

The last popular motivation for supplying access for all that I discuss here is *participation* or *social inclusion* in communities of all kinds. Here, the main problem of the digital divide is supposed to be that a large part of the population might be excluded from meaningful participation in the society of the future. This motivation is normative as well, although it is more neutral than the others because the details can be extremely different (as I explain in the following paragraphs) and because it can be empirically demonstrated whether people are included or excluded due to their use of new media in particular social contexts or communities.

The Stakes Highlighted in This Book

The position adopted in this book is that the primary motivation to supply access to all ought to be a combination of the last two (equal opportunities achieved by the distribution of particular resources and participation). To realize participation and social inclusion, specific resources that have been shown to be related to successive kinds of access may have to be distributed or stimulated among particular deprived groups. This is a necessary consequence of the preceding analysis if one chooses to act and help to close the digital divide. However, distribution and stimulation should be adopted with a very focused approach. For example, a general unfocused distribution of computers and Internet connections among those lacking access would be ineffective. However, public access provisions and conditional subsidies to particular motivated groups, such as the unemployed, who have to apply for jobs and take courses to improve their credentials, seem to be both reasonable and required for expansion of ICT skills and literacy. This position is fully explained in the next chapter.

That the position of participation or social inclusion can be explained extremely differently is demonstrated by the following list of concrete motivations. Corporations look for a large electronic market place. Consumers want access to this place to obtain new opportunities for shopping and trading. Politicians search for ways to extend their reach for political persuasion and a grip on new channels of political communication, bypassing traditional mass media. Civilians and other want to have a say in the political and other systems f these new channels. Military people and security erybody to be connected for purposes of control and the offliners of the future will create unknown risks.

Civilians want security, perhaps also through the use of electronic means. Educators are concerned about universal and public access to all learning resources, just like their pupils and students. Community builders want every citizen to be involved in online communications that are linked to offline local activities.

The absolute and relative measure of inclusion and exclusion in all of these contexts can be demonstrated empirically in principle. As it would require another book to do this for all parts of the world, in all of these contexts, I will leave it to arguments and references here. My efforts here are focused on demonstrating that, increasingly, the old media and other old means of information and communication will not be sufficient for full participation in a developed modern society. More and more, the new media will be used to develop a head start in all kinds of benefits and competitions. The result could be that we end up with first-, second-, and third-class citizens, consumers, workers, students, and other kinds of social actors. Increasingly, their status of participation in all important fields of society will depend, at least partly, on their type and level of access to the new digital media (of course, access to these media will not be the only factor affecting participation). In any case, a feedback relation to existing positions and resources will be created (see Figure 2.3). People with a high level of access to and participation in the new media will obtain better positions and more resources of all kinds. Access and participation provide increasingly important tools with which to acquire other resources in society.

I discuss the measure of inclusion and exclusion in the following seven contexts of participation: the economy (labor market and business), education, social relations (networking), public and private space (mobility), culture, politics and, finally, the official institutions of society (citizenship with entitlements). The expression *measure of inclusion and exclusion* means that I make a difference between absolute exclusion (no participation at all) and relative inclusion or exclusion (partial participation or participation at a particular, lower level).

❖ ECONOMIC PARTICIPATION

The command of digital skills has become a necessary condition for the acquisition of an increasing number of jobs in the developed countries (for plenty of evidence, see the U.S. Department of Labor's [2001] report on the American workforce). Not having any of these skills means absolute exclusion from these jobs. However, the kinds and levels of digital skills required diverge more and more. This is a matter of relative inclusion and exclusion. Polarization can be observed between relatively simple computer work in word processing and database maintenance, on the one hand, and, on the other, complex computer work in design, programming, and the use of decision support systems, management systems, and advanced information and communication means. Using the last-named applications might increase job complexity, autonomy, and opportunities to learn; using the simpler applications might lead to stagnation or degradation of the quality of labor. This type of work continually runs the risk of becoming completely automated, and that could lead to absolute exclusion for these workers.

In a number of occupations, information and communication technology does not play a role, or plays only a marginal one, now and in the foreseeable future. These occupations include a large part of the work in the sectors of care, traditional education, manual labor, simple services, transportation, and recreation, to mention the most important ones. It is not far-fetched to imagine that the characteristics of these occupations will become increasingly different from those occupations daily using ICTs. A first characteristic is the type of work: physical, manual, and face-to-face versus mental, intellectual, and face-to-interface. A second may be career opportunity. Physical, manual, and face-to-face communication jobs may result in far fewer career opportunities than the jobs of advanced intellectual labor (not the jobs of simple intellectual labor or computer work). This may lead to new class divisions, as most physical work requires relatively low-level educational credentials and most intellectual labor using ICTs demands high-level credentials. Thus the necessity of commanding digital skills may add to already existing differences between manual and intellectual labor. It may also help to widen the divide between intellectual labor in simple and advanced jobs.

There are a few odd exceptions to the rule that a career and the possession of a high position in the job hierarchy require digital skills. These are the positions of the old managing director or CEO of a firm, the lawyer or judge, the high public official, the political leader, or the media star. These people may have no experience with digital technology themselves and may leave it to secretaries or assistants to check their e-mail, to search on the Internet, to write letters, to work with databases, and so on. Within a few decades, this category will become almost extinct, as all new young leaders will have acquired a relatively high (necessary) level of digital skills in their school years and early jobs before they reach the top.

In the countries with the highest level of access (motivational, physical, skills, and usage) starting a business without access to the Internet, without a computer, and without a computer link to other businesses has become nearly impossible. Ordering and billing would be very awkward for most customers, supply chains would not reach the company, communication and advertising opportunities would be old-fashioned, and submitting obligatory electronic tax forms to the local and national government could only be left to expensive financial agents.

In the previous chapters, it was emphasized that having certain specific positions in labor can provide people with the resources to acquire motivational, physical, skills, and usage access. The higher career opportunities these types of access offer in turn are likely to result in a better labor position.

The unemployed and some of the disabled instinctively feel that having a computer and Internet access and acquiring digital skills could be very helpful in getting a job. In the second part of the 1990s, it could be observed in the statistics of many high-access countries that the physical and usage access to computers and the Internet among the unemployed and the disabled suddenly grew very fast (see Table 6.2). In these years, the computer and the Internet became part of the household equipment of many high-tech societies. The unemployed and the disabled do at least possess one type of scarce resource: time. More and more often, the Internet is used to find a job or to look for another one. Particularly in the United States, job vacancy sites are very frequently used. This also goes for people with a low level of education or of ethnic minority background. African Americans are among the heavy users of these sites (Howard et al., 2001). People with low levels of education and from the ethnic minorities also use the Internet relatively often to take all kinds of courses. The logical conclusion is that unemployed and disabled people who do not have a computer and an Internet connection at home are seriously deprived compared to their competitors in the job market who do have them. For some social- and Christian-democratic local governments in Western Europe, this was the prime motive to provide some categories of the unemployed with the benefit of a free computer and Internet connection: to be able to better apply for jobs.

❖ EDUCATIONAL PARTICIPATION

The second most important driving force that motivates people to get access to computers and the Internet is education. Increasingly, access to computers and the Internet will be necessary to achieve specific training. It has already become practically impossible to achieve a university degree in the Western countries without these technological means. This requirement is rapidly trickling down to lower levels of education. From regular education it will move to adult education. Within 10 years, computers and the Internet will have become indispensable in education throughout the developed world.

The inescapable result is that people who do not have physical access will be excluded from an increasing number of educational opportunities. Children in families lacking access are strongly disadvantaged compared to children who have computers and Internet connections at home. Access to computers and the Internet at school is only available during particular hours and for a limited number of children. Even in the developed countries, it is fairly common, even in 2005, that only one computer is available for every 10 to 20 pupils. Those who have the means at home are learning to work with computers much earlier, longer, and faster, even before they reach school years.

Of course, it is still possible to educate people using classical methods such as (exercise) books, calculators, chalkboards, and teachers of flesh and blood. These means will be used for a long time to come. However, increasingly, computers and Internet connections will be obligatory for drafting and delivering papers, searching for information, making assignments and calculations, taking tests, and so on. A popular view is that the teacher will become a coach, but this will only apply after students have the machines with which to work on their own and explore their knowledge and skills.

This argument concerns only the (partial) transformation of traditional education in computerized education. Exclusion becomes even sharper with the (im)possibility of taking advantage of new opportunities for distant education and special computer facilities for the disabled, such as speech recognition. Distant education is able to bring the best educational sources to the most remote places and to people who are immobile because they have a handicap, are chained to child care, or lack transportation. Unfortunately, as we observed repeatedly in the previous chapters, it is just these people—the disabled, full-time mothers with small children, and people living far away or in rural areas or developing countries—who have the lowest levels of access of all kinds.

The most serious problem in regard to educational participation and ICT access is adult education. In conventional schools, at least, there are regular provisions for hardware, software, courses, and staff. Adult education depends on public libraries and community access centers, which often lack adequate provision and are understaffed. People in the developed countries older than 35 or 40 years who have missed any training in digital skills during their school years and have not touched on computer work in their jobs have to rely on these public means or on private computer classes if they want to catch up. For them, acquiring digital skills is not a natural thing learned in the practice of a current job or training (see chapter 5). Most of these people learn to use the computer and the Internet by trial and error at their home connection. There are few stimulations at home, and no corrections. Only a minority learns from special computer courses and computer books. However, the large part of the population older than 35 or 40 still has to live in the information society—for another 40 or 50 years, at least in the developed countries. These people will be relatively excluded from its opportunities, compared to the younger generations. Some of them will be excluded absolutely.

The general conclusion has to be that absolute or relative exclusion from the educational opportunities of the new digital media has a negative feedback effect on mental, social, and cultural resources and on educational positions (maximum level of education attained).

❖ SOCIAL PARTICIPATION

The use of computers and the Internet can increase social capital in terms of social contact, civic engagement, and sense of community (Katz & Rice, 2002; Quan-Haase & Wellman, 2002). This does not mean that this will happen on all occasions (Nie & Erbring, 2000; Putnam, 2000). According to the research projects compiled in Wellman and Haythornthwaite (2002) and Katz and Rice (2002), however, the effects of Internet use on social capital are either neutral or positive. "The Internet complements and even strengthens offline interactions, provides frequent uses for social interaction and extends communication with family and friends" (Katz & Rice, 2002, p. 326). The Internet does not supplant existing communication modes but supplements them.

It serves as an extra medium or tool used to build social capital. More than a tenth of Internet users in the United States had established friendships via the Internet by the year 2000 (Katz & Rice, 2002, p. 327). A comparable number is known to be engaged in online dating in a number of countries.

The Internet adds new forms of social capital to the traditional ones (dinner parties, sporting events, club meetings, local bars, or dances, etc.). These are forms of selecting and contacting complete strangers with particular characteristics, types of online conversation, and the initiative to act both online and offline. The important issue in the context of this book is that some people have access to these new tools and others do not. In using them, some are capable of maintaining and extending their social networks, but others see these networks crumble if they cannot compensate for the increasing difficulties of maintaining pure offline social relationships in an individualizing and busy urbanized society. E-mail has become an important extension of the telephone.

The second most important issue here is that those who already have developed a large and dense social network through face-to-face communication, the telephone, and writing are more likely to extend this network with Internet use than those who have only a small network even though they also use the Internet. This is another instance of the Matthew effect. The tool of the Internet strengthens the socially strong more than the socially weak. This is a matter of relative inclusion and exclusion.

Because they use the Internet (more), the socially strong increase their advantage over the socially weak as they make more and better contacts and as they use the Internet for all kinds of opportunity hoarding and to obtain strategic pieces of information and decision. Perhaps surprisingly soon, this will even be true in the market of sexual relations and marriage. In this way, having more or less access (of all four kinds) has feedback effects on social and material resources and on positions occupied in the markets of labor, marriage, and even friendship.

❖ SPATIAL PARTICIPATION

Contrary to the expectations of some futurists in the 1980s, the use of information and communication technology did not reduce spatial mobility by means of the "electronic cottage" (Toffler, 1980) and telecommuting, but it did strongly reinforce this mobility (Graham & Marvin, 1996; van Dijk, 1999). However, it did so with very different strengths for the high and low social classes. In the previous chapter, it was argued that the lower social classes of the developed countries and whole populations of the developing countries are geographically and physically excluded from networks; that if they are not entirely excluded, they are only able to attain a marginal position inside the networks. They depend on local circumstances and are not able to benefit from the place- and time-transcending gains of networks.

The use of ICT supports not only spatial but also social mobility and, what is more important here, their interrelationship. Traditionally, the higher social classes have a higher number of weak ties across great distances. The use of digital media, from mobile telephones to the Internet, enlarges this number and helps to better maintain the ties. In this way, the "strength of weak ties" also is better exploited. Digital networking stimulates the early discovery of strategically important information, the selection of links that might be important for improving one's position, the participation in exclusive online and offline communities, and visits to crucial meetings of the "jet set" and other conference "tigers." In this way, selective community building is organized, both online and offline, even to the extreme of the manner of electronically fortified gated communities in city environments.

At the other end of the class spectrum, the lower social classes have few or no online or offline long-distance connections. This goes for work, social relations, and e-commerce. Instead, these people use the digital media to support mobility and communication at short distances with proximate family, friends, and colleagues in the same physical environment. E-commerce is used relatively more for the support of local shopping (in the shop and language they know) and for the occasional fully organized long-distance holiday trip.

In conclusion: Not having access to online environments increasingly also means absolute exclusion from particular offline environments and from a number of social, economic, and cultural opportunities. Having less access means relative exclusion from the most valuable places in social, economic, and cultural competition.

❖ CULTURAL PARTICIPATION

Digital media use has added a new branch to our culture: *digital culture* or *e-culture*. It is self-evident that those who have no physical, skills, or usage access to these media also miss new opportunities for cultural consumption and expression. These include new types of access to the incredibly voluminous cultural inheritance available on the Internet and on CD-ROM or DVD; new communication modes, such as e-mail, chatting, and instant messaging; new forms of transaction, such as e-commerce, online auctions, and online dating; and all kinds of digital creation, reproduction, and collage. This is the first reason why those people who claim that all of our cultural artifacts and expressions are available in the old media are simply wrong. A second reason is that in the old media, conditional access (pay services) has increased more than in the new media. I am talking about pay TV, increasing access fees for museums in many countries, and rising prices for print media (books, magazines, quality newspapers). A final reason is that more and more services offering information, communication, and transaction are only available on the Internet. Instances are additional files, video, audio, and pieces of information for newspapers, journals and digital broadcasting; communication systems using videoconferencing; and electronic transaction systems using self-service.

Cultural services that are scarce or have limited availability will provoke a new kind of absolute exclusion when they are completely open for electronic booking. I am talking about all kinds of cultural performances, journeys (flights and other public transport), and sporting events. Now or in the near future, they will be fully booked electronically. Those who have not one, but several (mobile) connections will have the best chances of getting a seat or service. Most likely, this will (negatively) motivate Internet nonusers to try to obtain a connection.

A final aspect of cultural participation is the necessity to speak the official language in a particular country and, on many occasions, the mother language of the computer world (English) to have access to digital culture. Here all kinds of cultural minorities are disadvantaged. They have to master two or three languages, their own and the foreign (inter)national ones, to fully participate. The skills of language are more important in using the new digital media than are numerical and technical skills (see chapters 5 and 6). The requirement of being able to speak two more or less foreign languages to have (usage) access to these media increases the chances of cultural exclusion, compared to the old media, which are often available in the native language of the user.

❖ POLITICAL PARTICIPATION

Contrary to popular expectations in the 1990s, the Internet is not drawing more people into the political process (Boogers & Voerman, 2002;

Delli Carpini & Keeter, 2003; Katz & Rice, 2002, p. 148; Quan-Haase & Wellman, 2002, p. 312; Wilhelm, 2003a). However, it does provide a platform for additional forms of political activity that are more difficult to realize in the offline world. These forms are additional opportunities to find political information and to create political interaction (sending and receiving e-mail to and from the government and candidates, using e-mail to support or oppose a candidate, taking part in online polls, and participating in online discussions). By far the most popular activity is browsing to find information about political parties or candidates, about their voting behavior, and about elections and political news (Boogers & Voerman, 2002; Cornfield, Rainie, & Horrigan, 2003; Katz & Rice, 2002). Information is much more popular than online discussion and campaigning (Cornfield et al., 2003).

In the Unites States and most other countries with data about political uses of the Web, it appears that between a tenth and a fifth of Internet users were engaged in some kind of online political activity at the end of the 1990s (Katz & Rice, 2002, p. 138). The total number of users of political information and news on the Internet is rising. In the United States, it rose to 46 million, or 39.4%, of the online population in 2002 (Cornfield et al., 2003). In the Netherlands, there were 2 million users of the electronic voting compass called *Stemwijzer* among an electorate of approximately 7 million Dutch in the 2002 elections (Boogers & Voerman, 2002). However, those already politically involved and those with high levels of education are much more likely to use these new forms of political information retrieval and activity than those who are less involved and have a low level of education (Boogers & Voerman, 2002; Robinson, DiMaggio, & Hargittai, 2003; Wilhelm, 2003). The only exception is a part of the younger generation that was less politically engaged in many Western countries during the 1980s and 1990s but which has now been attracted to politics via the practice of Web browsing (Boogers & Voerman, 2002; Cornfield et al., 2003; Katz & Rice, 2002).

Once again, we have met an instance of the Matthew effect. The already politically involved obtain a new powerful tool with which to reinforce their activity and their power to influence politics. It is not a matter of absolute exclusion. The traditional methods and channels of political activity are still available to all citizens. They remain effective. However, slowly but surely, the politically active on the Internet and those using computers are getting better informed than those who only read papers or watch TV. Moreover, they can be more influential, sending e-mails to politicians and public administrators and participating in electronic pressure groups.

❖ INSTITUTIONAL PARTICIPATION

For a long time to come, citizens without access to digital media will not be excluded from voting. This would be a strong and unacceptable form of institutional exclusion. However, in several Western countries, experiments in official online voting are on the agenda. Those allowed to participate in these experiments will have to spend less effort to vote. They are privileged, as they do not have to travel (sometimes) several miles to the nearest ballot box, and they are able to choose their own time (within limits) to vote. The underprivileged, who in the future will have to keep going to (fewer) geographical polling places, will be confronted with electronic means anyway. They will have to use electronic identity cards and electronic voting machines, requiring them to have a minimum of digital skills. It is not certain that these skills will be fewer than the skills required in the sometimes extremely complicated voting procedures of contemporary elections. Instead of making things easier, electronic voting may necessitate the use of additional skills when digital technology is used to extend opportunities to vote.

There are other fields of the welfare state and citizenship in which a full transition to digital media in public services might lead to the absolute exclusion of digital illiterates. These are the fields of government services, health care, and social insurances. Anyone who wants to use an electronic means of payment these days has simply to obtain a PIN card. In the near future, the same is going to happen with electronic citizen identity cards for government services, health identity cards for care, and social security cards for insurances and social benefits. To obtain the full benefit of these cards means the purchase of a personal computer and a connection to the Internet. In this way, not only can online transactions of services be realized but also particular communications with public servants and personalized information services.

Searching for health information on the Internet is the most popular activity after e-mail and looking for information about a particular product or service. In 2003, about half of American adults turned to the Internet for health information (Fox & Fellows, 2003). A quarter of adult Americans were able to ask family and friends to search on their behalf. Another quarter never received any online health information. On average, these last are less educated, poorer, male, and live in rural and inner city environments. It is well known that these people have relatively more health problems. Those Internet users who are wealthier, more highly educated, and have broadband are significantly more likely to have searched for health information, as are women in general (Fox & Fellows, 2003, p. 31). According to Fox and Fellows, an educated health-care consumer stands a better chance of getting good treatment, and the Internet can be a significant resource for health education.

The Internet can also be a significant aid for participation in health institutions. In a number of countries, there are waiting lists for surgery in hospitals. In some of these countries, patients are able to search on the Internet for the hospital with the shortest waiting list and apply for surgery in that hospital. It also helps patients to find the best hospitals, doctors, and medicines. Using health information on the Internet assists patients in preparing for talks with doctors and nurses. It empowers them to ask more informed questions during consultations and hospital visits. Finally, it enables them to claim their rights as patients and consumers of medicine.

❖ CONCLUSIONS

In this chapter, the social consequences of the digital divide have been discussed. They can be summarized under the categories of unequal benefits from technological progress, different stakes in economic growth and competition, and unfair distributions of societal resources, opportunities, and life chances. However, in this book, the social consequences of the digital divide are understood as greater or less participation in several fields of society and as matters of social inclusion and exclusion: These are neutral perspectives, which can be accepted by the majority of public opinion worldwide, and are broad in scope, as "fields of society" includes the economy and the labor market and the fields of education and of social and political life. Greater or less participation in these fields of society through use of digital media can be demonstrated empirically. The beneficial effects of digital media access on the mitigation, or at least the diminution of aggravation, of existing positional and personal inequalities can be shown to exist.

In this chapter, it was argued that not having access to ICTs will substantially diminish the chances of participation in all relevant fields of society. This happens ever faster and more definitely as the new media pervade society. Increasingly, the old media and face-to-face communications will become inadequate means of full participation in society. Progressively more people will even be entirely excluded from particular fields of society. The result will be first-, second-, and third-class citizens, consumers, workers, students, and community members.

This prospect is a serious problem, as it would lead to structural inequalities of both absolute and relative exclusion from current and future society. The term *structural* is a slippery one, of course. What exactly is *structural*? Absolute exclusion is a clear case of structural inequality that can be demonstrated empirically. Relative exclusion is more difficult to demonstrate, as it requires detailed investigations into the amount of participation in particular fields of society and its consequences for specific positions of affluence and influence. However, in the long run, relative exclusion can also lead to clearly perceptible structural inequalities.

The situation of structural inequality amplified by the digital divide can be portrayed in a simplified picture of a tripartite, instead of a two-tiered, society (see Figure 9.1).

This picture sketches a (developed) society with an information elite of about 15% of the population; a majority of 50% to 65% that participates to a certain extent in all relevant fields of society, with both social and media networks; and a class of outsiders that is excluded from the new media networks and has a relatively small social network. The information elite consists of people with high levels of education and income, the best jobs and societal positions, and a nearly 100% access to ICTs. This elite in fact makes all important decisions in society, although the other citizens are allowed to vote for those who will fill the political positions that formally make these decisions. The elite lives in dense social networks that extend to a large number of strategically important weak ties. Most people belonging to this elite are heavy users of computers and the Internet. Some of them form a "broadband elite" that works with these media all day.

In a second ring, we find the majority of the population, which participates significantly less. It contains a large part of the middle class and the working class. This majority does have access to computers and the Internet but also possesses fewer digital skills than the elite, information and strategic skills in particular. Moreover, it uses fewer and less diverse applications. These applications are less focused on a career, a job, study, or other ambition and more on recreational and entertainment uses. The majority has a smaller social network and fewer weak ties spanning large distances.

Largely excluded from participation in several fields of society and having no access to computers and the Internet, voluntarily or not, we find the unconnected and excluded outside the rings of the drawing. They comprise a quarter to a third of the populations of (even) the most

Figure 9.1   Tripartite Participation in the Network Society

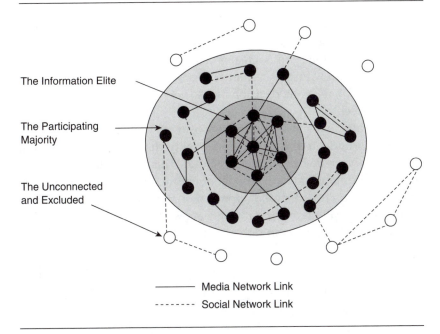

The Information Elite

The Participating
Majority

The Unconnected
and Excluded

——————— Media Network Link

- - - - - - - Social Network Link

advanced high-tech societies. Increasingly, they become equal to the lowest social classes, particular ethnic minorities, and a majority of (new) immigrants. At this stage of new media diffusion, the unconnected still contain a large proportion of elderly people of higher social class but isolated socially and without access to computers and the Internet.

This is a rather bleak picture of contemporary network society. Unfortunately, it is not far from reality when the access divides described in previous chapters are real. I do not intend to portray with this picture a sharp division between three classes. There are social and media links and social transfers between them. Regarding Internet access, I described an ever-shifting Internet population in chapter 3. I prefer the image of a spectrum or a continuum (chapter 1).

However, the spectrum or continuum is being stretched. The distance between the information elite and the unconnected or excluded is extending. The divide is deepening between the broadband elite, which uses about ten different computer and Internet applications every day, occupying the best positions in society and maintaining a large social network, and the unconnected or excluded, who are deprived of any experience in the computer world, possess low and marginal positions, and sustain a small network of proximate others. This means rising levels of social and information or communication inequality. Eventually, this creates a threat to democracy. It would decay into a purely formal system of electing political candidates every few years. All relevant decisions in society would be made by the information elite.

The main policy task for those choosing to prevent this situation is not only to mitigate the types of inequality discussed but to prevent them from becoming fixed and structural. This means, first of all, that the links and transfers in the model of Figure 9.1 have to be kept wide open. This requires a focused approach of attempts to close the digital divide, specifically removing the barriers with the four kinds of access described in chapters 3 through 6.

10

Policy Perspectives

❖ INTRODUCTION

After this long analysis of the digital divide, it is time to examine what can be done. Saying that something needs to be done about it assumes that the digital divide is a problem. The first section of this chapter deals with this assumption. Is it a problem? If so, is it a new or special problem? Is it mainly technical or social? Is it urgent? Can it be solved at all? What would happen if it were not solved? In this section, I summarize some of the main arguments of this book and make a number of my own views more explicit.

The second section is about the digital divide in the context of general trends of (in)equality worldwide. The digital divide should not be isolated from social and information inequality in general. It is inconceivable that the digital divide, in the broad interpretation of this book, can be closed without a lessening of general social and information inequality. Keeping this in mind, the message of this section is not optimistic, as the background of increasing, not decreasing, inequality will be discussed.

The third section will be a short exposé on the appearance of the digital divide in some of the most important regions of the world: North America, Europe, East Asia, and the Third World. The similarities of this appearance in these regions are greater than the differences. The divides among demographic groups are about the same, and everywhere the main approach to the problem is an emphasis on physical access and operational skills. The point of departure, the general level of development, the state of the economy, and the size of the digital divide are very different from country to country, of course. However, the first signs of diverging trends are perceivable. The dominant policy perspectives on the digital divide in these regions of the world also are growing apart.

This exposé is a stepping stone to the final section of this chapter, which will deal with all the policy instruments that can be used to confront the problem. The introduction of this section will refer to general policy options. Should the main option be a better distribution of the technology, income measures, general and computer education, or the stimulation of usage and applications? Subsequently, 26 concrete policy instruments that can assist in closing the divide will be discussed. They will be linked to the four kinds of access that are the core of this book: The instruments have been forged to improve them.

❖   THE DIGITAL DIVIDE AS A
COMPREHENSIVE SOCIAL PROBLEM

As I wrote this book, many people asked me, What is so special about the digital divide? Is it really a new problem? Isn't information inequality a problem of all times? Haven't people always been exposed unequally to access to media and used them in various ways? What is the difference between having and using digital media and having and using books, newspapers, magazines, televisions, radios, and telephones?

My usual answer was that information inequality is both an old and a new problem. It is old in the sense that people have always had to be motivated to adopt a particular medium, that they had to make an effort to obtain it, that they were obliged to develop the operating skills required, and that they used it for different purposes, from creating careers within and from it and using it in business to using it in social conversation and for leisure and entertainment. With all four kinds of access, inequality has been the rule throughout all ages. It is also an old problem because an unequal distribution of resources and positions in society has always been the primary cause behind these differences of access (to whatever new technology).

The digital divide is new as a type of inequality, however, for two basic reasons. The first reason is the *character of the new media* under consideration and their integration into social environments. The computer and the Internet are multifunctional technologies that are (increasingly) used for all kinds of purposes: information, communication, transaction, and entertainment. They are applied at work and in education, politics, culture, social relationships, and leisure time. In all these spheres of human life, computer and network applications are claiming to replace or add to a wide range of comparable, traditional, face-to-face activities in particular situations. Never before have we created media that were so all-embracing and that had such weight in all parts of society. A combination of social and media networks has become the nervous system of modern societies. It will not be long before access to the digital media becomes a necessary condition to taking part in them. I would defend the claim that they mean even more for current and future society than print media, literacy, and television did to the modern mass society of the recent past. Increasingly, all types of inequality that exist in society will be reflected in the deepening divide and its causes. New inequalities will be added, such as the differing mastery of the information and strategic skills discussed in this book. Clearly, the new media require more skills for use than do print media, broadcasting, and telephones.

The second basic reason is related to these *new inequalities and the development of new types of society.* Our societies are evolving into information and network societies. In these societies, media are not just tools, if media have ever been only tools. They contain the tools and raw material or substance of the information society, and they connect all positions in the network society. I have shown that information serves as a primary and a positional good in the information society. The people holding these goods, and holding more of them than others, are appropriating an increasing share of all value produced. To do this, they also need a specific, preferably strategic position in the network society. To achieve such a position, access to computers and their networks and the ability to insert them in social networks are more and more required.

Another characterization of the digital divide is that it is not a technological problem. In this book, I have tried to show that it is a social problem, with a large number of educational, cultural, economic, and political ramifications. The definition of the digital divide as a technological problem—that is, a lack of physical access and operational skills—has haunted the field of new media adoption long enough.

Unfortunately, this perspective is still dominant among policy makers, technicians, and economists. However, arguing that the divide is basically a social problem is too general. In this book, I have tried to demonstrate that the emphasis of new media adoption is shifting from motivational and physical access to skills and usage access. The more developed a society is, the greater the shift. In developing countries, physical access and the motivations to gain access and to use the new technologies remain the primary problems. In the previous chapters, I have related all four kinds of access to a long and detailed list of resources and positional or personal categories. In this chapter, I select the most important resources and categories related to each kind of access and derive from them the appropriate policy instruments for change that are specific to their kind.

A corresponding description of the digital divide is that it does not exist in isolation. All expressions of the problem have to be contextualized. Problems of motivational access are related to general attitudes about technology and change. A lack of material access is clearly linked to general socioeconomic inequality within or between particular societies. Deficiencies in digital skills cannot be solved without general educational resources and improvements. Feasible use of the digital media in local communities is unlikely to happen if it is not integrated into the general approach to community building in that particular environment.

On these issues, I have implicitly adopted the approach of social informatics and a mutual-shaping view on technology. Social informatics says ICT does not consist of isolated tools but constitutes a whole sociotechnical network. The technology cannot be separated from its use in particular social environments. ICTs do not solve things by themselves; additional social skills and effort are required to make them work. This is an ongoing process; the introduction of ICTs is not a one-shot implementation (Kling, 2000; also see Warschauwer, 2003b). Similarly, the digital divide is not necessarily closed when the stage of universal usage access has been reached.

A mutual-shaping view of technology (Bijker & Law, 1992; Feenberg, 1991; Ziman, 2000) assumes that ICTs are both *agents* of change, shaping their contexts of use, and *objects* of change, which are shaped and redesigned by users in their familiar contexts. On the one hand, the introduction of ICTs offers both opportunities and threats to users and imposes on them access problems of all kinds. On the other hand, these users make selections among these opportunities and threats and meet with access problems in adapting the technology to their own needs, resources, and environments. Crucial consequences are that individuals, organizations, and countries deal with the digital divide problem in various ways and that there are many policy options (discussion follows).

The next fundamental constituent of the digital divide problem is that it is urgent. The divides distinguished in this book will not automatically close by themselves. This is true even of physical access. The Americans Adam Thierer (2000) and Benjamin Compaine (2001) have recommended a "wait and see" attitude toward efforts to bridge the digital divide. Public intervention is a waste, they say. The problem will be solved by the market offering ever cheaper and simpler computer products. Via the so-called trickle-down principle, the deprived are getting access only some time later than the early adopters, just as occurred with other mass media, such as the radio, television, VCR, and telephone. I consider this to be the worst advice one can give at this stage of introduction of the new technology. Compaine and Thierer only focus on physical access. Moreover, they do not see the difference between the old and new media. In chapter 4, I noted that the physical access divide grew between 1985 and 2000 in the developed countries. After 2000, this divide began to close, partly and slowly, in the developed countries, but it is uncertain to what degree this will continue during the next two decades. Most likely, the digital divide within developing countries and between them and the developed world will continue to rise. In the mean time, subsequent digital technologies, such as broadband, have arrived, partly repeating the unequal adoption process. In this way, the unconnected not only continue to lag behind but lag behind in a cumulative sense, being deprived of all ensuing hardware, software, and applications. Meanwhile, the difference between the broadband elite described in chapter 6 and complete digital illiterates is about as big as the gap between the highly educated in the First World and traditional illiterates in the Third World.

It is evident that inequalities of motivational, skills, and usage access will not disappear by themselves. Of course, one is free to hold the view that intervention is not appropriate here anyway, as these kinds of access have to do with a person's individual choice—but to be consistent, this would mean bidding farewell to education as a public service or obligation and to any innovation policy that goes further than stimulating a free market. Any government adopting a policy of nonintervention will only help their countries to fail competitively in the world market of information and communication products and services, if not all technologically advanced products.

The problem of the digital divide is so comprehensive and so much entrenched in all aspects of society that it cannot be solved by governments alone. In the first place, individual citizens and consumers will have to become aware of the importance of participation in the information and network society and what this means in terms of the resources and skills they need. To help them, business and industry must accept their primary responsibility in developing and supplying ICTs. They should offer not only cheaper products in competition but also more user-friendly products that really present a surplus value and gain trust among consumers. Further, the introduction of ICTs into society requires the cooperation of all kinds of nonprofit organizations and the development of public-private partnerships. Both formal and informal educational institutions and community organizations have a special role in bridging the digital divide. In the final section of this chapter, the role of all these actors will be discussed at greater length.

The final and decisive question about the digital divide as a problem is, of course, why it is a problem at all. What are the stakes if it is not solved? In answering this vital question, one can take a more offensive *and* a more defensive stance. The more offensive position observes that if the problem is not solved, the full potential of digital technology will not be realized. There would be less support to the economic prosperity of a country in worldwide competition than that country requires. Productivity would be less. Innovation would be limited. The labor force would develop insufficient digital skills. The market of ICT products and services would be restricted. In politics, there would be less democratic experimentation and fewer new opportunities for civic engagement for all. In social and cultural life, particular new opportunities of expression, communication, and relationship building would not be seized by large parts of the population.

All this is true. Still, the attitude taken in this book is less ambitious. I advocate an attitude that is more defensive, that tries to prevent the rise of an unacceptable level of inequality (structural inequality). Structural inequality means systematic exclusion of parts of the population from several fields of society. They would become second- or third-class citizens, consumers, laborers, and community members. Participation in all fields of society is at stake. My expectation is that there is a very large base of support in all current societies to prevent this situation, which could keep the problem of the digital divide on the political agenda.

The defensive attitude is also more neutral. You do not have to be a fan of digital technology to acknowledge that its use is increasingly becoming vital for participation in society. Neither do you have to be in favor of achieving complete equality. Inequality, both social and information inequality, has always existed. It is extremely unlikely to disappear. Later it will become understandable why I have reconciled myself to a future of rising inequality worldwide and in most nations. The risk that must be controlled is lasting, structural inequality.

The defensive attitude can also be seen as neutral because when you adopt it, you do not have to force people, the information want-nots in particular, to gain access to computers and networks. You have only to give them every opportunity for access. These are, first of all, opportunities of *action,* not of equal distribution of all resources. This seems to come close to the views of Amartya Sen (1992) on inequality. However, Sen explicitly rejects the means or resource approach to (in)equality, which is a cornerstone of the digital divide theory in this book (see chapter 2). Instead, he emphasizes that humans have equal capability to act and equal freedom to achieve. I think that this is not sufficient. What the rather idealistic proponents of equal opportunities in terms of personal capabilities often forget is that particular resources and conditions are necessary to be able to act and to participate at all. Some (not all) resources and positions of personal and positional inequalities have to be (re)distributed or stimulated to realize the four kinds of access distinguished in this book.

Obviously, biological personal inequalities cannot be changed by policy (although social and cultural personal artifacts can) and neither can many deep-seated positional inequalities. General mental, material, temporal, social, and cultural resources cannot be (re)distributed easily either. Even if they could, this would prove ineffective in solving the concrete problems of the digital divide. I am looking for *specific* resources and conditions that are able to remove the barriers of access discussed in chapters 3 through 6. These resources and conditions will receive the whole focus of my attention in the proposals for policy instruments discussed in the last section.

❖   A BACKGROUND OF RISING GENERAL INEQUALITY

As I argued before, the digital divide cannot be isolated from other forms of social and information inequality. They are expressed in unequal divisions of all kinds of resources and the personal and positional inequalities that explain these unequal divisions. Thus when these divisions grow wider or smaller, this will automatically enlarge or reduce the digital divide in terms of unequal motivational, material, skills, and usage access. Unfortunately, I cannot escape the conclusion that social and information inequality in general is rising worldwide and that several economic, political, social, and cultural trends come together to accomplish this. The digital technology in question does not help very much. In chapters 7 and 8, it was explained that ICT has properties that are capable of both extending and limiting access. It is true that computer networks are able to support an unprecedented public diffusion of data, information, and knowledge in the world, but apparently this does not prevent ever more private and unequal appropriation in practice (Lessig, 2001; van Dijk, 1999, 2000).

There are a number of epochal trends and tendencies causing this rise in general inequality. The first is a *structural* one. It is the process of globalization, which is marked by combined and uneven development. This means that on the one hand, the whole world is connected in an exchange of goods, services, information, jobs, and technologies, but on the other hand, these connections, exchanges, and distributions are made ever more selective and unequal locally. The result is a network structure with nodes or hubs that are very strong but with other, perhaps geographically close, links that may be absent or very weak. For the diffusion of ICT, this means that the process starts in the most developed countries, and within them, in the urban, business, and educational centers (Graham & Marvin, 1996). Subsequently, the urban centers in less developed countries are connected and with them, the local information elite of computer programmers, business or government officials, and people at universities. However, the rest of the population in the developed countries lags behind, —and in the developing countries even far behind. There is no guarantee that this portion of these populations will be connected in the years to come. The interests of those connected are to serve the global economy and information infrastructure, preferably their rich and powerful centers.

Castells (1996, 1998) and I (van Dijk, 1999, 2001a) have tried to demonstrate that this global network structure supports global information exchange and diffusion and has the potential of greater spread but that currently, in practice, it does so in an extremely unequal way. Presently, it leads to more instead of less social and informational inequality.

The second theoretical tendency and empirical trend is a particular *economic* process. Since the middle of the 1980s, it has been marked by rising material inequality and income differences between countries and between individuals within countries worldwide. Facts and figures can be found in the annual Human Development Reports of the United Nations, notably the 1998 report (UNDP, 1998), Wolff (2002) for U.S. data, and in Nahuis and De Groot's (2003) discussion paper on the OECD countries, which used innumerable national sources. It goes without saying that rising income inequalities cause more unequal access to the new media, particularly in regard to physical and conditional access. For these kinds of access, income remains a decisive factor, especially in the developing countries. In chapter 4, it was emphasized that total media expenditure in households is rising almost everywhere because new media are added to the old ones, which do not disappear. Rising media expenditures in equal or shrinking household budgets lead to propensities to save on expensive new equipment, application software, and conditional access services. Low-income households tend to wait to purchase computers and expensive connections, to select the cheapest options for peripherals and applications, and to choose only one option among overlapping media such as television news and newspapers.

The third tendency is the increasing importance of *education* and the shortage of skills in both the developed and developing world. This is one of the main factors behind rising income inequalities. Economists Nahuis and de Groot (2003) have calculated the expanding skill premiums as a part of salaries over the last decades. They expect skill premiums to grow as a result of a widening gap between the demand for and the supply of skills among employees. Most likely, the rise of ICTs and the shortage of digital skills are the main cause of this gap. These conditions will contribute to the current polarization on most labor markets between classes of employees (highly skilled labor vs. labor requiring a low level of skills), with increasing wage differences. The rising expectations for skills required put pressure on the digital divide as a problem that should be solved, not only for economic reasons (innovation and competition) but for social reasons (the loss of social cohesion and the growth of social class disparity and ethnic conflict). All the better-paid jobs will require digital skills, and the number of jobs that do not require these skills will either shrink, or employees in them will be paid less and less.

The next tendency increasing inequality in general is *sociocultural:* the individualization and cultural differentiation of (post)modern society. ICT not only enables these processes, it supports them. The computer enables and supports individualization because it is a device that is, first of all, used and operated by individuals for their own purposes. Of course, it also connects individuals in groups and communities by means of networks, but this mainly occurs after these individuals have been deliberately selected. Cultural differentiation is both enabled and supported by computers and networks, as well. Their uniform digital (infra)structure helps to produce and spread all kinds of cultural artifacts in every quality and quantity desired. Thus increasing information inequality also is an aspect of general social-cultural differentiation and opportunities for choices in society. Of course, there is nothing wrong with this tendency. On the contrary, it is a source of freedom and emancipation. However, from a less normative and more objective point of view, it increases the chances that sociocultural inequality is not a matter of free choice because it is linked to the unequal material, temporal, and cognitive resources of individuals. Clearly, sociocultural differentiation is a primary cause of the usage gap described in chapters 6 through 9.

The final tendency that is increasing general inequality is *political*. It serves to tolerate rising inequalities. It is the policy of privatization and liberalization (of the free market economy) in most countries. It is leading to the commercialization of formerly public communication infrastructures and information supply and the upsurge in private education. Inevitably, these processes expand opportunities for information inequality. In regard to the provision of new communication infrastructures, traditional government initiative and spending is replaced by market investments. When regional and social disparities appear in specific types of connections, such as broadband connections, present-day governments expect that the market will solve these problems, and they hesitate to intervene. With the decline of public broadcasting and other public media accessible to all, the inequalities produced by conditional access and commercial services tend to rise. The expansion of private education also reduces equal opportunities for learning basic and advanced digital skills. The only opportunities available are, finally, basic facilities in compulsory and public education, libraries, and community centers. This may increase the already very large gaps of information and strategic digital skills and the growth of usage gaps.

Privatization and liberalization make the achievement of public goals such as the reduction of digital divides more difficult, but they do not rule out the possibility that societies can reach these goals by other than the traditional ways of government. Goals can be attained through clever regulation, public-private partnerships, and the mobilization of civil society and individual citizens. However, this requires sensible and sometimes new or inventive policies that societies are only beginning to discover. We now turn to the ways in which societies in different parts of the world have approached the problem of the digital divide and, on most occasions, have tried to solve it.

❖ THE DIGITAL DIVIDE IN NORTH AMERICA, EUROPE, EAST ASIA, AND THE THIRD WORLD

As I have noted before, the similarities in the approach to the digital divide in different parts of the world are greater than the differences. Everywhere there is a strong emphasis on technological diffusion and physical access. Moreover, there is a widespread belief that the market will solve most access problems, making digital technology cheaper, more powerful, and easy to use. The primary—and often the only—way to introduce the technology to users is to organize special courses and guidance so that they can learn the operational skills required. Social and contextual aspects are very much neglected, and differential usage is most often considered a matter of individual responsibility.

However, there are also differences of approach that reflect the political, economic, social, and cultural distinctions between countries. I expect they will grow when digital technology permeates deeper and deeper into societies, reflecting ever greater disparities of all kinds. A comparison of the ways in which different parts of the world use policy instruments to bridge the digital divide is shown in Table 10.1. Clearly, this table is not complete; I have focused on the most obvious trends in the policy discussions concerning the digital divide worldwide.

North America

The United States is the homeland of the digital divide concept and discussion. The concept was invented in 1998 (see Gunkel, 2003), but public discussion about unequal access had already started with the proliferation of PCs in the early 1980s. In 1995, it reached the political agenda with then–Vice President Al Gore's announcement of the National Information Infrastructure, which was supposed to be accessible to all Americans, and the publication of the first of the NTIA

Table 10.1   A Classification of Current Policy Instruments for Closing the Digital Divide

Orientation		Policy Instruments
Material access	Technical	*General* technology diffusion: Universal access (innovation and investment) *Focused* technology diffusion: Public access (libraries, CTCs, kiosks, other public places) Universal service (hardware connections by funding and regulation)
	Economic	Subsidies to disadvantaged groups
Motivational, skills, and usage access	Educational	Educational investment: Computer and network provisions in schools Special computer classes and courses Teacher training, curriculum adaptation Educational software development
	Psychological	Awareness programs (information campaigns) Model projects (demonstrations)
	Social and cultural	Content and application development

Note: CTC indicates computer technology center.

Falling Through the Net reports (NTIA, 1995). The subtitles of the NTIA series reveal the official political history of the digital divide problem in the United States. It started with the *A Survey of the "Have-Nots" in Rural and Urban America* (the subtitle of the 1995 NTIA report). In the 1998 NTIA report, the problem was given a name, *New Data on the Digital Divide*, to be followed by more conceptual and empirical analysis of a digital divide supposed to be growing: *Defining the Digital Divide* (NTIA, 1999). In 2000, the fourth report was a special call for action by the Clinton administration: *Towards Digital Inclusion* (NTIA, 2000).

After the installation of the Bush administration in 2001, the denomination of the problem suddenly took a giant turn (Dickard, 2002). The United States was becoming *A Nation Online: How Americans Are Expanding Their Use of the Internet* (NTIA, 2002). As may be seen, the assumption was that the problem was already being solved. The Bush administration concluded that government action was no longer needed. It proposed termination of programs like the Computer Technology Centers (CTC) program and the Technology Opportunities Program (TOP). (A discussion of this follows.)

The United States takes a clear market orientation toward technological innovation and diffusion. Governments may spend hundreds of billions of dollars in the defense, space, and aircraft industries, but the elaboration of innovation and diffusion is left to R&D departments and the industries themselves. This also goes for information and communication technology. The presumption is that the diffusion of ICTs will reach the whole population eventually, after market mechanisms have done their job.

There is only a small direct government investment left for the diffusion of ICTs. It mainly concerns educational investment in computers, network, and software for schools and teacher training. For example, in 2001, $872 million was invested in educational technology for secondary education according to the Elementary and Secondary Education Act (ESEA; U.S. Department of Education, 2001).

The largest amount of clearly identifiable investment in closing the digital divide of physical access comes from the Universal Service Fund, which flows into the so-called E-rate Program. In 2001, this Program spent $2.25 billion dollars to wire schools and libraries in poor and rural communities (Mossberger et al., 2003; Wilhelm, 2003b). It only concerns Internet and telephone connections, not computers or training. The Universal Service Fund is a unique outcome of the 1996 Telecommunications Act, extending universal service from plain old telephones to computerized telecommunications. The money comes from a small part of the tariffs paid by telephone users. The existence and focus of this fund clearly testify to the hardware orientation on this issue in American policy. The availability of connections is offered. No further public investment in the distribution of computers and staffing (training), except for education, is considered to be appropriate. Government programs to provide or subsidize computers and Internet access to low-income families and rural residents have been suggested by some politicians and business leaders, but they have not been realized, despite the support of about the half of the population, according to surveys (see Mossberger et al., 2003; Wilhelm, 2003b).

The direction of American policies to bridge the digital divide is heading toward the accomplishment of public access. Home access is not an official objective, although the temptation to use it as an objective (re)appeared with the uneven regional diffusion of broadband after 2000. Public access means the provision of libraries and community technology centers, next to public schools and hospitals, with connections, computers, and a limited number of staff. The Community Technology Centers Program has funded about 400 centers, and the Technology Opportunities Program provided grants to pilot projects with local innovative use of ICTs. These two federal programs only cost $110 million in 2001. Still, their funding was severely reduced, despite some opposition in Congress.

A very conspicuous U.S. trait is the important role of private and corporate donations of computers and Internet connections to schools, libraries, CTCs, and teacher training. Instances are the Bill and Melinda Gates Foundation, which spent between $200 and $250 million dollars for equipment and training in 2002 and 2003; the Cisco initiative for skill building in high schools; the AOL–Time Warner support for CTCs; and Intel's training of teachers. These forms of charity and public relations substitute for local and federal government spending.

A final characteristic feature of the U.S. situation is the small part played by public initiative in model projects, awareness programs, and special content and application development to stimulate underserved Americans, minorities, the disabled, and illiterates. The TOP is the only government exception. The rest is all corporate initiative by hardware and software producers and public-private initiative by software and service companies, sometimes in cooperation with community organizations. U.S. software and services industries are leading in the world, but they invest very little money in supporting the underserved with focused R&D.

Canada ran a close second to the United States in 2002 in the number of computer and Internet users, according to ITU estimates (ITU, 2002). The striking difference between Canada and the United States is Canada's much greater government initiative in promoting an information superhighway infrastructure and reducing the digital divide. Generally, Canada is somewhere between the United States and the European Union (EU) in social and information policies. The Canadian government strategy of the 1990s was called *Connecting Canadians*. It was based on a very broad program containing six "pillars" (Steinour, 2001). These pillars were policies that were intended not only to extend universal access to infrastructures and computers but also to support local communities in establishing pilot demonstration projects, to increase Canadian content online, to organize Canada's *SchoolNet*, and to promote e-commerce and e-government.

Another characteristic of the Canadian situation is the large urban-rural digital divide (Rural Secretariat, 2001). This was approached with universal access measures and a National Broadband Taskforce, established in 2000. In 2000, close to Can$1 billion in mandatory subsidies were collected from long distance carriers to fund local telephone (and Internet) service (National Broadband Taskforce, 2001). According to O'Brien (2001), government programs have been more successful in hardware diffusion than in the skills and content areas.

Europe

For a long time, Europeans thought they were far behind North America in the diffusion of ICTs. However, the current situation is actually mixed and marked by extremely uneven development. Northern Europe is ahead of the United States in computer possession and Internet access among the population. Southern Europe, however, is far behind, and the Eastern European countries belong to that group of low to medium development and penetration of computers and the Internet shown in Figure 4.4.

Officially and ideologically, the European Union (which has had 25 member states since May 2004) is very much occupied in building an all-inclusive information society. Documents with titles such as *An Information Society for All* have abounded since the middle of the 1990s. However, just like the United States, the EU has adopted a market orientation toward technological innovation and diffusion. This strongly applies to ICTs. Here the prime strategic orientation is the liberalization of telecommunications. The construction of new infrastructures and their general diffusion is left to the market. The EU and its member states try to stimulate and direct development with innovation funds and to correct by regulation.

In the tradition of welfare states, the (western) European countries are inclined to redistribute resources, in this case, hardware, software, services and training, among those having no or inadequate access. This tendency has declined considerably. The EU information society policy now vacillates between broader social concerns, such as social inclusion for all, and a more technology- and market-oriented focus (Henten & Kristensen, 2000, p. 83). Direct national and local government investment in closing the digital divide is limited to the field of education and the support of particular problem areas or groups. It focuses on educational investment, public access, community building (installing community access centers), and some assistance to the unemployed, people living on social benefits, and low-income families with school-age children. In some European countries or cities, these groups are provided with computers and Internet access on the condition that certain courses are taken, jobs are applied for, and so on.

Instead of direct government intervention, EU and member state policies now focus on the stimulation of information technology through their funding of R&D. The EU lags behind the United States and Japan in labor productivity and innovation expenditure. In the so-called Fourth, Fifth and Sixth Framework Programs of the EU, billions of euros are spend on research and innovation projects concerning, first of all, information technology. Some of them are dedicated to a diffusion of more and better hardware, software, and services among segments of the population and European regions that have a low level of access. However, the structural funds of the EU are rarely dedicated to closing the enormous gap between the northern and southern regions of Europe. The money is spend on transportation and building projects, not on computers and their networks.

In contrast to the United States, Europe has no Universal Service Fund or equivalent. The European Commission has made the creation of such funds possible, but practically no member state has taken this option. Instead, the EU tries to realize universal service by regulation (European Commission, 2003). A large number of obligations forces telecom operators to interconnect their networks, to open up their connections for access to the Internet and digital media by telephone subscribers, and to provide some public access points.

As in North America, Europe is oriented toward accomplishing public access first. National and local European governments have also started to connect schools, libraries, and all kinds of community buildings. However, since the year 2000, the attempts to stimulate and organize home access have become stronger. The main reason is that Europe is one of the most densely populated and wired regions of the world. To improve existing connections, the diffusion of broadband has reached number one priority within the EU as a whole as well as at the level of local government.

When total spending is considered, it seems that articulated government investment in closing the digital divide is considerably greater in the EU than it is in the United States. U.S. spending is mainly based in universal service funds, private investments, and charity. However, nobody is able to measure the precise difference. Most innovation funds, educational investments, and even the connection of public facilities are not focused solely on social inclusion but on technological diffusion in general. In theory, the entire population of a country takes advantage of the opportunity when that country moves to a state of universal access. In practice, this condition may never appear, and the higher social classes could benefit more than the lower social classes in using the provisions. Another difficulty is the exact distribution between the federal (union), state, and local levels of funding. It is certain that charity and private public relations improving access play a much smaller role in Europe than in the United States. Instead, the orientation of public-private partnerships in promoting all kinds of access is on the rise in Europe.

The most important difference in digital divide policy between the United States and the EU is the much larger role of public awareness building programs and promotion of the information society in general in Europe (Servaes & Burgelman, 2000). A large part of the money devoted generally to ICTs in Europe does not go to technical infrastructures but to model projects, information campaigns, and the development of content and applications with a popular appeal. More regulation has also been proposed to transform the Internet into a safer environment for users. In this way, Europe pays comparatively more attention to motivational and usage access issues than does the United States.

East Asia

East Asia has become the third stronghold of ICT production and diffusion in the world, next to Northern America and Europe. It specializes in hardware manufacturing and has become the main producer of computers, telephone equipment, and computer peripherals. The growth figures of ICT production in this region are impressive. Within a decade, not only Japan but Singapore, Hong Kong, and South Korea were computerized, with around 50% of the population having a PC and Internet access in 2003. South Korea has even become the number one in broadband diffusion in the world. However, a clear divide can be discerned between the more advanced countries in the region (Japan and the so-called newly industrializing economies of Hong Kong, Singapore, South Korea, and Taiwan) and the less developed countries, particularly in Southeast Asia (Wong, 2002). In 2002, the last-named group had computer penetration rates between 12 per 100 inhabitants (Malaysia) and 1.2 per 100 in Indonesia and Internet connections between 27 per 100 (Malaysia) and 1 per 100 in Indonesia. China is experiencing explosive growth in rates of ICT production and numbers of computer or Internet users (Giese, 2003).

The most important characteristic of the East Asian countries concerning the digital divide is their strong emphasis on general technology diffusion through government initiatives that stimulate the national private sector to manufacture ICTs. This is a consequence of their character as "developmental states" (Castells, 1998). Developmental states make strategic and selective interventions in the economy to promote and sustain development, but they leave execution to private enterprise. In all these countries, influential ministries have launched and coordinated nationwide plans to promote information technology in society, from the Technopolis Program in Japan, the Singapore One Project, and the Malaysian Super Corridor Project to the Cyber Korea 21 initiative. The ultimate aims of these plans was to accomplish universal service, not by funds and subsidies, as in the United States, or by regulation, as in the EU, but by letting the national telecom companies and electronics manufacturers roll out infrastructures and produce equipment that will finally reach every household.

The main presumption behind this method of general technology diffusion is that hardware diffusion will, first, boost industrial production of ICTs, will subsequently lead to large-scale adoption of ICT by the population at large, and will finally result in the development of digital skills, information services, and all kind of applications among the new computer users. It is as if the sequential scheme of kinds of ICT access in this book were being followed. Moreover, the whole process starts with stimulating motivational access in the public information campaigns that accompany the nationwide plans. Unfortunately, this stages approach may lead to stagnation after some time, as digital skills, user experience, and the local development of applications are needed to reap the fruits of ultimately much more profitable software, innovative design, and service supply (Wong, 2002, p. 169) and to build a fully mature information society.

The essential problem of the East Asian countries is their over-emphasis on ICT *production* as compared to *use*. Kraemer and Dedrick (2002) argue that the digital divide in use of ICT between Asian and non-Asian countries is growing. "Asian countries have lagged in adopting IT due to language barriers, organizational resistance, and in some cases, government policies that promoted computer production at the expense of use by raising trade barriers" (p. 35). They note one exception: "The only place in Asia where production and use have flourished has been Singapore, where government policies have explicitly pushed both supply and demand" (p. 37). The most strongly growing sectors of the information economy in East Asia also are software and services, but in Japan and Singapore, the proportion is negligible; for example, 11.8% in South Korea in 2001 (Ministry of Information and Communication, 2002) and 1% in China (Meng & Li, 2002).

There are serious consequences of this hardware and technology push orientation for digital divide policies. First, there is scarcely any focus on the inclusion of deprived groups and remote regions. National and business interests are at the core of ICT policies. Probably it is assumed that general technological diffusion ultimately includes everybody and all places. There are no subsidies for disadvantaged groups. The promotion of public access in a variety of access points has no priority. Although they are often severely controlled by the government, as in China, Malaysia, and Singapore, public access is left to private initiatives (Internet cafés and the like).

Second, the prime orientation is economic and technical, not social and educational. There is a lack of attention to human resources. A good illustration is the introduction of ICT in South Korea. The impressive results of the hardware diffusion of computers and Internet connections in this country were not accompanied by sufficient distribution of digital skills and usage applications (Park, 2002). Table 5.1 shows that more than 45% of the South Korean population had no or very few digital skills in 2000. Additionally, a usage gap of different applications appeared between Koreans with high and low levels of education and blue- and white-collar occupations (Park, 2002). I have no room to offer additional data here, but I would like to note that there are data to show that skills and usage access divides are bigger in East

Asian countries than they are in North America or in northern or western Europe. A massive technology push by governments does not automatically lead to sufficient digital skills and a diversity of locally attractive usage applications. In line with the main message of this book, it may be seen that skills access and usage access require more, not less, effort than does physical access. Efforts by governments to promote technology and to build skills should be made in parallel, not in succession.

A third consequence of the hardware orientation is less educational investment, other than supplying schools with computers and network connections, in East Asia than in North America and in Europe as a whole. In most East Asian countries, educational investment started in sections of higher education and industry and largely remains in these sections. Basic, secondary, and adult education lag far behind. Educational innovation (new didactics, curricula, and course software) is scarce.

A final characteristic of the East Asian digital divide is the modest attention to content and application development. Important exceptions are the translation of Western software and the production of contents and Internet hosts in the local language. This is done to promote local culture and because reading and writing English are a big problem in the large majority of the East Asian countries. This modest attention is a consequence of the relatively small effort to produce software and services (discussed earlier).

The Third World

In chapter 4, specifically in Figures 4.4a and 4.4b, it was emphasized that the digital divide of physical access between developed and developing countries increased from 1990 onwards (see Campbell, 2001; ITU, 2002; Kenny, 2002; and UNDP, 1998, for similar data). The same applies to the physical access divides within developing Third World countries. The gaps between urban and rural regions are growing. Connectivity grows much more intensively in the few big cities containing business centers, government departments, and universities than it does in the numerous villages of the Third World. Skills access and usage access lag still further behind the level of the developed world, even in places where physical access is available (see Kenny, 2002; Pigato, 2001).

This bleak picture looks somewhat better for the newly industrializing economies than it does for the least developed countries. Some East

Asian countries and a few others have at least raised ICT production, and India specializes in software development. However, even for these countries, the national and international divides are basically the same, although less pronounced. This was amply described in earlier paragraphs (also see Kraemer & Dedrick, 2002). From this state of affairs, one can draw the general conclusion that all kinds of access divides are *wider* in developing than in developed countries. However, in the evolving information and network societies of the developed world, divides may become *deeper*, as the title of this book says.

This account raises the fundamental strategic question: To what extent is the Third World able to support general technology diffusion in the form of universal access? Are the means of investment adequate to accomplish this aim in a few decades? Or should other priorities be preferred, such as literacy and better primary education, health, electricity, and universal access to old mass media such as newspapers and radio and television broadcasting? The discussion was even raised by the chief of computer promotion, Bill Gates (2000), in the following remarkable quote from a speech about development priorities:

> I am suggesting that if somebody is interested in equity that you wouldn't spend more than twenty per cent of your time talking about access to computers, that you'd get back to literacy and health and things like that. So the balance that makes sense is that more money should be spent on malaria.

A short list of opportunities and threats resulting from ICT diffusion in Third World countries may be required as an input to the strategic discussion. Opportunities can be listed at all levels (see Marker, McNamara, & Wallace, 2001). When properly used and broadly deployed at the micro level, ICTs in the Third World "can increase the access of the poor to information on market prices for their crops and other goods, to health and educational sources, to information about government services and their own rights as citizens" (Marker et al., 2001). At the intermediate level, ICTs are able to assist hospitals and universities in getting the latest international expertise; farms in finding the best information about new agricultural techniques, irrigation, and diseases; and schools in new educational resources and methods. Moreover, ICTs such as mobile telephone systems and Internet connections offer small entrepreneurs low-level entries to business start-ups in Internet cafés, mobile phone rental, computer training, data entry, and software services. Finally, at the macro level, it is simply necessary for Third World countries to have a reasonable level of access to computers and to the global information infrastructure when they want to participate in the current worldwide trend of outsourcing of production from the high-tech economies to the newly industrializing economies (Campbell, 2001, p. 130).

The most important threat to ICT diffusion in Third World countries is that unequal development will get even worse. When a nation-wide basis of development in technological infrastructure (electricity and reliable connections), educational resources (literacy, school attendance, participation of girls), and political institutions (regulation and a working system of law) is simply lacking, ICT diffusion will not fall on any fertile soil. For the mass of the population, it will simply be a waste, and only very small elites will take advantage of the new opportunities. Diffusion would increase inequality instead of decreasing it.

There are four main strategic reactions to this balance of opportunities and threats. The first reaction is to adopt some kind of stages approach, as is done in East Asia. This means, first, roll out the technical infrastructure and promote a local industry of ICT production and software development. The second stage is to invest in operational digital skills, first for those who need it most and then for the whole population. The final stage is to develop usage applications for the masses. A consequence of this strategy might be that government policy focuses on business access at the cost of equitable access (Kenny, 2002).

A second strategy is a strong version of a stages approach, useful when it is held to be possible that a Third World country can leapfrog stages of development and go directly to the production of ICT in enclaves of industrial regions linked directly to the world market, as in some East Asian countries and in Costa Rica (chip production) and India, which focuses on software programming (see Press, Foster, & Goodman, 1999, and Steinmüller, 2001). A technological infrastructure could be built very quickly using wireless technologies and cheap terminal devices (simple computers and mobile phones). James (2000, 2003) suggests this road as one of the solutions for the digital divide in the Third World.

The third strategy is a strong version of the stages approach from the opposite point of view. This version contends that Third World countries are able to evolve only gradually from their current stage of development. The massive introduction of ICTs is not a priority in this stage. Instead, all effort should be spent on the improvement of basic material and human resources. This means electricity, transportation, health, traditional education, and old mass media (the press, broadcasting, and the telephone system).

The final strategy is a rejection of all stage approaches in the suggestion that investment in technical infrastructures, education, and all kinds of usage applications should be made in parallel. Mansell and When (1998) have argued that "the developing societies will need to find ways of combining their existing social and technical capabilities if they are to benefit from the potential advantages of ICTs" (p. 256). Ideally, they say, investment in both capabilities should be undertaken simultaneously, but when this does not appear to be possible, investment in social capabilities should receive priority. Because of this doubt, they tend to endorse the third strategy.

Parallel investment in all four kinds of new media access and the resources required is the strategy that fits the analysis in this book. As has been explained several times before, the successive kinds of access in the model that serves as the backbone of this book should not be understood as stages of diffusion but as an analytic explanatory scheme: One kind of access cannot be satisfactorily accomplished without the others. The core statement is that all kinds of access require both social and technical investments.

The most important characteristic of ICT diffusion in Third World countries is a strong emphasis on public access. There is no other option, as universal access for homes, families, and individuals is unattainable now and will be for several decades to come. Therefore some countries have mitigated the principle and defined *universal access* as a telephone line within 20 kilometers (Burkina Fasso) or a traveling distance of 30 minutes (South Africa). India wants to connect at least every village. Computer and Internet access in the Third World largely is a matter of public access, beyond the very small information elite who have private access. This does not mean a preponderance of public or government investment is necessary. Private investment dominates. Public access does not have to be seen as a secondary option only; it offers the best opportunities to attend to the broader community development and education that are even more important in these countries than in the developed world. In this way, more attention can be paid to motivational, skills, and usage access that are adapted to local circumstances.

Currently there are four types of public access in Third World countries. First we have Internet or cyber cafés popping up in the main cities and tourist spots. Most often, they are private initiatives. The same goes for the phone shops that sometimes also provide a computer with Internet access. (In these countries, the diffusion of mobile telephone systems is much faster than computer and Internet diffusion.) The third type of public access is offered by telecenters, which most often are run by telecom operators and stimulated by universal service subsidies. Increasingly, they combine several types of other businesses (Falch, 2004). The final type is the community (technology) center or Internet kiosk run by the local government and supported by international agencies with development programs. These centers try to combine computer and Internet access with broader educational and community development purposes.

Contrary to the expectations of some, these public access sites are barely connecting the so-called ordinary people. Use of these sites also is a phenomenon of the elite, mainly the highly educated, wealthy, and male population that often has access elsewhere (Mwesige, 2004). To reach the mass of the population, the role of human intermediaries having access and passing digital information to their local environment is vital (Cecchini & Scott, 2003; Heeks, 1999). Strategically, the choices of these local intermediaries between the technology and the local population without sufficient resources may be called decisive for the prospects of ICT in developing countries. It is by no means sure that they will choose to assist in the development of their local environment. Instead, these people from the growing middle classes in many Third World countries may serve their own interests or careers and turn their eyes to the global information infrastructure and the interests of the advanced economies, multinational corporations, and the few national strongholds of industry and services. The ICT enclaves in these countries may have no impact on the rest of the population or the region concerned.

For ICTs to have a broader impact in Third World countries, educational investment at all levels and the development of sensible local usage applications are the most important steps required. Currently, Third World educational investment in digital skills is mostly confined to higher education. Basic, secondary, and adult education do not seem to have priority (see Press et al., 1999). This only increases the gap between the mass of the population and a large portion (close to half, on average) of illiterates. For illiterates, learning digital skills is nearly impossible. They have to learn to use the information and messages retrieved by proximate others.

In education, training and the adaptation of course and application material to local needs are more important than the provision of hardware. All experience of ICT projects in the Third World shows that they should never focus on technology as an end in itself. Instead, they should "use technology as an additional tool to promote social capital and community development" (Warschauer, 2003b, p. 172). A second lesson that can be learned from successful projects is that they are characterized by local ownership and participation of the community (Cecchini & Scott, 2003).

Addressing motivational and usage access awareness programs and the creation of practical local applications and cultural content are the prime objectives of local governments and of international agencies conducting development work. Awareness is a necessary condition, as the mass of the population in these countries has no understanding of the potential uses of computers and the Internet. They can only be convinced of their usefulness when sensible applications related to daily problems with food, trade, jobs, health, education, religion, and local community building can be demonstrated. Not having to travel far to hospitals, markets, libraries, and government institutions or simply being able to send messages to remote families and friends appear to be the most attractive applications (Best & Maclay, 2002). They should be framed in the local language, as few people in the Third World speak the official language of their country, let alone English.

❖ POLICY INSTRUMENTS FOR CLOSING THE DIGITAL DIVIDE

In this final section, I will present a large number of policy instruments that can be used to close the digital divide according to the analysis in this book. Before we begin, it must be affirmed that, on principle and for more practical reasons, it is impossible to close the divide completely. The principle is that, following the analysis in this book, the divide is deepening. In the information and network society, information and communication inequalities tend to grow. They are a part of differentiating individual human capabilities that are amplified by the use of technology. Therefore the stakes have been lowered in this book. They are to prevent structural inequality in terms of a first, second, and third class of participation in society—or no significant participation at all. It certainly is possible to mitigate information inequality to attain an acceptable level.

The practicality is that the wish to close the digital divide occurs in a situation of rising general inequalities, as was explained in an earlier section. If this situation does not improve, all practical policies to close the digital divide will have only limited results. When global inequality rises, when low incomes are stagnating or declining, or when educational inequality increases in certain countries, it will be very difficult to solve the digital divide problem. This problem has not been treated as a narrow technical or economic one in this book. Instead, it was portrayed as a very broad social, educational, and political problem. This means that general solutions in terms of more economic, educational, cultural, and political (citizen) equality would produce the best chances for solving it in the end.

However, such a conclusion would be very unsatisfactory after the detailed analysis in this book. It is not justified, either. Concrete policies for confronting the digital divide are possible. The import of the previous section was that different regions in the world have been able to choose diverging strategies and responses that deal with the digital divide problem. In this section, I focus on a large number of more or less concrete measures that can prevent structural inequality. These instruments are not only meant to be used by governments. We will see that businesses, nonprofit and civilian organizations, technical designers and producers, and individual citizens also have a responsibility to use them.

It will be no surprise that the policy instruments proposed are linked to the four successive kinds of access shaping the core of this book. There is a logic in their description that is summarized in the "wheel" of policy instruments shown in Figure 10.1. It starts with motivational access and finishes with usage access, with its apparent link to motivational access.

Motivational Access

To improve motivational access, we have to look at the reasons the information want-nots, dropouts, and intermittent users supply when refusing access (see chapter 3). Often they appear to be very sensible and rational reasons. In this case, the technology is to blame, not so-called laggards or backward people who have not yet discovered the miracles of the new technology. There is still a lot of improvement

Figure 10.1   A Wheel of Policy Instruments for Closing the Digital Divide

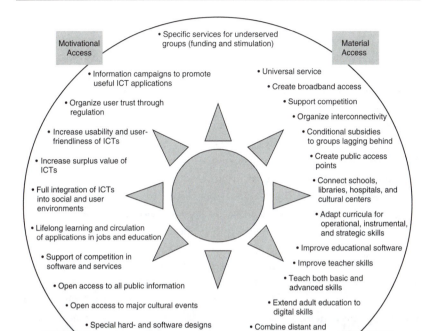

needed in the maturing information and communication technologies. *Increasing the surplus value of ICTs* for daily purposes of work, education, social living, and leisure time would be the best option to increase the attractiveness of this technology for the mass of the population. Many people are, rightfully, not convinced that the new media are better for a lot of uses than are the old media and meetings or face-to-face interaction. This specifically is true of those groups who regularly stay at the wrong side of the divide: the elderly, those with low levels of education, the disabled, some part of the female population, and many ethnic minorities. The problem is that it is exactly these people who are underserved with regard to applications that would motivate them to obtain computer access (see chapter 6). Working on programs, special information content (practical, local, own language), and communication services for these groups would increase the surplus value of ICTs.

The second solution for increasing motivation, again especially for these groups lagging behind, is to *increase the usability and user-friendliness* of ICTs. This is the best way to ease computer anxiety and technophobia. Many improvements are still needed in user interfaces to digital technology. Remember that it is only about a decade ago that we left the stone age of computer and network technology with the introduction of graphical interfaces and multimedia applications. The new media have a large potential in this regard. Their capacity of inter-activity, for example, increases user motivation (including disadvantaged groups), but it also requires more cognitive resources (Bucy, 2004). The interactivity of interfaces could be improved considerably.

Another barrier for the motivation of potential computer users is the wrong, offensive, dangerous, and outright criminal uses of computers and the Internet. Many people are worried about the invasion of privacy this technology of registration and control may produce. They fear online (child) pornography, racism, fraud, and credit card (identity) theft. They think PCs damage health, producing repetitive strain injury, stress, addiction, and social withdrawal. These fears are not irrational; all these problems are real. Therefore it is a primary task for governments and other institutions to *organize user trust by regulation* of the Internet and the computer world. Many governments, especially in Europe and North America, have adopted this task, among other reasons to extend the user populations of their countries and to close the digital divide.

When regulatory improvements are made, it becomes possible to raise awareness of the benefits of the new technologies. Both governments and businesses organize *information campaigns to promote useful applications of ICTs*. At the start of the diffusion of a new technology, mass awareness of its benefits (and potential threats) is not an automatic result of its adoption by innovators among the population and their influence on the mass media. Considerable effort has to be made to demonstrate its usefulness, for the later adopters in particular, and sometimes special campaigns are necessary. In the days of the Internet hype, this was comparatively easy. Now, in the first decade of the 21st century, the approach needs to be more critical and qualified, taking into account the fears and doubts of people with a lack of motivation.

The best way to accomplish this is to produce and promote *specific services for underserved groups* by funding and other stimulation. For the elderly, this might mean health and alarm services; services for the disabled, both for general purposes and for using computers; and simple

or low-income households, this could mean
;s of jobs and housing, low-cost child care,
·cost insurance, tax filing support, and the
 help wanted sites and online job training
 inorities might be motivated by computer
mation in their own language that presents
ow minority members in familiar cultural
_azarus and Mora (2000) for other examples.

Material access remains a necessary condition everywhere, even though the emphasis in the priority of kinds of access shifts to skills and usage access, at least in the developed countries. However, technology push does not help very much, as I have argued elsewhere in this book. Simply to provide deprived groups with boxes of computers and network connectors or even to stimulate a general, nationwide technology diffusion without sufficient attention to skills and usage is not a good digital divide policy. In contrast, the principle of *universal service*, which originated in the world of telecommunications, is a crucial policy instrument for realizing physical access for everybody who is able and willing to use computers and the Internet. Universal access may be defined as "access to a defined minimum service of specified quality to all users independent of their geographical location and, in the light of specific national conditions, at an affordable price" (European Commission, 1996). This telecommunications principle should be extended to the Internet, specifically e-mail, and, within a reasonable term, to broadband connections (Anderson, Bikson, Law, & Mitchell, 1995; van Dijk, 1997). We have seen how the United States, the EU, East Asia, and the Third World are trying to realize this principle in different ways—and without sufficient results. As realization seems to be impossible in the short term, all countries step back to reach principles of public access and public service. In the developed countries, this means access in schools, libraries, and other public buildings, and in many developing countries, this comes down to the attempt to connect at least every village or city neighborhood in telecenters, kiosks, or Internet cafés.

In the developed countries, universal access and service at home could be a reasonable policy goal. There are many ways to realize this goal: universal service funds; infrastructure competition between telephone and cable companies, leading to lower prices; regulatory obligations for these same companies to provide connections in remote places; and special public-private partnerships to connect places that want broadband capacity or where connection would be expensive.

Elsewhere I have proposed the principle that in a network and information society, every citizen should have *access to basic provisions* of information and communication (van Dijk, 1997, 2000). This means

1. Basic connections: extending universal service of telecommunications to Internet connections, e-mail, and (in a reasonable amount of time) broadband in all infrastructures (telephone systems, cable, and satellite)

2. Public information and communication: government information, vital community information services, and public broadcasting

3. Health information and communication, with basic alarm facilities

4. Compulsory education information: primary and secondary schools provided with computers, internet connections, and (subsidies for) home connections

The *promotion of broadband access* in advanced high-tech societies is no premature policy goal. In chapter 6, it was demonstrated that broadband makes a difference. It changes lifestyles and offers many useful applications for daily life that are very attractive for people from the lower social classes. These applications could motivate these people to use computers and the Internet. Instead, the opposite seems to happen: A broadband elite arises that increases the advance of computers and the Internet for this elite, but not for nonusers. Thus it is very reasonable that a growing number of cities and regions in the Western and East Asian worlds are starting community broadband projects, not waiting until the market installs them.

In the past decade, the market has lowered the price of computer hardware and connections, making the technology available to a much larger segment of the population in the rich countries. However, prices of software and most services have declined only slightly. This calls attention to the continuing importance of *support for competition* by all kinds of regulatory economic bodies. Other institutions should organize *better interconnectivity* of currently separate media channels. A transparent nationwide infrastructure reaching every household or community (Third World) is a great stimulus to close the digital divide of physical access.

A highly contested subject of debate is whether governments should directly subsidize physical access for disadvantaged groups by tax measures, vouchers, and (parts of) social benefits. This happens in some Western European countries, and it was raised in the U.S. Congress but did not pass. In the United States, this option has taken the road of private and corporate charity, although half of all Americans also backed government intervention to provide Internet access to low-income families and rural residents in 2001 (Mossberger et al., 2003, p. 135). According to my analysis, undirected provisions of computers to disadvantaged groups make no sense. *Conditional subsidies to particular groups lagging behind* are better. These groups are all in the lowest quartile of the income distribution. Special attention should be paid to (a) the unemployed; (b) people living on social benefits or with low income who have no access at work or at school and who are dependant on adult education; and (c) in some countries, particular ethnic minorities. The conditions could be that these groups take certain courses and use job-search or job training sites.

One of the most important lessons of the last decade is that simply providing people with hardware and software without adequate guidance, training, and contextualized usage opportunities is not a good solution to the digital divide problem. This lesson can be learned by observing the vast majority of public access points, Internet cafés, community technology centers, and libraries. The importance of these *public access places* in closing the digital divide cannot be overrated. They provide 90% of physical access in the Third World. In the developed countries, they help a large part of the "truly unconnected" and intermittent users to get access when they want it (Schement, 2003). They are the single most important means of starting to close the divide for the most disadvantaged groups.

Rarely are these public access venues dedicated solely to computer access and courses. They mix these activities with general social and vocational work; public information services; community building; and special educational, cultural, and health activities. Personal assistance, group instruction, and community networking, with staff not trained to teach more than just computer work, are the prime assets of CTCs, libraries, and public access points (Hull, 2003; Liff & Steward, 2003; Penuel & Kim, 2000). These assets remain, although the first (best) option is to have broader home access in the developed countries, as this is associated with much more frequent, intense, and comfortable use. The main problems with public access sites, in terms of physical and usage access, is that they "may require users to wait long periods for their turn, impose strict time limits on computer sessions, filter out useful websites deemed to have controversial content, and provide users with little privacy" (Mossberger et al., 2003, p. 129). In terms of staff, these sites have the problem of having too few employees with computer experience and the time to give personal assistance or computer courses. Another striking fact is that people who already have access somewhere use these public facilities more than people who do not have any access and who perhaps need them most.

Skills Access

A cornerstone of public access policy throughout the world is to *connect all schools* with at least one Internet connection and a number of computers. This is a necessary condition if all young people are to be taught how to work with computers. However, in chapter 5, we saw that the influence of schools on the level of digital skills is relatively low, at least at this point and in the developed countries. Children and young people learn more in practice, at home and from each other, than they do in class from teachers. In school, they learn fewer subjects with the help of ICTs than they do about learning to operate ICTs themselves. Operational skills are dominating computer classes at schools. Information and strategic digital skills are neglected.

The reason for this mismatch is twofold: Often teacher capabilities are inferior, and most educational software is inadequate. However, the most important task for schools to accomplish that will improve skills access in the long run is to *adapt their curricula* so that they teach not only operational but also information and strategic skills. These must be fully integrated into all school subjects, which means, first of all, a revision of the traditional subjects of language and mathematics. Language students need to acquire the capabilities of searching, processing, reproducing, and using information from an overabundance of increasingly digital sources. Mathematics should contain the elementary skills for processing computer data communication. Subjects with names like *media literacy* or *computer class* have to be expanded to deal with contents of television, the Internet, computer games, and multimedia in general and how to handle them. Is it not strange that the most important daily media reality for children, television and computer games, usually are not treated in schools at all? Instead, schools are a completely different world of books, writing, and calculating.

To complete this task, the preparation of *better educational software* is crucial. Many traditional teachers are, rightfully, not convinced that digital ways of learning are better than their own age-old didactics. It has yet to be proved that they are indeed better with much better software. This software needs to be made appropriate for girls, disabled children, children with learning problems, and those who come from a lower social or minority background. Even after this happens, most traditional methods of face-to-face instruction will not disappear. Information and strategic skills in particular are a matter of substance and understanding, to be exchanged in fully interactive communication.

When teachers are convinced of the surplus value of ICTs and their ability to improve education, the second basic problem can be solved. Teachers will be motivated to learn *better digital teaching skills.* They will be able to teach more to their pupils, who themselves often have much better operational skills to start with. The problem with learning from practice is that many operational skills that do not immediately appear to be relevant are not learned at all. This goes even more for information and strategic skills. Thus despite the fact that young people learn many digital skills outside school, this institution remains vital for learning all digital skills required. For children of poor families that have no computer or Internet connection at home, it may even be the only way to learn them.

Another step specifically focused on closing the digital divide in the long run is to teach all pupils in secondary education *both basic and advanced skills.* When one group of students learns only simple or so-called remedial drills for secretarial jobs and other groups learn advanced information searching and producing skills, the digital divide is perpetuated and leads to a lasting usage gap in employment.

Because age is a basic determinant of the digital divide, the *extension of adult education in learning digital skills* is one of the most important policy decisions to make for closing the divide. The problem is that most people who are more than 35 years old, even in the developed countries, have not learned any digital skills during their years of schooling. If they did not enter a job requiring computer work after finishing their schooling, they must learn these skills themselves if they are to learn them at all. They learn from computer books and courses, from their children or from other proximate persons, and most often at home. Unfortunately, governments offer no structural solutions for this problem. Talk about "lifelong learning" abounds, but investment in it is scarce. Community technology centers, libraries, and some subsidized social and cultural educational institutions that offer cheap computer courses are, most often, the only options. Only a small part of the adult population uses these provisions to learn digital skills. The image of these institutions is that they are made for "poor people" and minorities.

For this reason, there is room for public and private initiatives in adult computer education for much larger parts of the population, emphasizing both *distant education at home and a combination of distant education and classes or meetings* in attractive local surroundings. The presumption made here is that this type of education is required not only for people who have never touched a computer or had access to the Internet. The lack of digital skills is spread across a much larger part of the adult population, even in advanced high-tech societies. This is a hidden problem that could be brought to the surface by a far-sighted public educational policy and attractive commercial offerings.

Usage Access

As I have emphasized that practice is more important than formal education in learning digital skills, it will be no surprise that a number of the policy instruments I propose are appropriate for advancing both skills and usage access. The most general one is for assisting approaches that *support learning on the job and at home.* Basically this means two things. First, suitable software programs should be made that help not only in the execution of tasks at work and in homework for the job or for school in a straightforward manner but that also assist the user in learning more operations and applications. Second, to mitigate the usage gap, employees should be allowed to learn more advanced applications on the job than they need right away. For the same reason, students in the lower levels of secondary education should learn not only word processing and to fill databases or spreadsheets but also more advanced programs, such as those that will allow them to search and process information.

The following two instruments are focused on the groups lagging behind in skills. To motivate the disabled, (functional) illiterates, elderly, and children, especially girls, to use computers and the Internet, *more special hardware and software must be designed* for these groups. All of them have special preferences and mental, social, and cultural problems in handling interfaces. Unfortunately, not much investment is made in these special designs, as this market is not a priority for producers. Governments, special interest groups, and not-for-profit organizations should step in.

Perhaps the most important instrument for stimulating the skills and usage of groups lagging behind is the production of *special content for cultural minorities and socially deprived groups*. Language problems, minority cultural interests, and conditions of poverty serve as barriers for motivational, skills, and usage access. In chapters 5 and 6, we have seen that it is no surprise that the innovators and early adopters of the new technologies concerned follow their own preferences regarding the supply of and demand for particular contents and applications. The list of alternative Internet contents put together by Lazarus and Mora (2000) (see chapter 6) clearly shows the omissions in current mainstream Web site supply.

In this book, the rise of usage gaps has been stressed. It is a fundamental question whether policy instruments should be devised at all to reduce these gaps in an individualizing and differentiating society. Isn't use a matter of free choice, not to be directed by agents of policy "from above"? My answer would be that direction is allowed, as, soon, absolute and relative exclusion from certain types of usage will lead to structural information inequality. Moreover, does not every societal and government organization have the right to encourage particular types of usage and to drive back others? Hasn't this been the policy of governments and cultural institutions for ages?

I have explained that structural information inequality appears when particular segments of the population systematically use advanced and strategically important applications of ICTs, for their social positions and careers, and other segments use strategically unimportant applications, for recreation, entertainment, shopping, and simple communication. The most general policy option that can prevent a further rise in structural inequality is the strong support of open access to all relevant content in the new media. This means, first of all, *open access to all public and scientific information* in computer programs and on the Internet. It does not mean that these types of information should be without any cost to users. That should certainly be the case for the basic provisions of information and communication discussed earlier. However, open access to the kind of public and scientific information that has a particular market value means that a large part of it should be available as freeware and shareware. High-value, specialized information has to be available at reasonable prices for all those concerned. Open access to public and scientific information also means that the current trend to expand patents on software and all procedural and specialized information should be diverted. This trend allows monopolistic practices to hamper innovation and prevent vital types of access for all. To some, this call for open access may seem redundant, as they think the multimedia and the Internet are gigantic copying machines flooded by free music, programs, and every imaginable type of information. However, I am not convinced that this situation will stay as it is today. More often in history, we have seen that uncontrolled use marked the beginnings of a new media age. After some time, the radical potential of new media is suppressed and normalcy reappears. Presently, governments and business interests are working hard to safeguard future intellectual property rights through a strong combination of protection by law and by technology.

Increasingly, popular contents or contents for special interest groups are placed behind decoders and screens that ask for user names and passwords. To prevent further social and cultural divides in society, *open access to major cultural events* has to be safeguarded. This means events on national holidays, championship games in sports with mass appeal, and cultural highlights of certain countries. The European Union, for example, has given its member states the opportunity to file a list of protected national events.

Lower prices for computer hardware and Internet connection costs have been very beneficial in closing physical access divides in the developed countries. However, the prices for software and for many information and communication services have not and probably will not decline. *Supporting competition in software and services* and breaking up monopolies are important means of improving usage access. Support for the open source principle in operating systems and other vital software for every computer and Internet user may bring not only lower prices but also better software, perhaps even better software for users with low skill levels.

The last-named actions are measures aimed at preventing absolute exclusion. To mitigate the relative exclusion that is part of all usage gaps, the coupling of specific computer and Internet applications with particular social classes must stop. In jobs, this means better career opportunities, organization of *lifelong learning,* and vocational training in more digital skills than are immediately required, as well as offering *job rotation schemes* in computer applications. These are modern forms of human resources management. At schools, this also comes down to lifelong learning and a broad offer of computer courses for every student instead of narrow divisions in studies and the preparation for particular jobs.

Full integration of ICTs into social and user environments is, however, always the best option for improving usage access. As has been explained many times before, ICTs should never be introduced as an end in themselves. They should always be adapted to the local and specific needs of individual and collective users.

In the preceding argument, the focus on the support of particular groups that are lagging behind in computer access or that are underserved in terms of Internet applications shifted to open access for broader sections of the population. This is no coincidence. As the digital divide problem moves from motivational and physical access to skills and usage access, it deepens. This is the main message of this book. It means that the digital divide problem touches not only deprived and totally excluded groups but also the majority of the populations in the developed countries that participate more or less in the digital world. Among this majority, the distribution of skills and usage access is very unequal. Only the information elite escapes the deepening divide that threatens to become a primary aspect of the society of the future.

References

American Library Association. (1989). *American Library Association Presidential Committee on Information Literacy: Final report.* Washington, DC: Author. Retrieved September 28, 2004, from http://www.infolit.org/documents/89Report.htm

Anderson, R., Bikson, T., Law, S.-A., & Mitchell, B. (Eds.). (1995). *Universal access to e-mail: Feasibility and societal implications.* Santa Monica, CA: RAND.

ARD/ZDF-Arbeitsgruppe Multimedia. (1999a). ARD/ZDF-online-studie 1999: Wird online alltagsmedium? [ARD/ZDF online study: Is online becoming an everyday medium?]. *Media Perspektiven 1999*(8), 388-409.

ARD/ZDF-Arbeitsgruppe Multimedia. (1999b). Nichtnutzer von online: Einstellungen und zugangsbarrieren. Ergebnisse der ARD/ZDF-offline-studie 1999 [Online nonusers: Attitudes and access barriers. Results of the ARD/ZDF offline study 1999]. *Media Perspektiven, 1999*(8), 415-422.

Autor, D., Katz, D., & Krueger, A. (1998). Computing inequality: Have computers changed the labor market? *Quarterly Journal of Economics, 113*, 1169-1213.

Barabási, A.-L. (2002). *Linked: The new science of networks.* Cambridge, MA: Perseus.

Barabási, A.-L., & Albert, R. (1999). Emergence of scaling in random networks. *Science, 286*, 509-512.

Bartel, A.-P., & Sicherman, N. (1999). Technological change and wages: An interindustry analysis. *Journal of Political Economy, 107*, 285-325.

Beniger, J. (1986). *The control revolution: Technological and economic origins of the information society.* Cambridge, MA: Harvard University Press.

Berman, J. B., & Griliches, Z. (1994). Changes in the demand for skilled labor within U.S. manufacturing industries: Evidence from the *Annual Survey of Manufactures. Quarterly Journal of Economics, 109*, 367-365.

Bessière, K., Ceaparu, I., Lazar, J., Robinson, J., & Shneiderman, B. (2004). Social and psychological influences on computer user frustration. In E. Bucy & J. Newhagen (Eds.), *Media access: Social and psychological dimensions of new technology use* (pp. 91-103). London: LEA.

Best, M. L., & Maclay, C. M. (2002). Community Internet access in rural areas: Solving the economic sustainability puzzle. In World Economic Forum

(Ed.), *The global information technology report 2001-2002: Readiness for the networked world* (pp. 76-88). Oxford, England: Oxford University Press. Retrieved February 6, 2004, from http://www.cid.harvard.edu/cr/pdf/gitrr2002_ch08.pdf

Bijker, W., & Law, J. (Eds.). (1992). *Shaping technology/building society: Studies in sociotechnical change.* Cambridge MA: MIT Press.

Bikson, T., & Panis, W. (1999). *Citizens, computers, and connectivity: A review of trends* (No. MR-1109-MF). Santa Monica, CA: RAND.

Blackburn, R. (1999). Understanding social inequality. *International Journal of Sociology and Social Policy, 19*(9-11), 1-23.

Boneva, B., & Kraut, R. (2002). Email, gender, and personal relationships. In B. Wellman & C. Haythornthwaite (Eds.), *The Internet in everyday life* (pp. 372-403). Oxford, England: Blackwell.

Bonfadelli, H. (2002). The Internet and knowledge gaps: A theoretical and empirical investigation. *European Journal of Communication, 17*(1), 65-84.

Boogers, M., & Voerman, G. (2002, October). *Who visits political Websites, and why?* Paper presented at the Euricom Conference "Electronic Networks and Democratic Engagement," Nijmegen.

Bourdieu, P. (1986). The forms of capital. In J. G. Richardson (Ed.), *Handbook of theory and research for the sociology of education* (pp. 241-258). New York: Greenwood Press.

Brosnan, M. J. (1998). The impact of computer anxiety and self-efficacy upon performance. *Journal of Computer Assisted Learning, 14*, 223-234.

Brown, J. S., & Duguid, P. (2000). *The social life of information.* Boston, MA: Harvard Business School Press.

Buchanan, M. (2002). *Nexus: Small worlds and the groundbreaking science of networks.* London: W. W. Norton.

Bucy, E. (2004). The interactivity paradox: Closer to the news but confused. In E. Bucy & J. Newhagen (Eds.), *Media access: Social and psychological dimensions of new technology use* (pp. 47-72). London: LEA.

Bucy, E., & Newhagen, J. (Eds.). (2004). *Media access: Social and psychological dimensions of new technology use.* London: LEA.

Campbell, D. (2001). Can the digital divide be contained? *International Labour Review, 140*, 119-141.

Castells, M. (1996). *The information age: Economy, society and culture. Vol. I. The rise of the network society.* Oxford, England: Blackwell.

Castells, M. (1998). *The information age: Economy, society and culture. Vol. III. End of millennium.* Oxford, England: Blackwell.

Castells, M. (2001). *The Internet galaxy: Reflections on the Internet, business and society.* Oxford, England: Oxford University Press.

Cecchini, S., & Scott, C. (2003). *Can information and communications technology applications contribute to poverty reduction? Lessons from rural India.* Retrieved September 28, 2004, from http://www.eldis.org/static/DOC11916.htm

Chen, W., Boase, J., & Wellman, B. (2002). The global villagers: Comparing Internet users and uses around the world. In B. Wellman & C. Haythornthwaite (Eds.), *The Internet in everyday life* (pp. 74-113). Oxford, England: Blackwell.

The Children's Partnership (TCP). (2002). *About the Children's Partnership.* Retrieved September 9, 2004, from http://www.childrenspartnership .org/bbar/more.html

Cho, J., de Zúñiga, H., Rojas, H., & Shah, D. (2003, Spring). Beyond access: The digital divide and Internet uses and gratifications. *IT & Society, 1*(4), 46-72.

Chua, S. L., Chen, D. T., & Wong, A.F.L. (1999). Computer anxiety and its correlates: A meta-analysis. *Computers in Human Behavior, 15*, 609-623.

Coleman, J. S. (1988). Social capital in the creation of human capital. *American Journal of Sociology, 94*(Suppl.), 95-120.

Compaine, B. (Ed.). (2001). *The digital divide: Facing a crisis or creating a myth?* Cambridge, MA: MIT Press.

Cooper, J., & Weaver, K. D. (2003). *Gender and computers: Understanding the digital divide.* London: LEA.

Cornfield, M., Rainie, L., & Horrigan, J. (2003). *Untuned keyboards, online campaigners: Citizens and portals in the 2002 elections.* Washington, DC: Pew Internet and American Life Project and Institute for Politics Democracy and the Internet.

de Haan, J. (2003, Spring). IT and social inequality in the Netherlands. *IT & Society, 1*(4), 27-45.

de Haan, J., & Huysmans, F. (2002). Van huis uit digitaal: Verwerving van digitale vaardigheden tussen thuismilieu en school [Raised digital: The acquisition of digital skills between home and school environment]. The Hague, Netherlands: Sociaal en Cultureel Planbureau. Retrieved June 25, 2004, from http://www.scp.nl/publicaties/boeken/9037700896.shtml

de Haan, J., & Iedema, J. (in press). Models of access to the information society. *New Media & Society, 7.*

de Kerckhove, D. (1998). *Connected intelligence: The arrival of the Web society.* London: Kogan Page.

Delli Carpini, M., & Keeter, S. (2003). The Internet and an informed citizenry. In D. Anderson & M. Cornfield (Eds.), *The civic web: Online politics and democratic values* (pp. 129-154). Lanham, MD: Rowman & Littlefield.

Dickard, N. (2002, March). *Federal retrenchment on the digital divide: Potential national impact* (Benton Foundation Policy Brief No. 1). Retrieved September 30, 2004, from http://www.benton.org/publibrary/policybriefs/brief01.html

Doets, C., & Huisman, T. (1997). *Digital skills: The state of the art in the Netherlands.* 's-Hertogenbosch, Netherlands: CINOP.

Donnermeyer, J., & Hollifield, C. A. (2003, Spring). Digital divide evidence in four rural towns. *IT & Society, 1*(4), 107-117.

Dordick, H. S., & Wang, G. (1993). *The information society: A retrospective view.* Newbury Park, CA: Sage.

Dworkin, R. (1981). What is equality? Part 2: Equality of resources. *Philosophy and Public Affairs, 10,* 283-345. European Commission. (1996, March 12). *Communication of the commission about universal service for telecommunications* (COM [96]73). Brussels, Belgium: Author.

European Commission. (2003). *European electronic communications regulation and markets 2003: Report on the implementation of the EU electronic communications regulatory package* (COM [2003]715 final). Brussels, Belgium: Author.

Falch, M. (2004). Tele-centres in Ghana. *Telematics and Informatics, 21,* 103-114.

Fariña, F., Arce, R., Sobral, J., & Carames, R. (1991). Predictors of anxiety toward computers. *Computers in Human Behavior, 7,* 263-267.

Feenberg, A. (1991). *Critical theory of technology.* Oxford, England: Oxford University Press.

Fidler, R. (1997). *Mediamorphosis: Understanding new media.* Thousand Oaks, CA: Pine Forge Press.

Finn, S., & Korukonda, A. R. (2004). Avoiding computers: Does personality play a role? In E. Bucy & J. Newhagen (Eds.), *Media access: Social and psychological dimensions of new technology use* (pp. 73-90). London: LEA.

Fox, S. (2003). *Wired for health: How Californians compare to the rest of the nation.* Washington DC: Pew Internet and American Life Project. Retrieved August 28, 2004, from http://www.pewinternet.org

Fox, S., & Fellows, D. (2003). *Reports: Health.* Washington, DC: Pew Internet and American Life Project. Retrieved September 28, 2004, from http://www.pewinternet.org/reports/toc.asp?Report=95

Gates, W. H. (2000, October 18). *Remarks* (Digital Dividends Conference, Seattle). Retrieved March 8, 2004, from http://www.microsoft.com/billgates/speeches/2000/10-18digitaldividends.asp

Gaziano, C. (1983). The knowledge gap: An analytical review of media effects. *Communication Research, 10,* 447-486.

Gesellschaft Sozialwissenschaftlicher Infrastruktureinrichtungen (GESIS). (2004). The Eurobarometer Survey Series: Monitoring the public opinion in the European Union. Retrieved April 2, 2004, from http://www.gesis.org/en/data_service/eurobarometer/

Giese, K. (2003). Internet growth and the digital divide. In C. Hughes & G. Wacker (Eds.), *China and the Internet: Politics of the digital leap forward* (pp. 30-57). London: Routledge.

Gilster, P. (1997). *Digital literacy.* Chicester, England: Wiley.

Graham, S., & Marvin, S. (1996). *Telecommunications and the city: Electronic spaces, urban places.* London: Routledge.

Granovetter, M. (1973). The strength of weak ties. *American Journal of Sociology, 78,* 1360-1380.

Gunkel, D. (2003). Second thoughts: Toward a critique of the digital divide. *New Media & Society, 5*(4), 499-522.

GVU Center, Georgia University. (2001). *GVU World Wide Web user surveys* (1-10). Retrieved September 30, 2004, from http://www.gvu.gatech.edu/user_surveys/

Hamelink, C. (2001). *The ethics of cyberspace.* London: Sage.

Hargittai, E. (1999). Weaving the Western web: Explaining differences in Internet connectivity among OECD countries. *Telecommunications Policy, 23*(10/11), 701-718.

Hargittai, E. (2002). The second-level digital divide: Differences in people's online skills. *First Monday: Peer-Reviewed Journal on the Internet, 7*(4). Retrieved August 31, 2004, from http://firstmonday.org/issues/issue7_4/hargittai/

Hargittai, E. (2003). The digital divide and what to do about it. In D. C. Jones (Ed.), *The new economy handbook.* San Diego, CA: Academic Press. Retrieved August 31, 2004, from http://www.princeton.edu/~eszter/research/c04-digitaldivide.html

Heeks, R. (1999). *Information and communication technologies: Poverty and development* (Development Informatics Working Paper Series, Paper No. 5). Retrieved February 6, 2004, from http://wwwidpm.man.ac.uk/idpm/di_wp5.htm

Henten, A., & Kristensen, T. (2000). Information society visions in the Nordic countries. *Telematics and Informatics, 17,* 77-103.

Hirsch, F. (1976). *The social limits to growth.* London: Routledge & Kegan Paul.

Horrigan, J., & Rainie, L. (2002a). *The broadband difference: How online behavior changes with high-speed Internet connections.* Washington DC: Pew Internet and American Life Project. Retrieved August 28, 2004, from http://www.pewinternet.org

Horrigan, J., & Rainie, L. (2002b). *Getting serious online: As Americans gain experience, they pursue more serious activities.* Washington DC: Pew Internet and American Life Project. Retrieved August 28, 2004, from http://www.pewinternet.org

Howard, P., Rainie, L., & Jones, S. (2001). Days and nights on the Internet: The impact of a diffusing technology. In B. Wellman & C. Haythornthwaite (Eds.), *The Internet in everyday life* (pp. 45-73). Oxford, England: Blackwell.

Hudiburg, R. A. (1999). Preliminary investigation of computer stress and the big five personality factors. *Psychology Reports, 85,* 473-480.

Hull, B. (2003). ICT and social exclusion: the role of libraries. *Telematics and Informatics, 20,* 131-142.

Information Culture Center (ICC). (2000). *Kuk-min jeong-bo-saeng-hwal sil-tea mik jeong-bo-hwa insik cho-sa* [Survey on the information life and information awareness]. Seoul, South Korea: Author.

International Telecommunications Union (ITU). (2002). *World telecommunication development report: Reinventing telecoms* (6th ed.). Geneva: Author. Retrieved August 30, 2004, from http://www.itu.int/ITU-D/ict/publications/wtdr_02/

International Telecommunications Union (ITU). (2003). *ITU Internet reports: Birth of broadband.* Geneva: Author. Retrieved March 9, 2004, from http://www.itu.int/osg/spu/publications/sales/birthofbroadband

Jääskeläinen, P., & Savolainen, R. (2003). Competency in network use as a resource for citizenship: Implications for the digital divide. *Information*

Research, 8(3). Retrieved September 30, 2004, from http://informationr.net/ir/8-3/paper153.html

James, J. (2000). Pro-poor modes of technical integration into the global economy. *Development and Change, 31*, 765-783.

James, J. (2003). *Technology, globalization and poverty.* Cheltenham, England: Edward Elgar.

Katz, J. E., & Rice, R. E. (2002). *Social consequences of Internet use, access, involvement, and interaction.* Cambridge, MA: MIT Press.

Kenny, C. (2002). *The Internet and economic growth in least developed countries: A case of managing expectations?* (World Institute for Development Economics Research Discussion Paper No. 2002/75). Retrieved January 30, 2004, from http://www.wider.unu.edu/publications/dps/dps2002/dp2002-75.pdf

Kling, R. (2000). Learning about information technologies and social change: The contribution of social informatics. *Information Society, 16*, 217-232.

Kraemer, K., & Dedrick, J. (2002). Information technology in Southeast Asia: Engine of growth or digital divide? In C. S. Yue & J. J. Lim (Eds.), *Information technology in Asia: New development paradigms* (pp. 22-47). Singapore: Institute of Southeast Asian Studies.

Kumar, K. (1995). *From post-industrial to postmodern society.* Oxford, England: Blackwell.

Lave, J., & Wenger, E. (1993). *Situated learning: Legitimate peripheral participation.* New York: Cambridge University Press.

Lazarus, W., & Mora, F. (2000). *Online content for low-income and underserved Americans: The digital divide's new frontier.* Santa Monica, CA: Childrens Partnership. Retrieved March 8, 2004, from http://www.contentbank.org

Lazarus W., & Roberts, K. (2003). *The search for high-quality online content for low-income and underserved communities.* Santa Monica, CA: Childrens Partnership. Retrieved March 8, 2004, from http://www.contentbank.org

Lenhart, A., Fallows, D., & Horrigan, J. (2004). *Content creation online.* Washington, DC: Pew Internet and American Life Project. Retrieved August 28, 2004, from http//:www.pewinternet.org

Lenhart, A., Horrigan, J., Rainie, L., Allen, K., Boyce, A., Madden, M., et al. (2003). *The ever-shifting Internet population: A new look at Internet access and the digital divide.* Washington, DC: Pew Internet and American Life Project. Retrieved August 28, 2004, from http://www.pewinternet.org

Lessig, L. (1999). *Code and other laws of cyberspace.* New York: Basic Books.

Lessig, L. (2001). *The future of ideas: The fate of the commons in a connected world.* New York: Vintage Books.

Liff, S., & Steward, F. (2003, September). Shaping e-access in the cybercafé: Networks, boundaries and heteropian innovation. *New Media & Society, 5*(3), 313-334.

Machin, S., & Van Reenen, J. (1998). Technology and changes in skill structure: Evidence from seven OECD countries. *Quarterly Journal of Economics, 113*, 1215-1244.

Madden, M. (2003). *America's online pursuits: The changing picture of who's online and what they do* (L. Rainie, Ed.). Washington, DC: Pew Internet and American Life Project. Retrieved August 28, 2004, from http://www.pewinternet .org

Mansell, R., & When, U. (Eds.). (1998). *Knowledge societies: Information technology for sustainable development.* Oxford, England: Oxford University Press.

Marker, P., McNamara, K., & Wallace, L. (2001). *The significance of information and communication technologies for reducing poverty.* Retrieved February 7, 2004, from http://dfid.gov.uk/Pubs/files/ict_poverty.htm

Markus, L. (1990). Towards a "critical mass" theory of interactive media. In J. Fulk & C. Steinfield (Eds.), *Organizations and communication technology* (pp. 117-140). Newbury Park, CA: Sage.

Martin, S. P. (2003, Spring). Is the digital divide really closing? A critique of inequality measurement in A Nation Online. *IT & Society, 1*(4), 1-13.

Mason, S., & Hacker, K. (2003). Applying communication theory to digital divide research. *IT & Society, 5*(5), 40-55.

Maurer, M. M. (1994). Computer anxiety correlates and what they tell us. *Computers in Human Behavior, 10*(3), 369-376.

McChesney, R. (1999). *Rich media, poor democracy: Communication politics in dubious times.* New York: New Press.

Meng, Q., & Li, M. (2002). New economy and ICT development in China. *Information Economics and Policy, 14,* 275-295.

Merton, R. (1968). The Matthew effect in science. *Science, 159,* 56-63.

Milgram, S. (1967). The small world problem. *Psychology Today, 2,* 60-67.

Ministry of Information and Communication, Republic of Korea. (2002). *Information technology overview of Korea: Statistical profiles.* Retrieved February 22, 2004, from http://www.mic.go.kr/eng/jsp/res/res_300_03.jsp

Mossberger, K., Tolbert, C., & Stansbury, M. (2003). *Virtual inequality: Beyond the digital divide.* Washington, DC: Georgetown University Press.

Mulgan, G. (1991). *Communication and control: Networks and the new economics of communication.* Cambridge, England: Polity.

Mwesige, P. G. (2004). Cyber elites: A survey of Internet café users in Uganda. *Telematics and Informatics, 21,* 83-101.

Nahuis, R., & de Groot, H. (2003). *Rising skill premia: You ain't seen nothing yet* (CPB Discussion Paper No. 20). The Hague, Netherlands: Centraal Plan Bureau, Netherlands Bureau for Economic Policy Analysis. Retrieved February 7, 2004, from http://ideas.repec.org/p/cpb/discus/20.html

National Broadband Taskforce. (2001). *The new national dream: Networking the nation for broadband access.* Retrieved March 22, 2004, from http:// broadband.gc.ca

National Telecommunications and Information Administration (NTIA). (1995, July). *Falling through the Net: A survey of the "have nots" in rural and urban America.* Retrieved September 29, 2004, from http://www.ntia.doc.gov/ ntiahome/fallingthru.html

National Telecommunications and Information Administration (NTIA). (1998) *Falling through the Net II: New data on the digital divide.* Retrieved September 29, 2004, from http://www.ntia.doc.gov/ntiahome/net2/

National Telecommunications and Information Administration (NTIA). (1999). *Falling through the Net: Defining the digital divide.* Retrieved September 29, 2004, from http://www.ntia.doc.gov/ntiahome/fttn99/contents.html

National Telecommunications and Information Administration (NTIA). (2000). *Falling through the Net: Toward digital inclusion.* Retrieved September 29, 2004, from http://www.ntia.doc.gov/ntiahome/fttn00/contents00.html

National Telecommunications and Information Administration (NTIA). (2002). *A nation online: How Americans are expanding their use of the Internet.* Retrieved September 29, 2004, from http://www.ntia.doc.gov/ntiahome/dn/index.html

Nie, N. H., & Erbring, L. (2000). *Internet and society: A preliminary report.* Retrieved January 28, 2004, from http://www.stanford.edu/group/siqss

Norman, D. (1988). *The design of everyday things.* Hillsdale, NJ: Lawrence Erlbaum.

Norman, D. (1999). *The invisible computer.* Cambridge, MA: MIT Press.

Norris, P. (2001). *Digital divide, civic engagement, information poverty and the Internet worldwide.* Cambridge, England: Cambridge University Press.

O'Brien, R. (2001). *Research into the digital divide in Canada.* Retrieved September 29, 2004, from http://www.web.net/~robrien/papers/digdivide.html

Park, H. W. (2002). The digital divide in South Korea: Closing and widening divides in the 1990s. *Electronic Journal of Communication/Revue de Communication Electronique, 12*(1 & 2). Retrieved September 28, 2004, from http://www.cios.org/www/ejc

Parkin, F. (1979). *Marxism and class theory: A bourgeois critique.* London: Tavistock.

Penuel, W., & Kim, D. (2000). *Promising practices and organizational challenges in community technology centres.* Retrieved February 26, 2004, from http://www.sri.com/policy/ctl/assets/images/vStreets_Promising_Practices.pdf

Pew Internet and American Life Project. (2002). *Daily tracking survey data set.* Retrieved September 23, 2003, from http://207.21.232.103/dataset_download.asp?i=28&d=Decembe.2002

Pew Internet and American Life Project. (2004). *Data.* Retrieved September 15, 2004, from http://www.pewinternet.org/data.asp.

Pigato, M. (2001). *Information and communication technology, poverty and development in Sub-Saharan Africa and South Asia* (World Bank, African Region, Working Paper Series No. 20). Washington DC: World Bank.

Pool, I. de S., Inose, H., Takasaki, N., & Hunwitz, R. (1984). *Communication flows: A census in the US and Japan.* Amsterdam: North Holland.

Potter, W. J. (1998). *Media literacy.* London: Sage.

Powell, W. (1990). Neither market nor hierarchy: Network forms of organizations. In B. Slaw (Ed.), *Research in organizational behavior* (Vol. 12, pp. 295-336). Greenwich, CT: JAI.

Press, L., Foster, W., & Goodman, S. (1999). The Internet in India and China. *First Monday: Peer-Reviewed Journal on the Internet, 7*(10). Retrieved February 6, 2004, from http://www.firstmonday.dk/issues/issue7_10/press/

Putnam, R. (2000). *Bowling alone: The collapse and survival of American community.* New York: Simon & Schuster.

Quan-Haase, A., & Wellman, B. (with Witte, J. C., & Hampton, K.). (2002). Capitalizing on the Net: Social contact, civic engagement, and sense of community. In B. Wellman & C. Haythornthwaite (Eds.), *The Internet in everyday life* (pp. 291-324). Oxford, England: Blackwell.

Rainie, L., Fox, S., Horrigan, J., Lenhart, A., & Spooner, T. (2000, March-May). *Tracking online life: How women use the Internet to cultivate relationships with family and friends.* Washington, DC: Pew Internet and American Life Project. Retrieved August 28, 2004, from http://www.pewinternet.org/pdfs/New_User_Report.pdf

Rawls, J. (1971). *Theory of justice.* Cambridge, MA: Harvard University Press.

Robinson, J., DiMaggio, P., & Hargittai, E. (2003, Summer). New social survey perspectives on the digital divide. *IT & Society, 1*(5), 1-22.

Rockwell, S., & Singleton, L. (2002). The effects of computer anxiety and communication apprehension on the adoption and utilization of the Internet. *Electronic Journal of Communication/Revue de Communication Electronique, 12*(1). Retrieved June 12, 2004, from http://www.cios.org/www/ejc

Rojas, V., Straubhaar, J., Roychowdhury, D., & Okur, O. (2004). Communities, cultural capital and the digital divide. In E. Bucy & J. Newhagen (Eds.), *Media access: Social and psychological dimensions of new technology use* (pp. 107-130). London: LEA.

Rosen, L., & Maguire, P. (1990). Myths and realities of computerphobia: A meta-analysis. *Anxiety Research, 3,* 175-191.

The Rural Secretariat. (2001). *Rural and remote broadband access: Background report to the National Broadband Task Force.* Retrieved February 10, 2004, from http://broadband.gc.ca/english/resources/ruralsec_report.pdf

Savolainen, R. (2002). Network competence and information seeking on the Internet: From definitions towards a social cognitive model. *Journal of Documentation, 58*(2), 211-226.

Schement, J. (2003, Spring). Measuring what Jefferson knew and de Tocqueville saw: Libraries as bridges across the digital divide. *IT & Society, 1*(4), 118-129.

Schement, J., & Scott, S. C. (2000). Identifying temporary and permanent gaps in universal service. *Information Society, 16*(2), 117-126.

Schiller, H. (1996). *Information inequality: The deepening social crisis in America.* London: Routledge.

Sen, A. (1976). Real national income. *Review of Economic Studies, 43,* 19-39.

Sen, A. (1985). *Commodities and capabilities.* Amsterdam: North-Holland.

Sen, A. (1992). *Inequality reexamined.* Oxford, England: Oxford University Press.

Servaes, J., & Burgelman, J.-C. (2000). In search of a European model of the information society. *Telematics and Informatics, 17,* 1-7.

Shapiro, A. (1999). *The control revolution: How the Internet is putting individuals in charge and changing the world we know.* New York: Century Foundation.

Silverblatt, A. (1995). *Media literacy: Keys to interpreting media messages.* Westport, CT: Praeger.

Silverstein C., Henzinger, H., Marais, H., & Moricz, M. (1999). Analysis of a very large Web search engine query log. *SIGIR Forum, 33*(1), 6-12.

Sociaal en Cultureel Planbureau (SCP). (2001). *Trends in de tijd* [Trends in time]. The Hague, Netherlands: Author.

Spink A., Jansen, B., Wolfram, D. & Saracevic, T. (2002). From e-sex to e-commerce: Web search changes. *IEEE Computer, 35*(3), 107-109.

Stanley, L. (2001). *Beyond access.* Retrieved March 11, 2004, from www.media manage.net/Beyond_Access.pdf

Steijn, B. (2001). *Werken in de informatiesamenleving* [Working in the information society]. Assen, Netherlands: Koninklijke van Gorcum.

Steinmüller, W. (2001). ICTs and the possibilities of leapfrogging by developing countries. *International Labour Review, 140*(2), 193-210.

Steinour, D. (2001). *Canada's policies and programs to reduce the digital divide.* Retrieved January 12, 2004, from http://www.apii.or.kr/apacdata/telwg/23tel/dcsg_03.html

Steyaert, J. (2000). *Digitale vaardigheden: Geletterdheid in de informatiesamenleving* [Digital skills: Literacy in the information society]. The Hague, Netherlands: Rathenau Instituut.

Thierer, A. (2000, April 20). How free computers are filling the digital divide. *Heritage Foundation Backgrounder, 1361.* Retrieved September 30, 2004, from http://www.heritage.org/Research/InternetandTechnology/BG1361.cfm

Tichenor, P. J., Donohue, G., & Olien, C. (1970). Mass media flow and differential growth in knowledge. *Public Opinion Quarterly, 34,* 159-170.

Tilly, C. (1999). *Durable inequality.* Berkeley, CA: University of California Press.

Toffler, A. (1980). *The third wave.* London: Collins.

United Nations Development Programme (UNDP). (1998). *Human development report 1998.* Oxford, England: Oxford University Press.

United Nations Development Programme (UNDP). (2003). *Human development report 2003: Millennium development goals: A contract among nations to end human poverty.* Oxford, England: Oxford University Press. Retrieved March 8, 2004, from http://hdr.undp.org/reports/global/2003/

United Nations Statistics Division. (2004a). *Millennium development indicators: World and regional groupings.* Retrieved September 30, 2004, from http://millenniumindicators.un.org/unsd/mi/worldbank.htm

United Nations Statistics Division. (2004b). *Millennium indicators database: Goals, targets and indicators.* Retrieved March 11, 2004, from http://millenniumindicators.un.org/unsd/mi/mi_goals.asp

United Nations Statistics Division. (2004c). *Millennium indicators database: Internet users per 100 population (ITU estimates)*. Retrieved March 11, 2004, from http://millenniumindicators.un.org/unsd/mi/mi_indicator_xrxx .asp?ind_code=48

United Nations Statistics Division. (2004d). *Millennium indicators database: Personal computers per 100 Population (ITU estimates)*. Retrieved March 11, 2004, from http://millenniumindicators.un.org/unsd/mi/mi_indicator_ xrxx.asp?ind_code=48

U.S. Department of Education. (2001). *Education budget history table*. Washington, DC: Author. Retrieved December 12, 2003, from http://www .ed.gov./offices/OUS/budnews.html

U.S. Department of Labor. (2001). *Report on the American workforce*. Washington, DC: Author. Retrieved January 17, 2004, from http://www.dol.gov/opub/ rtawhome.htm

University of California, Los Angeles, Center for Communication Policy. (2000). *The UCLA Internet report 2000: Surveying the digital future*. Los Angeles: Author. Retrieved March 2, 2004, from http://www.ccp.ucla.edu/ pages/internet-report.asp

University of California, Los Angeles, Center for Communication Policy. (2001). *The UCLA Internet report 2001: Surveying the digital future, year two*. Los Angeles: Author. Retrieved March 2, 2004, from http://www.ccp .ucla.edu/pages/internet-report.asp

University of California, Los Angeles, Center for Communication Policy. (2003). *The UCLA Internet report: Surveying the digital future, year three*. Los Angeles: Author. Retrieved March 2, 2004, from http://www.ccp.ucla.edu/pages/ internet-report.asp

van Dijk, J.A.G.M. (1997). *Universal service from the perspective of consumers and citizens: Report to the Information Society Forum*. Brussels, Belgium: European Commission/ISPO.

van Dijk, J. (1999). *The network society: Social aspects of new media*. London: Sage.

van Dijk, J. (2000). Widening information gaps and policies of prevention. In K. Hacker & J. van Dijk (Eds.), *Digital democracy: Issues of theory and practice* (pp. 166-183). London: Sage.

van Dijk, J.A.G.M. (2001a). *De netwerkmaatschappij: Sociale aspecten van nieuwe media* [The network society: Social aspects of new media] (4th ed.). Houten, Zaventem: Bohn Stafleu van Loghum/Alphen aan den Rijn: Samsom.

van Dijk, J.A.G.M. (2001b). *Netwerken, het zenuwstelsel van onze maatschappij. Oratie* [Networks, the nervous system of our society. Inaugural lecture]. Enschede, Netherlands: University of Twente, Department of Communication.

van Dijk, J. (2004). Divides in succession: Possession, skills, and use of new media for societal participation. In E. Bucy & J. Newhagen (Eds.), *Media access: Social and psychological dimensions of new technology use* (pp. 233-254). London: LEA.

van Dijk, J., & Hacker, K. (2003). The digital divide as a complex and dynamic phenomenon. *Information Society, 19,* 315-326.

van Dijk, Liset, J., de Haan, J., & Rijken, S. (2000). *Digitalisering van de leefwereld: Een onderzoek naar informatie en communicatietechnologie en sociale ongelijkheid* [Digitization of everyday life: A survey of information and communication technology and social inequality]. The Hague, Netherlands: Sociaal en Cultureel Planbureau. Retrieved June 25, 2004, from http://www.scp.nl/publicaties/boeken/905749518X.shtml

van Eimeren, B., Gerhard, H., & Frees, B. (2002). Entwicklung der online-nutzung in Deutschland: Mehr routine, weniger entdeckerfreude [Development of online use in Germany: More routine, less joy of discovery]. *Media Perspektives, 2002*(8), 346-362.

Warschauer, M. (2002). Reconceptualizing the digital divide. *First Monday: Peer-Reviewed Journal on the Internet, 7*(7). Retrieved December 13, 2003, from http://www.firstmonday.dk/issues/issue7_7/warschauer

Warschauer, M. (2003a). Dissecting the "digital divide": A case study in Egypt. *Information Society, 19,* 297-304.

Warschauer, M. (2003b). *Technology and social inclusion: Rethinking the digital divide.* Cambridge, MA: MIT Press.

Watts, D. J., & Strogatz, S. (1998). Collective dynamics of "small world" networks. *Nature, 393,* 440-442.

Weber, M. (1968). *Economy and society: An outline of interpretative sociology* (G. Roth & C. Wittich, Eds.). New York: Badminster.

Webster, F. (1995). *Theories of the information society.* Londen: Routledge.

Webster, F. (2001). *The information society revisited: Handbook of the new media.* London: Sage.

Wellman, B. (2000). Changing connectivity: A future history of Y2.03K. *Sociological Research Online, 4*(4). Retrieved September 30, 2004, from http://www.socresonline.org.uk/4/4/wellman.html

Wellman, B. (2001, September 14). Computer networks as social networks. *Science, 293,* 2031-2034.

Wellman, B., & Berkowitz, S. D. (Eds.). (1988). *Social structures: A network approach.* Greenwich, CT: London: Jai Press.

Wellman, B., & Haythornthwaite, C. (Eds.). (2002). *The Internet in everyday life.* Oxford, England: Blackwell.

Wenglinsky, H. (1998) *Does it compute? The relationship between educational technology and student achievement in mathematics.* Princeton, NJ: Educational Testing Service. Retrieved February 20, 2004, from http://www.ets.org/pub/res/technolog.pdf

Wilhelm, A. (2003a). Civic participation and technology inequality: The "killer application" is education (pp. 113-128). In D. Anderson & M. Cornfield (Eds.), *The civic web: Online politics and democratic values.* Lanham, MD: Rowman & Littlefield.

Wilhelm, A. (2003b). Leveraging sunken investments in communications infrastructure: A policy perspective from the United States. *Information Society, 19*, 279-286.

Wolff, E. (2002). The impact of IT investment on income and wealth inequality in the postwar US economy. *Information Economics and Poverty, 14*, 233-251.

Wong, P.-K. (2002). ICT production and diffusion in Asia: Digital dividends or digital divide? *Information Economics and Policy, 14*, 167-187.

Ziman, J. (Ed.). (2000). *Technological innovation as an evolutionary process.* Cambridge, England: Cambridge University Press.

Zuurmond, A. (1994). *De infocratie: Een theoretische en empirische heroriëntatie op Weber's ideaaltype in het informatietijdperk* [Infocracy: A theoretical and empirical reorientation to Weber's ideal type in the information age]. The Hague, Netherlands: Phaedrus.

Index

About the Author

Jan A.G.M. van Dijk is an internationally recognized expert in the field of communication, his specific interest being new media studies. He is the author of *The Network Society: Social Aspects of the New Media* (Sage, 1999) and coeditor of *Digital Democracy: Issues of Theory and Practice* (Sage, 2000). As Full Professor of Communication Science at the University of Twente, van Dijk teaches and investigates the social aspects of information and communication technology; in particular, the social-cultural, political, and organizational aspects. His teaching chair is called *The Sociology of the Information Society*. He earned his Ph.D. in social sciences at the Catholic University of Nijmegen, the Netherlands. Van Dijk also is an advisor for a number of Dutch ministries and for the European Commission. Personal Web site: http://www.gw.utwente.nl/vandijk